EMORY *Seasons*

ENTERTAINING ATLANTA STYLE

EMORY UNIVERSITY WOMAN'S CLUB • ESTABLISHED JANUARY 18, 1919

The Emory University Woman's Club was established in 1919 to foster social interaction among faculty and to promote service to the University.

Library of Congress Catalog Card Number – 93-073052
ISBN 0-9637471-0-X

First edition

Printed by
Wimmer Brothers
Memphis Dallas

To order copies of
EMORY SEASONS write:

EMORY SEASONS
Houston Mill House
849 Houston Mill Road
Atlanta, Georgia 30329

Proceeds from EMORY SEASONS will be used to fund scholarships and other charitable projects serving the Emory community.

Table of Contents

*I*n EMORY SEASONS, the Emory Woman's Club has compiled a tempting array of recipes collected over the past four years from faculty, staff, students and friends. These dishes reflect traditions of many cultures, befitting a university that currently welcomes students from 90 different nations and has faculty, staff and neighbors from all parts of the world. In this treasury of recipes, each of which has been tested by the Woman's Club, you will find not only an international flavor, but also a healthy respect for sound nutritional guidelines.

On behalf of the University, I extend congratulations to the Emory University Woman's Club both for this happy resource and, in January 1994, for 75 years of service to and friendship within the Emory community. I am grateful for these years of fruitful colleagueship, and look forward to many, many seasons to come.

James T. Laney
PRESIDENT
EMORY UNIVERSITY

*A*s there are four seasons, so there are four tastes: bitter, sour, salt, and sweet. So say the physiology books. But who among us, intrigued by the gustatory subtleties of a salmon mousse or a sole Florentine, could describe the experience merely as some combination of those four tastes. Not I. The fascinating duet of taste and smell that occurs when we prepare, then eat, food is too complex to describe in those terms.

The ancients believed that four elements made up their world: earth, air, fire, and water. Were I to modify those elements, I'd add at least two more: food (the preparation of which requires all the others) and Art (with a capital A, to include all the arts). For of what possible use are all the other elements without Art? Including the art of food.

But if we are so easily to modify the elements that make up the world, we ought to include love, too. Let me explain. We know, when we listen to live performances of Vivaldi's *The Four Seasons*, that each one will be different from all others we've heard. So it is with food and the fixing of it. And so it is with love. We relish our favorite foods, our favorite music, the people we love, precisely because they are not always exactly the same through the years. And surely that is one of the joys of cooking—and of loving. An inspired choice of appropriate "spices" can at times make food, love or music mysteriously better. In the happiest of circumstances, they may even be combined, as Shakespeare knew full well: "If music be the food of love, play on."

The best foods can be as complex as music. Or as simple (though as hard to explain) as love. Food is both timeless and new, memory and the future, requirement and ritual. As all chefs know instinctively, the best foods are artful, art for the palate and art for the palette as well. Virginia Woolf asserted that "A Beethoven quartet is the truth about the world." Yes. But the world has many truths. And food is one of the best of them. May the most flavorful and provocative of such culinary truths grace your table. Play on!

John Stone
Cardiologist, poet, and writer
Emory University

EMORY UNIVERSITY
WOMAN'S CLUB

*T*he Emory University Woman's Club was organized January 18, 1919. At that time the Atlanta campus of Emory consisted of only a few buildings; the main campus was, until the following October, located at Oxford, Georgia. The purposes of the club, as outlined in the minutes of that first meeting, were twofold: to foster social interaction among the faculty and to provide service to the University.

The club has contributed to a variety of projects, including scholarship endowments, the Emory Libraries, the establishment of a wildflower trail at Lullwater, Christmas gifts for the Children's Medical Services of Georgia, and service at Egleston Children's Hospital and Emory University Hospital. In 1984 the club arranged for the establishment of a specific, named scholarship fund at Emory, and Commencement 1984 marked the first presentation of the Emory Woman's Club Memorial Award in Graduate Research.

In addition, for many years the Emory University Woman's Club has sponsored the Druid Hills Home and Garden Tour along with the Druid Hills Civic Association and in conjunction with the Atlanta Dogwood Festival.

Early in the administration of President James T. Laney, the Woman's Club was offered the challenge of supervising the renovation of the Houston Mill House to provide a faculty center and a meeting place for the club as well as other University groups. Utilizing capital outlay from the University and profits from a series of fund-raising projects, the club accomplished the refurbishing of the house and grounds, developed policies for use of the facility, and established a nonprofit corporation to manage the house on a continuing basis.

In September 1979 the Houston Mill House opened for business. Many faculty and alumni gatherings of educational and social interest are held there.

Since 1980 its in-house caterers, Epicurean, have served many guests for luncheons, faculty dinners, private receptions and weddings. The house, which will accommodate 250 people, is open to the public Monday through Friday for lunch.

Epicurean has graciously shared its recipes and menus for the publication of EMORY SEASONS.

Menus for the Four Seasons
by
Epicurean

Fall Seated Dinner for 12

Yellow Squash Bisque
Roasted Quail with Cornbread Stuffing and
Watercress Salad
Broccoli and Baked Tomatoes
Pear Custard Tart
Hot Breads
Coffee and Tea

Winter Buffet for 36

Greek Salad
Lamb Moussaka
Chocolate Nut Cake with Hot Fudge
Sauce or Berries and Cream
Hot Breads
Coffee and Tea

Spring Cookout for 30

Grilled Fish with Papaya Salsa
and Grilled Boneless Chicken Breasts
Wild Rice Salad with Herb Vinaigrette
Sliced Tomatoes and Cucumbers
Blanched Asparagus
Lemon Pound Cake with All Berry Topping
Hot Breads
Iced Tea

Summer Dinner for 25

Chilled Cucumber Vichyssoise
Poached Fresh Salmon
Blanched Vegetables and Bibb Lettuce
Fresh Fruit and Assorted Cookies
Bread Basket
Iced Tea

The Houston Mill House caterers, Epicurean, graciously shared recipes for each season of the year.

*W*e proudly dedicate this book to Emory University Woman's Club members past and present, in celebration of our 75th anniversary January 18, 1994.

CREDITS:

Art (Drawings)	Vicky Holifield
Emory University Publications	
Graphic Design	Joseph Alcober
Photography	Tommy L. Thompson
	University Photography
Word Processing	Martha Catherwood

Vicky Holifield's drawings in EMORY SEASONS represent botanicals indigenous to the Emory campus and architectural details of historic Emory buildings.

The recipes in EMORY SEASONS were chosen from more than 600 recipes submitted by the Emory community and from two earlier Emory University Woman's Club cookbooks. We do not claim these recipes to be all original but they are favorites that have been tested and enjoyed by friends and family. We thank everyone who shared in this project. All recipes have been triple-tested.

SYMBOLS USED IN EMORY SEASONS

Easy	recipe may be completed in one hour or less
◔	recipe will take several hours or overnight to complete
♥	emphasis on heart-healthy ingredients
★	contains uncooked egg

Appetizers

Dips and Spreads

Little Savories

Refrigerator and Freezer Do Aheads

*A*ppetizers introduce the meal. Their purpose is to excite our interest and to stimulate the taste buds for what is ahead. In French, these little tidbits are called "amuse-gueule" — literally, they entertain the tongue. At best they have a freshness and clarity of flavor that pique our interest. This is our chance to use our most attractive serving dishes and to add the little garnitures that bring brightness and eye appeal to the table.

How much or how many to make? We suggest planning 3 - 4 pieces per person for a pre-dinner cocktail hour and 6 pieces per person for a cocktail party. Aim for a variety of colors, textures and temperatures and include some raw or crisp vegetable crudites.

Most of these recipes can be quickly assembled and can be made ahead of time and frozen. We have learned to work from our cupboard shelves, our freezers and the deli counter and to plan ahead when cooking and shopping. Appetizers for an after-work party might consist of a dish of glossy black olives, a tray of crisp red radishes and 1 or 2 cheeses along with 1 or 2 frozen hors d'oeuvres popped into the oven.

For days when there's no time to shop (or you simply can't face the idea!) we suggest keeping a variety of staples in your "pantry." Keep on your shopping list fresh foods (such as cheese, fruits and vegetables) that will hold their flavor and are always healthful appetizers.

Here are a few practical suggestions for almost instant appetizers, one step beyond the bag of tortilla chips and jar of salsa!

APPLES AND PEARS: Toss slices of crisp apple or pear with lemon, lime or grapefruit juice and serve with softened blue cheese spread. Toss pears with freshly grated Parmesan cheese.

MELON: Wrap small cubes of melon with a strip of salami or prosciutto and secure with a toothpick.

CREAM CHEESE: Surround a block of cream cheese (low fat is great) with hot pepper jelly or chutney and serve with crackers.

CHILI DIP: Brown one-quarter to one-half pound of ground beef, add a can of chili, heat and serve with tortilla chips. Top with grated Cheddar or Monterey Jack cheese.

HOT DOGS: Cut the all-American hot dog into bite-size pieces and heat for 10 minutes in a fondue pot with a can of beer and a few drops of hot pepper sauce. Add toothpicks to serve and mustard for dunking.

VEGETABLES: Serve steamed, grilled or raw with flavored mayonnaise (process mixed chopped herbs, curry powder to taste and drained oil-packed sun-dried tomatoes with mayonnaise in blender or food processor).

SNOW PEAS: Lightly steam or blanch and stuff with a soft flavored cheese — boursin, rondele, pimiento or your own cream-cheese mixture.

Hot Crab Dip

Easy

1	pound lump crab meat
10	ounce can condensed cream of celery soup
8	ounces cream cheese
⅓	cup minced olives

- Remove any bits of shell from crab meat.
- Blend cream cheese and soup.
- Add olives and fold in crab meat.
- Put in 2-quart casserole dish.
- Bake 30 minutes at 350°F.

Serve with sesame crackers or toast points.

Cold Crab Dip

Easy

6	ounces frozen snow crab meat
8	ounces cream cheese, softened
½	cup mayonnaise
➤	dash of Worcestershire sauce
¼-⅓	cup chopped onion

- Thaw and drain crab meat.
- Mix remaining ingredients. Add crab meat.
- Refrigerate until serving.

Best if made an hour or so ahead.

Hot Clam Dip

Easy

½	cup butter or margarine
2	(6 ounce) cans minced clams, undrained
1	tablespoon lemon juice
1	onion, minced
1	red or green bell pepper, minced
1	stalk celery, minced
1	tablespoon minced fresh parsley
1	clove garlic, minced
➤	dash each of pepper, oregano and thyme
¾	cup seasoned bread crumbs
8	drops hot pepper sauce
➤	grated Parmesan cheese

- Sauté undrained clams with lemon juice in butter 15 minutes.
- Add everything but Parmesan cheese. Mix well.
- Put in baking dish.
- Sprinkle Parmesan cheese over top.
- Cover and bake 30 minutes at 350°F.

SHRIMP MOLD

🕐

1	envelope plain gelatin
⅓	cup cold water
10	ounce can condensed tomato soup
8	ounces cream cheese, softened
1	cup mayonnaise
½	cup each chopped celery and onion
2	(6 ounce) packages frozen shrimp or 2 (4 ounce) cans shrimp, drained

- Dissolve gelatin in cold water. Set aside.
- Bring undiluted tomato soup to boil. Stir in cold gelatin mixture.
- Using electric mixer, slowly add soup mixture to cream cheese.
- Add mayonnaise. Fold in onion, celery and shrimp.
- Grease 3 - 5-cup mold.
- Pour mixture into mold. Refrigerate overnight.
- Unmold and serve with crackers.

SALMON BALL

🕐

16	ounce can red or pink salmon, drained
8	ounces light cream cheese
1	tablespoon lemon juice
1	tablespoon finely chopped onion
1	teaspoon prepared horseradish
¼	teaspoon liquid smoke
¼	cup finely chopped fresh parsley
½	cup finely chopped pecans

- Remove skin and bones from salmon. Flake and mash.
- Blend first 6 ingredients (a food processor is ideal).
- Refrigerate until mixture is firm to touch.
- Mix parsley and pecans.
- Form salmon mixture into ball. Roll in parsley-nut mixture.
- Wrap in plastic. Refrigerate until serving.

Sesame or wheat crackers are an especially good accompaniment.

CHEF'S NOTE

Greasing a dish, pan or mold is fast and easy with a vegetable cooking spray.

HUMMUS

Easy

¼   **cup tahini (sesame paste)**
1   **teaspoon ground cumin**
½   **teaspoon salt**
3   **large cloves garlic, minced**
4   **tablespoons lemon juice**
3   **tablespoons hot water**
16   **ounce can chick-peas or garbanzo beans, drained**
➤   **chopped fresh parsley**

- Combine tahini, cumin, salt and garlic. Slowly add lemon juice and hot water.
- Purée chick-peas.
- Add tahini mixture to puréed chick-peas. Process or mix well.
- Adjust seasonings to taste.
- Spread hummus on large plate.
- Sprinkle with chopped parsley.

BABA GHANNOUJ

2   **medium eggplants**
⅓   **cup lemon juice**
½   **cup olive oil**
⅓   **cup tahini (sesame paste)**
2   **cloves garlic, mashed**
¾   **teaspoon salt**
➤   **fresh parsley or pomegranate seeds**

- Prick the skin of eggplant in several places.
- Grill unpeeled eggplant over low flame or bake in 425°F oven 1 hour.
- Remove skin and mash pulp.
- Beat in lemon juice and oil alternately. Stir in tahini, garlic and salt.
- Pour into serving dish. Garnish with parsley or pomegranate seeds.

CHEF'S NOTE

Hummus and Baba Ghannouj are Middle-Eastern and usually are served with pita bread and raw vegetables.

SHRIMP SPREAD

Easy

8	ounces light cream cheese, softened
3	tablespoons cocktail sauce with horseradish
2	tablespoons lemon juice
2	(4 ounce) cans shrimp, drained

- Mash cream cheese with cocktail sauce and lemon juice, mixing well.
- Combine with shrimp.
- Refrigerate until serving.

SPINACH AND ARTICHOKE DIP

May do ahead — bake later

16	ounces light sour cream
1	envelope ranch dressing party dip mix
14	ounce can artichoke hearts, drained, chopped
10	ounces frozen chopped spinach, thawed, drained
2	ounce jar diced pimientos, drained
1½	pound loaf of crusty bread, preferably round

- Combine sour cream and dip mix. Stir in artichokes, spinach and pimientos.
- Slice off top of bread loaf. Hollow out center. Reserve bread chunks for dipping.
- Heat oven to 400°F.
- Spoon dip into shell. Place on baking sheet.
- Bake 20 - 25 minutes.
- Serve with carrot and celery sticks, other raw vegetables and bread from center.

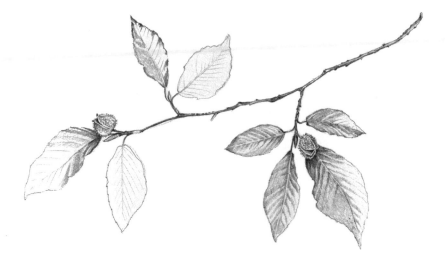

Salmon Mousse with Dill

🕐

1	envelope plain gelatin
½	cup cold water or clam juice
⅓	cup chopped fresh dill or 1 teaspoon dried dill weed
2	tablespoons grated onion
1	tablespoon lemon juice
1	teaspoon salt
➤	dash of hot pepper sauce
¾	cup low fat yogurt
½	cup low fat sour cream
½	cup finely chopped celery
16	ounce can red sockeye salmon, drained

- Sprinkle gelatin over cold water in small pan. Let stand 5 minutes to soften.
- Heat over medium heat until gelatin is dissolved. Cool to room temperature.
- Stir in dill, onion, lemon juice, salt, pepper sauce, yogurt, sour cream and celery. Mix well.
- Refrigerate mixture until it begins to set.
- Remove skin and bones from salmon. Mash well; mix with gelatin mixture.
- Spoon into 4-cup mold. Cover and refrigerate until firm, 3 - 4 hours.
- Unmold on serving plate. Garnish with decorative vegetables or parsley. Serve with crackers.

Potted Rumaki Spread

🕐

Sauce:

4	teaspoons light soy sauce
1	tablespoon white wine vinegar
1	tablespoon Dijon mustard
½	teaspoon each garlic powder, onion powder and white pepper
¼	teaspoon hot pepper sauce

Spread:

6	slices lean bacon
4	tablespoons vegetable oil, divided
¾	pound fresh chicken livers, soaked 1 hour in skim milk to cover
2	green onions, chopped
6	ounce can water chestnuts, drained

- Mix sauce ingredients thoroughly. Set aside.
- Cook bacon to crisp. Drain and crumble.
- Drain chicken livers. Sauté in oil 3 - 5 minutes, until centers are no longer pink. Drain.
- In food processor finely chop bacon, onions and water chestnuts.
- Remove mixture and then process cooked livers.
- Combine all of these with sauce in mixing bowl.
- Refrigerate overnight before serving.
- May be served cold or warmed gently in microwave. Serve with toast points.

MUSHROOM PÂTÉ

🕐 ★

½	pound fresh mushrooms, chopped
2-4	tablespoons butter
1½	teaspoons plain gelatin
1	tablespoon sherry
¼	cup cold chicken broth
1	egg, separated
1½	drops of hot pepper sauce
¼	cup mayonnaise
1	teaspoon drained capers
1½	tablespoons chopped onion
½	teaspoon lemon juice
¼	teaspoon garlic powder or 1 small clove garlic, chopped
¼	teaspoon salt
➤	pinch of white pepper
½	cup heavy cream

- Sauté mushrooms in butter in large skillet. Set aside.
- Soften gelatin in sherry and broth. Heat gently to dissolve.
- Put gelatin mixture in blender or food processor. Process 1 minute.
- Add mushrooms, egg yolk, hot pepper sauce, mayonnaise, capers, onion, lemon juice, garlic, salt and pepper. Blend until smooth. Add cream.
- In small bowl beat egg white until stiff. Fold into mushroom mixture.
- Pour into serving container.
- Refrigerate until serving.

Best made two days ahead.
Serve with crackers and champagne!

BAKED ARTICHOKE DIP

Easy

14	ounce can water-packed artichoke hearts, drained, chopped
½	cup grated cheese (Cheddar or other full-flavored cheese)
1	cup mayonnaise
1	cup grated Parmesan cheese
¼	cup finely minced onion
➤	minced red bell pepper or sliced olives (optional)
2	tablespoons dry sherry (optional)

- Mix all ingredients. Put in ovenproof dish.
- Bake 15 - 20 minutes until bubbling at 350°F.
- Let stand 5 minutes before serving.

Egg Salad Surprise

Easy

6	hard-cooked eggs
1	small onion, chopped
8	ounces soft cream cheese
➢	dash of cracked pepper

- Grate eggs or chop in food processor.
- Add onion, cream cheese and pepper. Mix.
- Refrigerate until serving.

Traditionally served at Emory Bookstore autographing parties.

Caviar and Egg Spread

Easy

3	hard-cooked eggs
➢	salt, pepper and mayonnaise to taste
½	cup sour cream
3-4	ounce jar caviar, either red or black
➢	chopped green onion

- Mash eggs with salt, pepper and mayonnaise.
- Put into small bowl. Chill.
- Unmold onto serving dish. Cover mound with sour cream.
- Top with caviar and then green onion.
- Refrigerate until serving.

Guacamole

Easy

2	large ripe avocados, peeled, pitted
4	ounce can chopped green chilies
2	tablespoons lemon or lime juice
1	tablespoon finely chopped onion
➢	pinch of sugar
¼	teaspoon ground cumin
¼	teaspoon garlic powder or 1 clove garlic, crushed
1	large ripe tomato, seeded, finely chopped
➢	salt and black pepper to taste

- Mash avocado roughly and mix with lemon juice.
- Add other ingredients.
- Cover with plastic wrap and refrigerate.

For a creamier dip, add 2 tablespoons of sour cream or mayonnaise.

CHIPPED BEEF AND PECAN SPREAD

Easy

2½	ounces sliced dried beef
8	ounces soft cream cheese
2	tablespoons milk
1	tablespoon minced onion
½	teaspoon pepper
½	teaspoon minced garlic
½	cup sour cream
½	cup coarsely chopped pecans

- Chop dried beef.
- Blend cream cheese and milk.
- Stir in beef, seasonings and sour cream.
- Spoon into shallow baking dish.
- Sprinkle nuts over top.
- Bake 20 minutes at 350°F.

CUCUMBER YOGURT DIP

♥   *Easy*

3	medium cucumbers
1	tablespoon minced green onion
1	clove garlic, minced
¼	teaspoon ground cumin
½	teaspoon salt or 1 teaspoon No-Salt Herb Seasoning (page 69)
⅛	teaspoon white pepper
1½	cups plain low fat yogurt

- Peel, seed and coarsely grate cucumbers. Drain liquid or squeeze dry.
- Combine with remaining ingredients.
- Serve room temperature or chilled.

  This may be enjoyed as a salad dressing as well.

CREAMY FRESH DILL DIP

♥   *Easy*

¼	cup chopped fresh dill or 2 teaspoons dried dill weed (If using dried dill weed add additional 3 tablespoons chopped fresh parsley)
2	tablespoons chopped fresh parsley
8	ounces low fat cottage cheese
3	tablespoons plain low fat yogurt
➢	salt and freshly ground pepper to taste

- Chop dill and parsley in food processor.
- Add cottage cheese, yogurt, salt and pepper.
- Process briefly. Refrigerate.
- Serve with raw vegetables for dipping.

Sicilian Eggplant Caponata

🕐 ♥ *4 - 6 cups*

1	medium eggplant (1¼ pounds)
➤	salt
½	cup olive oil, divided
2	medium onions, chopped
3-4	cloves garlic, finely chopped
3	stalks celery, chopped
16	ounce can Italian plum tomatoes, coarsely chopped
10	large green olives, rinsed, pitted, chopped
¼	cup drained capers
¼	cup red wine vinegar
2	tablespoons sugar
3	tablespoons pine nuts

- Cut unpeeled eggplant into ½-inch cubes. Salt and set aside in colander to drain.
- In large sauté pan, cook onion, garlic and celery slowly in ¼ cup olive oil until tender, about 10 minutes. Remove to bowl.
- Pat eggplant dry.
- Add remaining ¼ cup oil to pan. Turn heat to medium.
- Stir-fry eggplant cubes until tender, about 5 minutes.
- Return onion mixture to pan. Add remaining ingredients and simmer, uncovered, 15 - 20 minutes. Stir occasionally.
- Adjust seasoning.
- Serve warm or room temperature with crisp bread or crackers.

May be served on lettuce or radicchio leaf as a cold first course.

Chinese Chicken Wings

🕐 *This is a sure crowd pleaser*

3	cloves garlic, minced
½	cup butter, margarine or oil
¼	cup soy sauce
½	cup honey
½	teaspoon Chinese 5-spice powder (optional)
3	pounds chicken wings, tip joint removed

- Sauté garlic in butter until fragrant and golden.
- Add soy sauce, honey and 5-spice powder.
- Brush chicken wings with sauce.
- Bake 1 hour at 350°F, basting often.

History Note

Emory College began with the Georgia Methodist Conference in Washington, Georgia, in 1834. Ignatius Alphonso Few planned and promoted the establishment of both the school and the town of Oxford, named after Oxford, England, where John and Charles Wesley had attended Oxford University.

SAVORY SPINACH SQUARES

2	tablespoons olive or vegetable oil
1	cup finely chopped onion
1	clove garlic, minced
2	(10 ounce) packages frozen chopped spinach, thawed, drained
4	large eggs or egg substitute
½	cup skim milk
1	cup lightly packed fresh bread crumbs
2	cups (8 ounces) shredded Monterey Jack cheese
1	cup grated Parmesan cheese
¼	pound Italian salami, finely chopped (about 1 cup)
½	cup minced fresh parsley
½	teaspoon mixed Italian herb seasoning, crumbled
¼	teaspoon rubbed sage
¼	teaspoon ground nutmeg

- Heat oven to 325°F and grease 13x9x2-inch baking pan.
- Sauté onion in oil until golden. Add garlic and cook 30 seconds. Stir.
- Squeeze spinach to remove excess moisture. Add to onion.
- In large bowl whisk eggs lightly with milk.
- Stir in spinach onion mixture and bread crumbs. Mix well.
- Stir in cheeses. Add remaining ingredients. Mix and spread mixture in pan.
- Bake 40 minutes or until knife inserted into center comes out clean. Cool on wire rack.
- Serve warm or room temperature. Cut into squares or diamonds.

May be cooled and refrigerated. Reheat uncovered in 350°F oven 15 - 20 minutes.

HOT CLAM PUFFS

Easy

10	ounce can minced clams, drained (save juice)
4	tablespoons butter or margarine
¾	cup sifted flour
2	eggs
1	teaspoon salt
➤	dash of pepper
½	teaspoon dried thyme
½	teaspoon chopped chives or green onion

- Heat oven to 400°F and grease baking sheet.
- Heat butter with ½ cup clam juice to boiling.
- Reduce heat; pour in flour. Stir vigorously until mixture leaves side of pan. Remove from heat. Transfer to large bowl.
- Beat in eggs one at a time. Fold in clams and seasoning.
- Drop by teaspoonful onto baking sheet.
- Bake 20 minutes or until browned.

May be frozen, tightly wrapped, and reheated.

SMALL TURNOVERS FOR COCKTAILS

 Makes 18-20 4-inch pastries or 26-28 3-inch pastries

Dough:

1¼	**cups flour**
½	**teaspoon salt**
¼	**teaspoon baking powder**
½	**cup butter**
8	**ounces cream cheese**

Glaze:

1	**egg, beaten with 1 teaspoon water**

- Combine flour, salt and baking powder in bowl.
- Cut in butter and cream cheese until mixture is coarse. Knead dough a few times until it comes together. If necessary add ½ - 1 teaspoon water to form dough.
- *Processor Method:* Cut butter and cream cheese into small pieces. Put all ingredients into bowl of processor. Process until dough just comes together, adding drops of water if necessary.
- Form dough into 2 balls.
- Refrigerate at least 1 hour.
- Roll out dough ⅛-inch thick and cut with a round biscuit cutter into 3- or 4-inch circles.
- Put 1 teaspoon of filling (more for 4-inch ones) in center of each circle.
- Paint edge on 1 side with water. Fold over and seal. Form additional pastries in same way, rerolling scraps of dough as necessary.
- Place on baking sheet and paint with egg glaze.
- Bake 20 - 25 minutes until golden brown at 400°F.

OPTIONAL VARIATIONS FOR FILLING

Cheese Filling:

4	**ounces crumbled Roquefort or Gorgonzola cheese**
½	**cup chopped walnuts**
1	**egg**
➢	**pinch of cayenne pepper**

- Combine ingredients. Mash well. (It will be lumpy.)

Mushroom Filling:

3	**tablespoons butter**
1	**large onion, finely chopped**
¼	**teaspoon dried thyme**
½	**teaspoon salt**
½	**teaspoon pepper**
2	**tablespoons flour**
¼	**cup sour cream**
½	**pound fresh mushrooms, chopped**

- Sauté onion in butter until soft.
- Add thyme, salt, pepper and flour. Stir well. Cook 1 minute to eliminate raw flour taste.
- Add sour cream and stir.
- In separate pan, sauté mushrooms until they yield most of their liquid and it evaporates.
- Combine mushrooms and sour-cream mixture. Adjust seasoning to taste.

Spinach Filling:

3	**tablespoons butter or olive oil**
¼	**cup chopped onion**
10	**ounces frozen chopped spinach, thawed, drained**
½	**cup ricotta, feta or soft goat cheese**
➤	**salt and pepper to taste**
1	**egg, beaten**

- Sauté onion in butter until soft.
- Add spinach and cook 1 - 2 minutes until excess water is evaporated.
- Remove from heat and stir in cheese. Adjust seasoning depending on the saltiness of cheese used.
- Stir in beaten egg.

This recipe is time-consuming but relatively easy.

TOASTED PARMESAN CANAPÉS

Easy

6-8	slices thin white bread
8	tablespoons freshly grated Parmesan cheese, divided
1	cup mayonnaise
¼	cup finely minced onion

- Cut 4 rounds from each slice of bread with small cookie cutter. Toast bread rounds on 1 side.
- Mix 4 tablespoons Parmesan with mayonnaise and onion. Place dollop of mixture on untoasted side of each round.
- Top with generous pinch of Parmesan.
- Brown under broiler. (Watch so they don't burn!) Serve piping hot.
- *Variation:* Use cocktail round rye instead of white bread.

May be prepared ahead, covered and refrigerated until baking.

ARTICHOKE SQUARES

Easy

2	(6 ounce) jars marinated artichoke hearts
1	small onion, chopped
1	clove garlic, minced
4	eggs, beaten, or egg substitute
1	tablespoon lemon juice
⅛	teaspoon dried oregano
⅛	teaspoon hot pepper sauce
¼	teaspoon salt
⅛	teaspoon black pepper
¼	cup seasoned bread crumbs
2	tablespoons chopped fresh parsley

- Drain artichokes, using oil to sauté onion and garlic.
- Combine remaining ingredients. Stir in drained onion, garlic and artichokes.
- Turn into 8x8-inch baking dish.
- Bake 30 minutes or until firm at 325°F.
- Cut into bite-size squares.

HISTORY NOTE

Emory College was named for Bishop John Emory of Maryland, who had presided at the Washington, Georgia, conference and who had been killed in a carriage accident.

STUFFED MUSHROOMS

Easy

18	medium mushroom caps
➤	melted butter or margarine
3	ounces cream cheese, softened
¼	cup grated Parmesan cheese
2	tablespoons milk
18	almond slices for garnish

• Grease baking sheet and brush caps inside and out with melted butter.
• Cream the cream cheese until light.
• Beat in milk and Parmesan cheese.
• Fill mushroom caps with cheese mixture. Top each with a slice of almond.
• Bake 15 minutes until tops are lightly browned at 350°F.

May be prepared ahead, covered and refrigerated until baking.

HOT ASPARAGUS CANAPÉS

🕐

8	ounces light cream cheese, softened
3	ounces blue cheese
1	egg or egg substitute
20	slices thin white bread, crusts removed
20	spears canned asparagus or blanched fresh asparagus
½	cup unsalted butter or margarine, melted

• Mix cheeses and egg.
• Flatten bread slices between wax paper with rolling pin.
• Spread each slice with cheese mixture.
• Roll 1 asparagus spear in each slice and secure with toothpick.
• Generously brush each roll with melted butter.
• Arrange on baking sheet and freeze. Take out toothpicks when rolls are firm. Leave frozen until ready to bake.
• Cut each roll into 3 pieces.
• Bake 15 minutes or until browned at 400°F.

HISTORY NOTE

On December 10, 1836, Governor William Schley signed the charter: "An Act to Incorporate Emory College, to be located in the County of Newton."

SAUSAGE BALLS

1	pound quality sausage, preferably highly seasoned
2	cups biscuit baking mix
8	ounces sharp Cheddar cheese, grated

- Crumble sausage. Add grated cheese and biscuit mix. Blend well.
- Knead briefly. Lightly form into small balls.
- Bake 10 - 15 minutes until lightly browned at 350°F.
- Drain on paper towels and serve hot.

May be frozen and baked later in small quantities. They may be served at brunch also!

SPINACH BALLS

Make — Freeze — Bake later

2	(10 ounce) packages frozen chopped spinach, thawed, drained
2	cups herb seasoned stuffing mix
6	eggs, beaten, or egg substitute
2	large onions, finely chopped
¾	cup butter or margarine, melted
½-¾	cup grated Parmesan cheese
¾	tablespoon garlic powder
½	teaspoon dried thyme
1	teaspoon black pepper
½	cup chopped fresh parsley

- Combine ingredients in large bowl.
- Lightly form mixture into small balls. Place on flat surface to freeze.
- Store in plastic bags in freezer.
- When ready to use, place frozen balls on baking sheet.
- Bake 20 minutes until lightly browned at 375°F.
- Serve hot.

STUFFED BABY POTATOES

24	new potatoes, about 1½ - 2 inches in diameter
6	ounce can chunk-style tuna, drained
⅓	cup mayonnaise
3	tablespoons butter or margarine
¼	cup finely chopped celery
2	tablespoons finely chopped onion
2	tablespoons finely chopped fresh parsley plus additional for garnish
2	tablespoons chopped pimiento-stuffed green olives
1	tablespoon fresh lemon juice
➤	salt and pepper to taste

- Pierce each potato with fork. Arrange on glass pie plate. Microwave at HIGH 8 minutes. Turn each over and rotate plate one quarter. Microwave an additional 8 minutes. Potatoes should be slightly soft to touch. Cover with towel and allow to stand 10 minutes.
- Mix other ingredients.
- Using sharp knife, slice top off each potato. Use melon baller or grapefruit spoon to scoop out center, leaving thin shell.
- Mash approximately 1 cup of potato. Mix with other ingredients.
- Spoon mixture into each shell, mounding. Sprinkle with parsley.
- Arrange on microwave-safe plate. Cook up to 4 minutes at HIGH or until hot.

Chopped cooked chicken breast, canned salmon or crab may be substituted for tuna.

Alternative Chicken Filling:

1	cup cooked chicken breast, skinned, boned, chopped
⅓	cup plain low fat yogurt
3	tablespoons butter or margarine
¼	cup finely chopped toasted walnuts
3	tablespoons minced green onion
1	tablespoon lemon juice
➤	zest of ½ lemon, grated
¼	teaspoon curry powder
➤	salt and pepper to taste
➤	finely chopped walnuts for garnish

- Mix as above recipe.

SUN-DRIED TOMATO CROSTINI

Easy

- ➢   **French or Italian bread**
- 6   **oil-packed sun-dried tomatoes, drained and julienne cut**
- 6   **ounces fontina cheese, sliced**
- ➢   **freshly ground pepper**

- Heat oven to 425°F.
- Cut diagonally 8 slices of bread ½-inch thick.
- Lightly toast one side. Lay slices on baking sheet, toasted side down.
- Top each slice with tomato strips and then cheese.
- Bake in upper third of oven 5 minutes until cheese melts.
- Season with pepper. Serve hot.

CREAMED SCALLOPS AND MUSHROOMS

Serves 4

- 2   **slices firm-textured white bread, crust removed**
- 4   **tablespoons unsalted butter**
- ¼   **pound large mushrooms, sliced**
- ½   **pound bay scallops**
- 1   **cup heavy cream**
- ⅓   **cup Cognac or brandy**
- ➢   **salt and pepper to taste**

- Toast bread and cut diagonally in half to form 4 triangles.
- In large skillet, melt butter over medium heat.
- Add mushrooms and sauté until tender, about 4 minutes. Remove to bowl.
- Put scallops and cream in skillet. Heat until scallops are barely opaque. Remove scallops with slotted spoon, leaving cream.
- Return mushrooms to skillet. Add Cognac and cook over medium heat until liquid is reduced to 2 tablespoons.
- Drain liquid from scallops into skillet. Continue cooking to reduce.
- Season to taste with salt and pepper.
- To serve, place toast points on plate. Return scallops to skillet to heat briefly. Spoon mixture over toast.

HISTORY NOTE

The first class began September 17, 1838, with a total of 15 students under the direction of President Few. In addition to their particular academic specialties, all faculty members of the first class of Emory College were Methodist preachers.

ZUCCHINI BARS

Easy

3	cups unpeeled finely chopped or grated zucchini
1⅓	cups buttermilk biscuit mix
½	cup finely chopped onion
⅔	cup Parmesan cheese plus additional for topping
2	tablespoons chopped fresh parsley
2	tablespoons chopped fresh basil
2	teaspoons No-Salt Herb Seasoning (page 69)
½-1	teaspoon Italian seasoning or oregano
⅛	teaspoon ground pepper
⅓	cup vegetable oil
4	eggs or egg substitute

• Put all ingredients in mixing bowl.
• Use electric mixer to mix thoroughly.
• Heat oven to 375°F and grease 13x9x2-inch pan.
• Put mixture in pan. Sprinkle with additional Parmesan.
• Bake 20 - 30 minutes, until lightly browned.
• Allow to cool about 15 minutes.
• Cut as desired. Serve hot or cold.

May be frozen and reheated.

CHEESE CRISPIES

Easy

1	cup butter or margarine
2	cups grated sharp Cheddar cheese
2	cups flour
1	teaspoon minced garlic (optional)
1	teaspoon minced onion or shallot (optional)
1	teaspoon cayenne pepper
2	cups plain crispy rice cereal

• Heat oven to 350°F and grease baking sheet.
• Cream butter. Add grated cheese. Mix. Add flour and seasonings. Blend.
• Stir in cereal and form mixture into balls an inch or less in diameter.
• Place on pan, pressing to flatten slightly with hand (or tines of a fork).
• Bake 10 - 12 minutes. Serve hot.

May be frozen.

COLD DEVILED SHRIMP

🕐 *Serves 15 - 20*

1	pound cooked and cleaned medium or medium-large shrimp
1	lemon, thinly sliced
1	onion, thinly sliced
1	cup drained pitted black olives
2	tablespoons chopped pimiento
½	cup fresh lemon juice
¼	cup vegetable oil
1	clove garlic, minced
1	tablespoon dry mustard
¼	teaspoon ground pepper
1	teaspoon salt

- Add lemon, onion slices, olives and pimiento to shrimp.
- Toss with marinade of remaining ingredients.
- Cover and refrigerate at least 2 hours. Stir once or twice.
- Elegant when served in a glass bowl. (Offer toothpicks.)

May be served on lettuce as first course for 6 - 8 people.

Cooking Note: If using fresh shrimp, buy 2 pounds. Bring 1 quart water to boil. Add shrimp and cook 3 minutes. Shrimp will turn pink. Drain at once. Plunge into bowl of ice cubes.

MARINATED SHRIMP AND VEGETABLES

🕐 *Serves 20*

1	pound cooked and cleaned medium shrimp
1	cup fresh cauliflower florets
4	ounces small whole fresh mushrooms, cleaned, dry
1	cup sliced summer squash (yellow and/or green)
1	large red or green bell pepper, cut in squares
½	cup fresh lemon juice
1	tablespoon chopped green onion
1	teaspoon sugar
¾	teaspoon salt
½	teaspoon dill weed
5	drops of hot pepper sauce
¼	cup vegetable or olive oil

- Place shrimp and vegetables in shallow dish.
- Combine remaining ingredients.
- Pour over shrimp and vegetables. Cover and refrigerate at least 6 hours. Stir occasionally.

Guests will need small plates and forks.

PICKLED MUSHROOMS

🕐

½	cup vegetable or olive oil
⅔	cup tarragon vinegar
1	clove garlic, crushed
1	tablespoon sugar
1½	teaspoons salt
➤	dash of freshly ground black pepper
➤	dash of hot pepper sauce
1	medium onion, sliced in rings and separated
¾	pound fresh mushrooms, cleaned, dry

- Combine oil, vinegar and seasonings in large bowl or wide-mouthed jar.
- Add onion and mushrooms to marinade.
- Cover. Refrigerate 8 hours, stirring or shaking several times.
- Drain. Serve room temperature.

STUFFED CHERRY TOMATOES

Easy

30	cherry tomatoes
10	ounces mild soft goat cheese
½	cup (minimum) coarsely chopped fresh herbs: parsley, dill, cilantro, basil, oregano, chives, mint or a mixture
3-4	tablespoons liquid (cream, milk or olive oil)
➤	salt and freshly ground black pepper
➤	extra herbs for garnish

- Slice top off each tomato. Hollow with melon baller or grapefruit spoon.
- Combine cheese and herbs in food processor or with electric mixer.
- Thin with drops of liquid to workable consistency.
- Salt and pepper to taste.
- Stuff tomato shells using small spoon.
- Garnish with sprig of fresh herb.

CHEF'S NOTE

If cherry tomatoes are unavailable, cut small plum tomatoes in half to make little cups. These will hold more stuffing; plan accordingly. If time is unavailable, stuff tomatoes with anything from the deli that looks appealing, such as chicken or tuna salad, rice salad, tabbouleh, guacamole, herbed goat cheese or boursin, or try our Shrimp Spread (page 23).

Vegetable Garden Pizza

🕐

2	tube packages crescent rolls (dairy counter)
2	(8 ounce) packages whipped or light cream cheese
3	tablespoons mayonnaise or light sour cream
1	teaspoon dill weed
¼	teaspoon garlic powder
1	teaspoon seasoned salt or No-Salt Herb Seasoning (page 69)
2	cups cut-up fresh vegetables of choice:
	green onion
	red, green or yellow bell pepper
	zucchini
	carrot
	cucumber
	broccoli florets
	tomato
	green or black olives
2-3	tablespoons chopped fresh herbs (parsley, basil, chives or a mixture)

- Heat oven to 375°F.
- Roll out crescent rolls on ungreased 15x10x1-inch jelly-roll pan.
- Press dough to fill pan.
- Bake 11 minutes. Cool.
- Mix cream cheese, mayonnaise and seasonings. Thin if necessary with additional mayonnaise or sour cream to spreading consistency. Spread over cooled crust.
- Arrange chopped vegetables and herbs decoratively over cheese. Press down lightly.
- To serve, cut in 2 - 3-inch squares.

Prepare ahead. Wrap in plastic for later serving. Refrigerate.

Spiced Pecans

🕐

1½	cups firmly packed brown sugar
¼	cup sherry
2	tablespoons light corn syrup
1	teaspoon pumpkin pie spice
5	cups pecan halves
➤	granulated sugar

- In large saucepan, over low heat mix first 4 ingredients until sugar dissolves.
- Add nuts. Stir to coat.
- Remove from heat. Spread pecans on wax paper.
- Sprinkle with granulated sugar. Allow several hours to dry.
- Store in airtight container.

Wonderful hostess gift.

GLAZED PECANS

½	cup sugar
1	teaspoon instant coffee
2	tablespoons water
½	teaspoon ground allspice or cinnamon
⅛	teaspoon salt
3	cups perfect fresh pecan halves

- Put all but pecans in medium saucepan. Bring to boil.
- Add pecans and stir constantly 3 minutes.
- Spread on wax paper to cool and dry.
- Store in airtight container.

SUGARED PEANUTS

Easy

2	cups raw peanuts
1	cup sugar
½	cup water
➤	salt to taste

- Heat oven to 300°F and grease jelly-roll pan.
- Cook peanuts, sugar and water over medium heat. Stir.
- Mixture will crystallize and coat peanuts (about 10 minutes).
- Spread mixture in pan. Sprinkle with salt.
- Bake 15 minutes. Turn with spatula. Bake additional 15 minutes.
- Cool. Store in covered container.

CHEESE STRAWS

1	cup sifted all-purpose flour
½	teaspoon salt
¼	teaspoon dry mustard
½	teaspoon cayenne pepper (more if you like spicy food)
⅓	cup butter, melted
1	cup shredded sharp Cheddar cheese
1½	tablespoons ice water, or as needed
➤	celery or poppy or sesame seed

- In medium bowl, sift flour with salt, dry mustard and cayenne pepper.
- With pastry blender, cut in butter and cheese until mixture resembles coarse crumbs.
- Add water. Stir to blend. Shape into ball.
- Heat oven to 350°F.
- On lightly floured surface, roll out ¼-inch thick. Cut into strips about 3-inches long and ½-inch wide.
- Sprinkle with celery seed. Transfer to ungreased baking sheet.
- Bake 12 minutes or until crisp.

Salads

Salads

Salads

Frozen Salad

Molded Gelatin Salads

Dressings

Seasoning Mix

Epicurean

*S*alad—the word conveys many possibilities! Where once our availability of greens and vegetables was limited to the summer growing season, now we have access to the markets of the world the year round. Added to that abundance is our increased knowledge of nutrient values and our demand for variety and quality.

Salads range from lettuce and tomato to the most elaborate centerpieces of exotic greens, fruits and vegetables. One is as likely to encounter grilled meat, warm cheese and unusually shaped pastas here as in a main course. Indeed, many salads are the "main course" of lunch or supper.

Crisp leafy greens are basic to many salads, though they may serve primarily as a frame for more substantial ingredients. Cooked ingredients are usually preferred al dente; no one wants overcooked rice or pasta. Dressings are generally essential but again may range from a splash of fresh lemon juice to a blend of fragrant fresh herbs, delicate oil and tangy vinegar that tantalizes our taste buds, enhancing the meal and complementing the entrée.

In planning and preparing your menu we encourage you to choose contrasting colors, textures and flavors. Select greens and reds, and yellows too, that are fresh, crisp and flavorful. Wash them thoroughly but gently. Dry them well. Wrap in paper towels or a dish towel (or pillow case) and store in the refrigerator. Transfer to a plastic bag for storage of more than one day.

Attractive serving dishes enhance even the simplest effort. Try one of our chicken salads in a hollowed-out tomato cup. Garnish squares of Frozen Strawberry Salad with fresh strawberries and parsley or mint leaves; add an extra bit of crunch and texture with a sprinkle of crisp croutons, Chinese noodles or chopped nuts. Pine nuts, walnuts, hazelnuts, pecans and macadamias are a piquant and welcome addition to many salads.

Make a habit of combining familiar ingredients with new fruits and vegetables. Have fun! Salad is ideal for guilt-free indulgence and creativity!

MARINATED ASPARAGUS

🕐   ♥   *Serves 8*

2-2½	pounds fresh asparagus spears, trimmed, cut in 4-inch pieces
➤	13x9x2-inch pan of cold water and ice cubes
1	cup olive oil and vinegar salad dressing
➤	lettuce (shredded or whole leaves)
2	ounce jar chopped pimiento, drained
14	ounce can hearts of palm, drained, cut in rounds

- In large (5-quart) cooking pot bring to boil 8 or more cups water.
- Add asparagus and cook only 2 - 3 minutes, until just fork tender.
- Quickly drain asparagus. Put in ice water to stop cooking process. Let cool.
- Drain asparagus and place in shallow storage container.
- Pour salad dressing over asparagus to marinate.
- Cover and refrigerate 8 - 12 hours. Stir occasionally.
- To serve, arrange asparagus on lettuce on individual salad plates or large platter.
- Garnish with pimiento and hearts of palm.

Marinated Asparagus is also a wonderful appetizer.

BROCCOLI SALAD

Easy   *Serves 8 - 12*

Dressing:

1	cup mayonnaise
3	tablespoons cider vinegar
3	tablespoons sugar

Salad:

5-6	cups broccoli florets
½	pound bacon, cooked, crumbled
1	medium Bermuda or Vidalia onion, chopped
¾	cup seedless raisins
¾	cup pecan pieces (optional)
½	cup grated sharp Cheddar cheese

- Prepare dressing and set aside.
- Separate florets. Cut in bite-size pieces.
- Mix salad ingredients and toss with dressing.
- Chill at least 1 hour for best flavor.
- Top with cheese and serve.

Apple-Walnut Butter Lettuce Salad

Easy   *Serves 8*

2	tablespoons unsalted butter
2	cups walnut halves
2	heads butter lettuce, torn in bite-size pieces
2	Granny Smith apples, cored, sliced

- Sauté walnuts in butter over medium heat, stirring, for 5 minutes.
- Drain and cool on paper towels.
- Toss lettuce with just enough Raspberry Walnut Vinaigrette to lightly coat leaves.
- Divide lettuce onto 8 salad plates.
- Arrange apples on lettuce. Top with walnuts.

RASPBERRY WALNUT VINAIGRETTE

1½ cups

1	small red onion, peeled, coarsely chopped
1	clove garlic, peeled
1	tablespoon coarse grained mustard
1	teaspoon sugar
½	teaspoon freshly ground black pepper
¼	teaspoon salt
2	tablespoons raspberry vinegar
1	cup walnut oil

- Process onion and garlic in blender or food processor until almost puréed. Scrape sides.
- Add mustard, sugar, pepper, salt and raspberry vinegar. Blend.
- With blender on, add oil slowly until blended. Dressing is thick and creamy.

CABBAGE SALAD WITH AN EASTERN ACCENT

🕐   *Serves 4 - 8*

Dressing:

2	tablespoons sugar
3	tablespoons balsamic or red wine vinegar
½	cup canola or other vegetable oil
1	teaspoon freshly ground pepper
➤	seasoning packet from chicken-flavored ramen noodles
⅓	cup shelled sunflower seeds

Salad:

2	tablespoons sliced almonds
2	tablespoons sesame seed
½	head cabbage (red or green), chopped
1	package chicken flavor ramen noodles
2	green onions, finely chopped
➤	finely chopped red or green bell pepper or parsley for topping (optional)

- Prepare dressing day ahead and refrigerate.
- Toast almonds and sesame seed lightly and set aside.
- Several hours before serving stir cabbage and dressing together.
- Break up ramen noodles and mix in.
- When ready to serve, stir in almonds, sesame seed and onion. Toss.
- Use large spoons to transfer salad to decorative server and top with complementary topping if desired.
- *Variation:* This vegetarian salad may be quickly changed to a superb entrée with the addition of 2 cups cut-up cooked chicken.

Another cook's variation:
- Use 2 cooked whole chicken breasts, skinned, boned and carefully shredded.
- Substitute Chinese cabbage.
- Add 1½ tablespoons soy sauce.
- Substitute 3 tablespoons rice vinegar.
- Substitute 2 tablespoons sesame oil and ⅓ cup vegetable oil.

CHEF'S NOTE

Cabbage may be chopped 1 day ahead if tightly bagged and refrigerated so as not to dry and darken.

OLD FASHIONED SWEET-SOUR COLE SLAW

Serves 10 - 12

1½	pounds green cabbage, shredded
1	teaspoon salt
⅔	cup sugar
⅓	cup vinegar
1	cup heavy cream

- Place shredded cabbage in ice water in refrigerator 30 minutes. Drain.
- Mix remaining ingredients in order 30 minutes before serving. Pour over cabbage.
- Refrigerate until served.

JIMMY CARTER COLE SLAW

Serves 6 - 8

1	medium head green cabbage, cored, finely shredded
1	cup shredded carrot
1	cup finely chopped onion
3	cloves garlic, crushed
1	cup cider vinegar
2	tablespoons celery seed
1	tablespoon Worcestershire sauce
1	tablespoon Dijon mustard
1	tablespoon salt
¼	teaspoon ground white pepper
1	tablespoon sugar
1½	cups mayonnaise
2	tablespoons chopped fresh parsley

- Wash cabbage in cold water. Drain well and dry.
- In large bowl combine cabbage, carrot, onion and garlic.
- In small bowl combine vinegar, celery seed, Worcestershire sauce, mustard, salt, pepper and sugar. Pour over vegetables and mix well.
- Let stand 30 minutes with a plate pressing down vegetables in bowl to assist absorption of marinade.
- Drain excess marinade.
- Mix in mayonnaise a few tablespoons at a time until vegetables are evenly coated.
- Transfer to serving bowl. Sprinkle with chopped parsley.
- Refrigerate several hours. Serve cold.

HISTORY NOTE

Former President and Emory University Distinguished Professor Jimmy Carter has been a faculty member since 1982. His presence at the Carter Center of Emory University has brought many world leaders to Atlanta to focus on world affairs and human rights issues.

CHICKEN SALAD WITH RED GRAPES AND PECANS

Serves 6 - 8

4	whole chicken breasts, skinned, boned
14	ounce can chicken broth
1	cup chopped celery
1½	cups halved red seedless grapes
¾	cup chopped pecans
1¾	cups light mayonnaise
1	cup crumbled Roquefort or blue cheese
½	teaspoon salt
➤	freshly ground black pepper to taste

- Simmer chicken breasts in broth until done, about 15 - 20 minutes.
- Cut chicken in chunks.
- In large bowl combine chicken, celery, grapes and pecans.
- Stir in mayonnaise, cheese and seasonings.
- Serve on lettuce leaves or in ½ cantaloupe slightly hollowed. Prepare cantaloupe and wrap tightly in plastic for picnicking. Keep chicken mixture chilled.

Alternative cooking method for chicken: Place in jelly-roll pan and cover with foil. Bake 20 - 25 minutes at 350°F. Cool.

SUPER CHICKEN SALAD

A favorite for luncheons   Serves 8

2	cups shredded coconut
4	whole chicken breasts, cooked
2	cups chopped celery
1	cup pecans, toasted
1	teaspoon salt
2	cups drained pineapple tidbits
2	cups halved seedless grapes
1	cup mayonnaise
1	cup sour cream
➤	cantaloupe rings

- Toast 1 cup coconut.
- Remove skin and bones from chicken. Cut in small pieces.
- Toss together chicken, celery, pecans, salt, pineapple, grapes and remaining 1 cup coconut.
- Blend mayonnaise and sour cream. Stir into salad.
- Serve on cantaloupe rings. Sprinkle toasted coconut over top just before serving.
- *Variation*: Substitute cashews or walnuts; add 1 teaspoon curry powder, 2 - 3 tablespoons chutney and ¼ teaspoon grated fresh ginger.

This is good served with Marinated Asparagus (page 46) and biscuits.

CHEF'S NOTE

Toast coconut on baking sheet in 300°F oven 10 - 15 minutes or until lightly browned.

Nifty 50's Supper Dish

Hot Turkey Salad   *Serves 6*

½   cup slivered almonds
2   cups cooked and cubed turkey or chicken
2   cups sliced celery
1   cup mayonnaise (or ½ cup light mayonnaise and ½ cup plain low fat yogurt)
2   tablespoons lemon juice
2   teaspoons grated onion
½   teaspoon salt
½   cup grated mild Cheddar or American cheese
1   cup crushed potato chips

- Toast almonds lightly.
- Combine turkey, celery, mayonnaise, lemon juice, onion and salt. Toss.
- Put in shallow baking dish.
- Sprinkle with cheese, potato chips and almonds.
- Bake 10 - 12 minutes at 450°F.

Serve with tossed salad for easy family meal.

RICE AND ARTICHOKE SALAD WITH SHRIMP OR CHICKEN

Easy   *Serves 6 - 8*

6	ounce jar marinated artichoke hearts, drained (save liquid)
6	ounce package Chinese-style chicken-flavored rice vermicelli mix
1	green bell pepper, chopped
4	green onions, chopped
12	pimiento-stuffed green olives or black olives, sliced
1	pound fresh shrimp, cooked, peeled, cleaned or 1½ cups chopped cooked chicken
4	ounces fresh mushrooms, sliced
½	cup sliced almonds
1	cup finely chopped raw cauliflower or broccoli
➤	chopped hard-cooked egg for garnish

Dressing:

1	teaspoon curry powder
½	cup mayonnaise
➤	liquid reserved from artichoke hearts

- Halve artichoke hearts.
- Prepare rice mix according to package directions.
- Add other ingredients.
- Mix dressing. Add to salad and stir mixture well.

HISTORY NOTE

During the Civil War the buildings at Oxford were used as a hospital center by Confederate authorities for both Northern and Southern soldiers. Many died and were buried there.

MILLION DOLLAR MARINATED SALAD

🕐 *Serves 8 - 10*

Dressing:

1	cup vegetable oil
½	cup cider vinegar
3	cloves garlic, minced
1½	teaspoons thyme
2	teaspoons salt
½	teaspoon pepper
¾	cup chopped fresh parsley

• Mix dressing ingredients and set aside.

Salad:

½	pound fresh shrimp, cooked, peeled, cleaned
8	ounce can bamboo shoots, drained
8	ounce can artichoke hearts, drained, quartered
14	ounce can hearts of palm, drained, cut in rounds
8	ounces fresh mushrooms, sliced
1	pint cherry tomatoes, halved

• In large bowl combine salad ingredients.
• Pour dressing over salad and toss. Cover and marinate several hours in refrigerator.

Serve on individual beds of lettuce.

St. Louis Salad

🕐 *Serves 10*

14	ounce can artichoke hearts, drained, cut in half
14	ounce can hearts of palm, drained, cut in rounds
4	ounce jar diced pimiento, drained
⅓	cup sliced red onion
½	cup freshly grated Parmesan cheese
½	cup vegetable oil
⅓	cup red wine vinegar
➢	salt and freshly ground black pepper to taste
1	head romaine lettuce, torn in bite-size pieces
1	head iceberg lettuce, torn in bite-size pieces

- Combine all but lettuce.
- Marinate in refrigerator several hours.
- Toss with lettuce. Serve.

SOUTH OF THE BORDER SALAD

♥   *Easy*   *Serves 10*

Colorful on buffet table when served in glass bowl

1	jicama, peeled, cut in ½ x 4-inch sticks
➤	juice of 4 limes
1	red bell pepper, cut in strips
1	green bell pepper, cut in strips
1	mango, peeled, cut in strips
1	orange, peeled, cut in cross slices and then in half
½	small onion, finely chopped

- Put jicama and lime juice in self-sealing bag. Shake and set aside.
- Layer remaining ingredients in shallow serving bowl. Add jicama and juice.

Dressing:

¼-⅓	cup balsamic or red wine vinegar
½	teaspoon ground cumin
½	teaspoon chili powder
1	tablespoon sugar
1-2	tablespoons vegetable oil (optional)

- Mix dressing ingredients together until blended.
- Pour dressing over salad and gently mix.

  To make dressing separately, remember to add lime juice.

  May be prepared ahead, covered with plastic wrap and refrigerated. Add dressing just before serving.

VITAMIN A CARROT SALAD

♥   *Easy*   *Serves 12 - 14*

Nutritious and economical!

2	pounds carrots, peeled, grated
1	pound apples, peeled, grated
⅓	cup raisins
2	tablespoons lemon juice
1	teaspoon vanilla
⅓	cup firmly packed brown sugar
1½	cups orange juice

- Mix carrot, apple and remaining ingredients.
- Chill before serving.

  May prepare 2 - 3 days ahead. Keep refrigerated.

Manhattan Deli Salad

🕐 *Serves 12 - 16*

12	ounce package spiral pasta
1¼	cups sliced pitted ripe olives
1	cup chopped red or green bell pepper
¼	pound hard salami, cut in thin strips
¼-½	cup grated Parmesan cheese
¼	cup finely chopped fresh parsley
8	ounces Italian dressing
1	tablespoon drained capers (optional)
1	can garbanzo beans, drained (optional)

• Cook pasta according to package directions. Drain.
• In large bowl combine other ingredients.
• Add pasta and toss together.
• Serve room temperature or chilled.

Try using several colors of bell pepper — red, yellow, orange and green.

SMOKED SALMON SALAD

Easy   *Serves 4*

2	tablespoons fresh ginger, julienne cut
⅓	cup vegetable oil
2	tablespoons red wine vinegar
1	tablespoon lemon juice
4	teaspoons drained capers
4	cups loosely packed fresh spinach, cleaned
¼	pound smoked salmon
➢	salt and freshly ground pepper to taste

- Bring 2 cups water to boil; plunge in the ginger and boil 2 minutes. Drain and set aside.
- Combine oil, vinegar, lemon juice, capers, salt and pepper to make vinaigrette.
- Toss spinach with half of dressing. Divide among 4 plates.
- Arrange smoked salmon on the spinach.
- Sprinkle ginger over all and lightly moisten with remaining dressing.

Smoked trout may be substituted for salmon.

SPINACH PARTY PLATTER

♥   *Easy   Serves 6 - 8*

½	pound fresh spinach, cleaned
2	large yellow bell peppers, sliced in rings
2	large tomatoes, thinly sliced in rings
¼	cup chopped fresh green onion
1	cup finely chopped fresh basil leaves
½	cup chopped fresh parsley
3	ounces Gorgonzola cheese, crumbled
➢	Balsamic Vinegar Dressing (page 65) or Dijon Vinaigrette (page 67)

- Layer spinach leaves on serving platter, putting a few extra in center.
- Arrange pepper and tomato lengthwise. (Make 2 lines slightly overlapping, a line of yellow pepper and a line of tomato.)
- Sprinkle green onion, basil and parsley in center overlap area.
- Cover with plastic wrap.
- Just before serving sprinkle with cheese and then dressing.

A milder cheese such as blue or feta may be substituted.

Day Ahead Spinach Salad

🕐 *Serves 6*

½-¾	pound fresh spinach, cleaned, torn in bite-size pieces
½	medium cucumber, thinly sliced
½	cup thinly sliced radishes
¼	cup thinly sliced green onion
2	hard-cooked eggs, sliced
¾-1	cup thick blue-cheese dressing
5	slices bacon, crisply cooked, crumbled
½	cup salted Spanish peanuts (optional)

- Arrange spinach evenly in shallow salad bowl.
- Layer cucumber, radish, onion and egg in order.
- Spread dressing over top. Cover and chill overnight.
- Just before serving, sprinkle with bacon and peanuts.
- To serve, lift out portions with salad servers, being careful to pick up all layers.

Spinach Salad

🕐 *Serves 4*

1	pound fresh spinach, cleaned, torn in bite-size pieces
3	hard-cooked eggs, sliced
1½	cups fresh bean sprouts
8	slices bacon, crisply cooked, crumbled

Dressing:

⅓	cup ketchup
¼	cup vinegar
¾	cup sugar
1	tablespoon Worcestershire sauce
¾	cup vegetable oil
1	medium onion, chopped

- Toss together spinach, egg and bean sprouts. Cover and refrigerate.
- Mix dressing ingredients in blender. Set aside.
- Just before serving, add dressing and bacon to salad.

Low-Cal Red Skin Potato Salad

♥   *Easy   Serves 10*

6	medium-large red potatoes, scrubbed
½	cup low fat sour cream
½	cup low fat plain yogurt
¼	cup finely chopped chives or green onion
➢	salt and pepper to taste
½	cup chopped celery, olives or radishes (optional)

- Boil potatoes in skins until fork tender.
- Drain and shake pan briefly over medium heat to dry potatoes.
- Cut in ½-inch cubes. Cool.
- Combine other ingredients and add to potatoes.
- Refrigerate until ready to serve.

GERMAN POTATO SALAD

♥ 🕐 *Serves 6*

1½	pounds red potatoes
½	cup vegetable oil
½	cup cider vinegar
2	teaspoons sugar
½	teaspoon salt
½	teaspoon dry mustard
⅛	teaspoon pepper
4	slices bacon, crisply cooked, crumbled
2	tablespoons chopped chives or green onion

- Cook potatoes in boiling salted water 20 minutes or until tender.
- Drain, peel and slice ¼-inch thick.
- Combine oil, vinegar, sugar, salt, mustard and pepper. Add to warm potatoes. Toss lightly.
- Refrigerate several hours.
- Garnish with bacon and chives just before serving.

INDIAN RAYATA

Easy   *Serves 4 - 6*   *A yogurt "salad"*

2	cups plain yogurt
2	medium cucumbers or 3 - 4 baby dill cucumbers, peeled, grated (seeding optional)
½	teaspoon each sugar and salt
½	teaspoon freshly crushed mustard seed
½	teaspoon freshly crushed cumin seed

- Mix all ingredients.
- Recipe may be varied by adding or substituting other vegetables or fruits such as chopped onion, bell pepper, tomato, mango, grapes, pear or apple.

CHEF'S NOTE

Seeds are easily crushed using flat side of meat mallet.

FROZEN STRAWBERRY SALAD

🕐 *Serves 8 - 10*

Perfect for the Bridesmaids' Luncheon

8	ounces cream cheese, softened
¼	cup honey
8	ounces vanilla low fat yogurt
10	ounce package frozen sliced strawberries, partly thawed
8	ounce can crushed pineapple, undrained
1¼	cups thinly sliced ripe banana
½	cup halved seedless grapes

- Using electric mixer cream the cheese and honey; add yogurt.
- Scrape sides of bowl and mix until smooth. Add strawberries, pineapple and banana. Mix on medium speed. Stir in grapes.
- Turn into loaf pan. Cover with foil and freeze.
- To serve, slice with medium-sharp knife rinsed with hot water.
- Garnish each slice with fresh strawberries and green grapes.

This can also be a dessert.

EMORY'S COCA-COLA SALAD

🕐 *Serves 6 - 8*

3	ounce package lemon gelatin
1	cup boiling water
¾	cup Coca-Cola
¼	cup finely chopped celery
½	cup drained crushed pineapple
1	tablespoon chopped maraschino cherries
¼	cup chopped pecans
➤	endive and lemon slices for garnish

- Dissolve gelatin in boiling water. Add Coca-Cola.
- Refrigerate until set slightly.
- Add remaining ingredients, stirring gently.
- Pour into 1-quart mold or individual molds.
- Chill until firm.
- Serve on endive with lemon slice garnish.

CHEF'S NOTE

Individual salad molds should be rinsed with cold water before filling to ease unmolding.

SOUR CHERRY SALAD

🕐 *Serves 10 - 12*

1	**orange**
1	**lemon**
20	**ounce can pitted tart red cherries, drained (save juice)**
8	**ounce can crushed pineapple, drained (save juice)**
¾	**cup sugar**
3	**ounce package cherry gelatin**
1	**teaspoon plain gelatin**
1	**cup chopped pecans**

- Remove and discard stems and seeds from orange and lemon. Finely chop orange and lemon, including skins.
- In medium saucepan, combine cherry juice, pineapple juice and sugar. Bring to boil.
- Dissolve cherry gelatin and plain gelatin in this mixture.
- Add orange and lemon to gelatin. Cook until mixture thickens slightly. Remove from heat.
- Add cherries, pineapple and nuts. Pour into 2-quart mold.
- Chill until set.

CRANBERRY SALAD

🕐 *Traditional with turkey*   *Serves 8 - 10*

12	ounce package cranberries (about 3½ cups)
1	cup water
1½	cups sugar
2	teaspoons plain gelatin
2	tablespoons cold water
3	ounce package lemon gelatin
1	cup boiling water
1	cup chopped pecans
1	cup chopped celery
➤	pinch of salt
1	tablespoon lemon juice
➤	mayonnaise for garnish (optional)

- Cook cranberries in 1 cup water 15 minutes over medium heat.
- Add sugar and cook 15 minutes longer. Let cool.
- Soak plain gelatin in 2 tablespoons cold water to dissolve.
- Dissolve lemon gelatin in boiling water. Add plain gelatin and let cool.
- Combine cranberries, gelatin, pecans, celery, salt and lemon juice. Chill in lightly oiled 2-quart ring mold until firm.
- Unmold and top with mayonnaise if desired.

STRAWBERRY SURPRISE

🕐 *Serves 12*

1¾	cups crushed pretzels
3	tablespoons sugar
½	cup (1 stick) margarine, melted
8	ounce package light cream cheese, softened
8	ounce package light frozen whipped topping, softened
½	cup sugar
6	ounce package strawberry gelatin
2	cups boiling water
16	ounce package frozen sliced strawberries

- Mix pretzels, 3 tablespoons sugar and margarine and press into bottom of 13x9x2-inch dish.
- Bake 10 minutes at 350°F. Allow to cool.
- Mix cream cheese, whipped topping and ½ cup sugar. Spread gently on cooled crust. Refrigerate.
- Dissolve gelatin in boiling water. Add frozen strawberries and stir until thawed.
- Refrigerate until nearly set.
- Pour gently over cream cheese layer. Cover with plastic wrap and refrigerate until set before serving.

MOLDED ASPARAGUS SALAD

🕐 *Serves 10*

¾	cup sugar
1	cup water, divided
½	cup white vinegar
2	envelopes plain gelatin
2	tablespoons lemon juice
2	tablespoons grated onion
½	cup chopped celery
1	cup chopped pecans
½-¾	cup chopped pimiento-stuffed olives
2	(10 ounce) cans asparagus tips, drained
➢	lettuce for garnish

- Mix sugar, ½ cup water and vinegar in 2-quart saucepan.
- Bring to boil, dissolving sugar.
- Dissolve gelatin in ½ cup water. Add to vinegar mixture. Cool slightly.
- Add lemon juice, onion, celery, pecans and olives. Stir.
- Add asparagus tips and mix gently.
- Transfer to 2 - 3-inch high 2-quart casserole. Refrigerate overnight to set.
- Cut in squares. Serve on lettuce leaf.

Easy Tomato Aspic

🕐 *Serves 6*

1¾	cups vegetable juice
3	ounce package lemon gelatin
¼	cup white vinegar
➢	options:

        dash of hot pepper sauce
        avocado
        chopped onion
        chopped celery
        olives
        shrimp

- Heat 1 cup vegetable juice to boiling.
- Add boiling juice to gelatin. Stir until dissolved.
- Add remaining ¾ cup vegetable juice and vinegar. Stir.
- Chill until partially set.
- Gently stir in any optional ingredients.
- Pour mixture into 3 - 4-cup mold. Refrigerate until set before serving.

Recipe can easily be doubled.

Balsamic Vinegar Dressing

Easy   2 cups

½	cup balsamic vinegar
1	tablespoon sugar
1	teaspoon each chopped fresh basil, thyme and oregano
½	teaspoon salt, or to taste
½	teaspoon freshly ground pepper, or to taste
¼	teaspoon dried mustard
1	cup garlic olive oil

- Mix all ingredients except olive oil.
- Allow to sit 15 minutes to absorb flavors before adding oil.
- Refrigerate if not used within 1 day.

This is wonderful with fresh fruit and greens.

Chef's Note

Garlic olive oil is easily made by adding 2 cloves garlic, peeled and sliced, to 1 cup olive oil. Store in covered glass jar in refrigerator. Replenish garlic and oil as used.

CAESAR SALAD DRESSING

★   *Easy*   *Serves 6 - 8*

⅓	cup olive oil
2	tablespoons wine vinegar
2	shakes of Worcestershire sauce
2	shakes of hot pepper sauce
1	tablespoon grated Parmesan cheese
2	tablespoons lemon juice
1	egg
2	cloves garlic
1	can anchovies, drained (optional)

• Mix all ingredients in food processor or blender.
• Toss with romaine lettuce and croutons for salad.

Super easy and delicious!

DIJON SALAD DRESSING

♥   *Easy*   *Serves 6 - 8*

½	cup cider vinegar, tarragon or other herbal vinegar
➤	juice of 1 lemon
1	tablespoon Dijon mustard
1	tablespoon sugar
½	teaspoon salt
1	teaspoon No-Salt Herb Seasoning (page 69) or Italian seasoning mixture
½	cup olive oil

• In medium bowl whisk together vinegar, lemon juice, mustard, sugar, salt and herb seasoning.
• Allow to sit briefly before adding olive oil.
• Dressing is ready to use; flavor improves if made a day in advance.

Dijon Vinaigrette

Easy   *Serves 6 - 8*

4	tablespoons Dijon mustard
3	tablespoons red wine vinegar
1	tablespoon white wine vinegar
¼	teaspoon salt
1-2	cloves garlic
½	teaspoon dried basil
⅛	teaspoon black pepper
2	drops of hot pepper sauce
1	tablespoon grated onion
¾	cup safflower or olive oil

- Combine mustard and vinegar in blender.
- Add salt, garlic, basil, pepper, hot pepper sauce and onion.
- Blend 10 seconds.
- With machine running, add oil slowly.
- Pour into container. Keep in refrigerator.

History Note

Atticus Green Haygood (president 1875-1884) delivered a Thanksgiving sermon in 1880 from which he was quoted widely. He declared that slavery was an evil thing and that with its abolition the South faced a brighter future. He later devoted years to the John F. Slater Fund for Negro education.

POPPY SEED DRESSING

Easy   *Serves 12 - 14*

⅓	**cup sugar**
1	**teaspoon salt**
1	**teaspoon dry mustard**
⅓	**cup red wine vinegar**
2	**teaspoons bottled onion juice**
1	**cup olive oil**
1½	**tablespoons poppy seed**

- Dissolve sugar, salt and mustard in vinegar.
- Add onion juice and oil.
- Combine in blender.
- Add poppy seed. Blend.
- Refrigerate.

ZESTY DRESSING

Easy   *Serves 6*

¼	**cup sugar**
¼	**cup red wine vinegar**
1	**large clove garlic, crushed**
½	**teaspoon dry mustard**
¼	**teaspoon salt**
¼	**teaspoon Worcestershire sauce**
⅓	**cup vegetable oil**

- Put all ingredients except oil into blender.
- Start blender on next to highest speed. Remove top and slowly add oil.
- Blend 15 - 30 seconds.
- Chill until ready to serve.

No-Salt Herb Seasoning

♥   *Easy*

1	teaspoon dried basil
½	teaspoon ground black pepper
½	teaspoon cayenne pepper
1	teaspoon garlic powder
1	teaspoon mace
1	teaspoon dried marjoram
1	teaspoon onion powder
1	teaspoon dried oregano
1	teaspoon dried parsley
1	teaspoon rubbed sage
1	teaspoon dried savory
1	teaspoon dried thyme

- Combine seasonings in small bowl.
- Makes about ⅓ cup of healthful no-salt seasoning.
- Store unused portion in airtight container.
- Use in casseroles, stews, fresh vegetable dishes or salad dressings.

A great gift idea (with contents listed).

EPICUREAN WINTER BUFFET FOR 36

GREEK SALAD

Serves 36

6	large heads lettuce (romaine and Bibb), cleaned, torn
➤	Potato Salad (recipe below)
6	tomatoes, each cut in 6 wedges
4	cucumbers, peeled, cut lengthwise in 8 fingers
4	avocados, peeled, cut in wedges
2	pounds feta cheese, crumbled
4	green bell peppers, each cut in 8 rings
36	slices canned cooked beets
36	anchovy fillets
36	fresh shrimp, cooked, peeled, cleaned
36	black olives (Greek style preferred)
36	radishes, fancy cut
36	whole green onions, cleaned, trimmed
1	cup white vinegar
1	cup olive oil

- Line serving platter with lettuce, gently mixing the two varieties.
- Place potato salad in center of platter.
- Place tomato wedges around edge of salad and cucumber fingers between tomatoes, making a solid base for salad.
- Place avocado slices around the outside.
- Sprinkle feta cheese and green pepper slices over top of salad.
- Top with sliced beets.
- Place a shrimp on top of each beet and an anchovy fillet on each shrimp.
- Arrange olives, radishes and green onions as desired.
- Just before serving, sprinkle entire salad with vinegar and then olive oil.

POTATO SALAD

10	pounds small red potatoes
1½	cups chopped green onion
¾	cup white vinegar
4	cups mayonnaise
1	teaspoon salt
½	teaspoon white pepper

- Boil potatoes until barely cooked. Drain and cool.
- Slice in ¼-inch slices. Sprinkle with onion.
- Mix vinegar, mayonnaise, salt and pepper. Stir gently with potatoes and onion.
- Refrigerate until ready to combine with Greek Salad greens.

EPICUREAN SPRING COOKOUT FOR 30

WILD RICE SALAD

Serves 30

1½	pounds uncooked brown rice
¾	pound uncooked wild rice
1	cup diced yellow squash
1	cup diced red bell pepper
1	cup chopped fresh parsley
¾	cup chopped green onion
½	pound fresh mushrooms, sliced

- Cook all rice according to package directions. Cool.
- Mix rice and vegetables. Refrigerate.
- Before serving toss with Herb Vinaigrette.

HERB VINAIGRETTE

1	cup (2 ounces) fresh basil
1	tablespoon sugar
2	large cloves garlic
½	cup (2 ounces) chopped onion
1	teaspoon salt
½	teaspoon white pepper
1½	cups white cider vinegar
3	cups vegetable oil

- Process all but oil and vinegar in food processor or blender.
- Add vinegar. Process.
- Add oil in slow steady stream while processing.

This vinaigrette is called for with several Epicurean recipes.

Soups

HOT

84 1-2-3 Asparagus Leek Soup
89 Apple-Acorn Squash Soup
79 Bay Scallop Chowder
78 Black Bean Soup
79 Broccoli Bisque
94 Brunswick Stew
84 Carrot Soup
88 Cream of Peanut Soup
76 Curried Pea Soup
91 French Market Bean Soup à la New Orleans
83 French Onion Soup with Cheese
85 Grandmother's Chicken Soup
77 Gumbo from the Gulf
82 Hearty Lentil Soup
87 Italian Sausage Soup
86 Lemon Chicken Soup
90 Mexican Corn and Cilantro Soup
80 Minnesota Wild Rice Soup
86 Peasant Soup
82 Ramen Noodle Microwave
92 Tortilla Soup
89 Vegetable Beef Barley Soup
80 Vegetable Cream Soup
81 Vegetarian Split Pea Soup
81 Yellow Split Pea Soup
93 Zucchini Vegetable Soup

COLD

96 Georgia Peach Soup
95 Spanish Gazpacho
95 Strawberry Soup

HOT OR COLD

98 Norwegian Fruit Soup (Sotsuppe)
97 Red Pepper Soup
97 Zucchini Soup

EPICUREAN

99 Chilled Cucumber Vichyssoise
99 Yellow Squash Bisque

*T*here is great satisfaction in preparing a pot of soup. Soup is soothing and sustaining; soup is nourishing and filling; soup warms you when you're cold, cools and refreshes when you're hot. Soup is for every palate and every table. A soup can be made from the most ordinary and least expensive of ingredients and yet may be the perfect mood setter for an elegant dinner.

Few soup recipes require split-second timing or indeed much attention at all. Most soups, except those with egg yolk, freeze beautifully, so soup is the ideal way to capture the flavors of summer fruits and vegetables at their peak, to cope with the excess of zucchini or peppers from your own or a neighbor's garden or to get a head start on a party or a family celebration.

In this chapter we give you a selection of our favorite soups. You will find many classics of the Southern kitchen, including hearty "meal in a bowl" favorites like Seafood Gumbo and New Orleans Bean soup and our own Georgia Cream of Peanut Soup. Our Brunswick Stew hails from Macon, Georgia, courtesy of Emory President James T. Laney.

There are a few notable omissions in these recipes: flour thickenings and egg yolk and cream enrichments rarely appear. Instead these soups rely on legumes, grains and puréed vegetables for body and substance. The result is that they are both more flavorful and more healthful than their predecessors.

We offer this idea for a neighbor get-acquainted party: begin with an invitation for Stone Soup. The host/hostess has meat or bone simmering when each neighbor brings a vegetable to contribute to the pot. While many hands prepare the soup and contribute to it as it simmers, a spirit of fellowship and conviviality builds along with the rising aroma. Supply an array of bowls and mugs, crusty breads and a variety of drinks. This would be a great time for a jug of Georgia's fresh apple juice! Enjoy!

CURRIED PEA SOUP

♥   *Serves 8 - 10*

3	tablespoons butter or margarine
2	cloves garlic, minced
2	onions, chopped
2	stalks celery, chopped
2	medium potatoes, chopped
1	carrot, chopped
2½	cups fresh shelled peas or frozen peas
¼	teaspoon sugar
2	teaspoons curry powder
3-4	cups chicken broth
2	cups half and half or milk
➣	salt and pepper to taste

- In medium saucepan sauté garlic, onion, celery, potato and carrot in butter until tender.
- Add peas, sugar, curry and 2 cups chicken broth.
- Cover and simmer 15 - 20 minutes until vegetables are very tender.
- Purée.
- Pour back into cooking pan. Add remaining chicken broth and enough milk for desired consistency.
- Heat gently on low heat. Do not allow to boil.
- Salt and pepper.
- Serve hot or cold.

Soup is best if prepared a day ahead, allowing the flavor to develop.

CHEF'S NOTE

Curry powder strength can vary greatly. Test several brands.

GUMBO FROM THE GULF

🕐   *Serves 6 - 8*

⅓	cup vegetable oil
6	tablespoons flour
2	onions, finely chopped
1½	cups finely chopped celery
¼	cup chopped fresh parsley
1	green bell pepper, chopped
4	or more large cloves garlic, minced
➤	bay leaf
28	ounce can tomatoes, undrained
6	cups turkey, chicken or ham stock with any meat from bones
10	ounce package frozen okra, thawed, chopped
2	pounds andouille sausage or shrimp or crab
1	pint oysters
3	tablespoons Worcestershire sauce
1	teaspoon hot pepper sauce
3	teaspoons salt
➤	gumbo-filé powder (optional)

- Roux: Heat oil in heavy cooking pot. Stir flour into oil until smooth. Cook slowly, about 20 minutes, until browned. This will take careful watching and stirring.
- Stir in onion, celery, parsley, pepper and garlic. Brown gently.
- Add bay leaf, tomatoes and stock. Simmer 1 hour or more.
- Add okra and preferred ingredients:
  - Brown andouille sausage and cut in chunks before adding.
  - Crab and oysters need a short cooking time. Stir into pot about 15 minutes before serving.
  - Shrimp should first be boiled or steamed with desired seasoning and then added to cooked gumbo about 5 minutes before serving.
- Add Worcestershire and hot pepper sauce. Salt and pepper to taste.
- Stir well and serve on steamed rice. Platter of rice surrounded with chopped parsley is very attractive.
- ½ teaspoon gumbo-filé powder per bowl may be used at serving time to thicken if needed.

CHEF'S NOTE

For shrimp stock simmer fresh shrimp shells in water to cover — easy, fast and a flavorful substitute for meat stock.

BLACK BEAN SOUP

Easy   *Serves 4 - 6*

2	**(15 ounce) cans black beans, undrained or ½ pound dried beans, prepared according to directions**
1	**cup water**
½	**cup chopped celery**
½	**cup chopped onion**
1	**clove garlic, minced**
½	**teaspoon dry mustard**
¼	**teaspoon ground cumin**
1	**teaspoon olive oil**
1	**beef flavored bouillon cube**
¼	**teaspoon ground pepper**
¼	**cup dry white wine (optional)**
➢	**garnishes:**

> **lemon or lime slices**
> **fresh parsley or cilantro**
> **chopped egg white or onion**
> **sour cream or yogurt**

- Combine everything but wine in medium pan. Simmer 20 minutes.
- Purée half to all of mixture in blender according to taste.
- Return to pan. Add wine and warm gently.
- Serve with your favorite hot pepper sauce!

Black bean soup varies within the different Spanish-speaking cultures, each one individual and interesting!

BROCCOLI BISQUE

♥   *Easy   Serves 6 - 8*

1½	pounds fresh broccoli, trimmed, chopped or 2 (10 ounce) packages frozen chopped broccoli
3½	cups chicken broth
½	cup white wine
1	medium onion, quartered
2	tablespoons butter or margarine
1	teaspoon salt
2	teaspoons curry powder
➢	dash of pepper
2	tablespoons lime juice
➢	light cream or milk (optional)
➢	sour cream and chives for garnish

- Combine broccoli, broth, wine, onion, butter, salt, curry and pepper in large cooking pot.
- Bring to boil. Reduce heat and simmer, covered, about 10 minutes until tender.
- Purée in blender.
- Stir in lime juice.
- If desired, thin with light cream.
- Garnish with sour cream and chives.
- Serve hot or cold.

BAY SCALLOP CHOWDER

♥   *Serves 6*

3	medium potatoes, peeled, chopped
2	large carrots, sliced
2	large stalks celery, chopped
1	medium onion, chopped
3	cups chicken broth
1	bay leaf
¼	teaspoon ground pepper
1	cup half and half or milk
1	egg yolk
2	tablespoons chopped fresh parsley
➢	dash of paprika
1½	tablespoons butter or margarine
1	pound fresh mushrooms, thinly sliced
½	cup white wine
1	pound fresh bay scallops

- Cook potato, carrot, celery, onion, chicken broth, bay leaf and pepper until vegetables are tender. Remove bay leaf. Purée vegetables in blender. Return to cooking pot.
- Mix egg yolk with half and half in small bowl. Add parsley and paprika.
- In separate pan, sauté mushrooms in butter 1 minute. Add wine and scallops, stirring frequently 1 minute more.
- Whisk egg yolk mixture into vegetables.
- Add scallop mixture. Heat very gently about 10 minutes and serve. Do not allow to boil.
- *Variation*: Clam juice may be substituted for chicken broth.

MINNESOTA WILD RICE SOUP

Serves 10 - 12

2	cups cooked wild rice (about ½ cup uncooked)
1	large Bermuda onion, chopped
1	cup sliced fresh mushrooms
½	cup butter or margarine
1	cup flour
8	cups hot chicken broth
➢	salt and pepper to taste
1	cup light cream or half and half
¼	cup sherry or dry white wine

- Prepare wild rice as directed.
- Sauté onion and mushrooms in butter about 3 minutes.
- Sprinkle flour over vegetables, stirring until mixed. Do not brown.
- Slowly add broth, stirring constantly until blended.
- Add rice. Season to taste. (May be refrigerated at this point for 2 - 3 days.)
- Heat thoroughly. Stir in cream. Add sherry. (Don't skimp!)

Heat gently. Do not allow to boil.

VEGETABLE CREAM SOUP

♥   *Easy*   *Serves 4 - 6*

A soothing supper soup with fresh taste!

¼	cup butter or margarine
1	cup finely chopped carrot
½	cup finely chopped celery
¼	cup finely chopped green onion
1	clove garlic, minced
4	ounces fresh mushrooms, sliced or chopped
1	cup cooked, chopped broccoli
¼	cup flour
4	chicken bouillon cubes
3½	cups hot water
1	cup milk

- Melt butter in 3-quart pot.
- Sauté carrot, celery, green onion and garlic until tender.
- Add mushrooms and broccoli. Stir well.
- Reduce heat and blend in flour.
- Stir 5 minutes to prevent scorching.
- Dissolve bouillon cubes in hot water.
- Whisk while adding broth gradually to flour mixture.
- Simmer 15 minutes. Add milk. Stir well and serve.

Other vegetables may be substituted for the mushrooms and broccoli.

May be prepared in advance. Reheat, covered, over low heat 10 minutes.

VEGETARIAN SPLIT PEA SOUP

♥   *Serves 8 - 12*   *Hearty, nutritious and inexpensive!*

16	ounce package dried green split peas
2	quarts water
1	teaspoon salt
1	teaspoon thyme
2-3	cloves garlic, minced
1	cup chopped onion
1-2	bay leaves
1½	cups diced potato
1½	cups chopped carrot
1	cup chopped celery
2	tablespoons dried parsley
2	tablespoons lemon juice
¼	cup dry white wine

- Wash and prepare peas according to package directions.
- Simmer in large, heavy pot with water, salt, thyme, garlic, onion and bay leaves 1 hour.
- Add remaining ingredients. Cook until tender.
- Remove bay leaves. Purée if desired.

Ham bone or ham hock may be added.

YELLOW SPLIT PEA SOUP

♥   *Serves 6 - 8*

2	tablespoons peanut or other vegetable oil
1	tablespoon curry powder
1	cup finely chopped onion
1	cup finely chopped carrot
1	cup finely chopped celery
2	quarts water
16	ounce package dried yellow split peas
1	teaspoon liquid smoke
½	teaspoon salt (optional)
¾	teaspoon pepper
1	medium potato, peeled, chopped
¼	cup chopped fresh cilantro for garnish

- In large pot, cook curry in oil 1 minute.
- Stir in onion, carrot and celery. Cover and cook 5 minutes.
- Add water, peas, liquid smoke, salt and pepper. Reduce heat and simmer partially covered until peas are tender, about 1 hour.
- Transfer 3 cups of mixture to blender or food processor and purée.
- Return purée to soup and add potato. Cook 30 minutes on low.
- Garnish with chopped cilantro.

Ramen Noodle Microwave

Easy   20 Minute Chinese Soup   Serves 1 - 2

3	ounce package Ramen noodle soup (shrimp or chicken)
1	chicken bouillon cube
2	cups boiling water
➤	options:
	½ cup sliced fresh mushrooms
	2-4 green onions, chopped
	snowpeas
	zucchini
	broccoli
	bean sprouts
2	tablespoons soy sauce
➤	seasoning to taste

- Mix soup seasoning packet, bouillon cube and boiling water in deep 4-cup microwave safe container.
- Crush noodles and add along with your choice of vegetables and seasoning.
- Cover loosely with plastic wrap.
- Microwave at HIGH 3 minutes. Add seasoning if desired.

Hearty Lentil Soup

♥   *Serves 8*

1	pound dried lentils
2	(14 ounce) cans chicken broth
4	cups water
1	large onion, thinly sliced
5	medium to large carrots, chopped
5	stalks celery, chopped
➤	juice of 3 lemons
2	teaspoons dried dill weed
➤	salt and pepper to taste
➤	sour cream, grated cheese and scallions for garnish

- Put all ingredients in large pot. Simmer (low heat) until lentils are soft and mixture has thickened, about 2 hours. Stir occasionally.
- If mixture seems too thick, add water.
- Garnish with sour cream, grated cheese and scallions if desired.

This is good as a main course with crusty peasant-style bread.

FRENCH ONION SOUP WITH CHEESE

Serves 6

6	medium onions, thinly sliced
6	tablespoons butter or margarine
2	teaspoons sugar
1	teaspoon salt
➤	dash of ground nutmeg
7	cups strong beef broth
¼	cup sherry, port or dry red wine
6	thick pieces French bread, dried in oven (bake at low oven heat 15 minutes)
➤	grated Swiss cheese (about ½ cup)
➤	grated Parmesan cheese (about ½ cup)

- Sauté onion in butter until soft.
- Add sugar, salt and nutmeg. Toss well.
- Cook down slightly until onions are golden brown.
- Add hot broth and bring to boil.
- Reduce heat. Simmer 10 minutes.
- Add wine and adjust seasoning.
- Ladle soup into 6 small ovenproof casseroles or bowls. Top each with a piece of French bread.
- Spoon grated cheese on top of each.
- Cook in slow oven (300°F) 10 minutes, or until cheese is melted and bubbly.
- Serve with additional cheese if desired.

CARROT SOUP

Easy   *Serves 6 - 8*

3	tablespoons butter or margarine
1	pound carrots, chopped
1	small onion, chopped
1	medium potato, peeled, chopped
½	teaspoon salt
¼	teaspoon pepper
½	teaspoon sugar
3	cups beef broth or 2 (14 ounce) cans
➤	chopped fresh parsley or chervil for garnish

- Melt butter in large saucepan. Add vegetables and seasoning. Cover and cook over low heat 15 minutes.
- Add broth and simmer additional 15 minutes.
- Purée in blender or food processor.
- Serve garnished with chopped parsley or chervil.

1-2-3 ASPARAGUS LEEK SOUP

♥   *Easy   Serves 2 - 4*

1	boxed envelope dried leek soup
1	cup cold water
10	ounce package frozen asparagus
¼	teaspoon pepper
3	cups milk (skim is fine)
➤	sour cream or plain yogurt for garnish

- In medium saucepan, combine soup mix with water. Set aside.
- Cook asparagus in microwave or on stove top.
- Purée asparagus in blender until smooth. Transfer to soup mixture.
- Cook on low, stirring frequently, about 10 minutes.
- Add milk and pepper. Simmer gently 2 - 3 minutes.
- Top each serving with dollop of sour cream or yogurt.

GRANDMOTHER'S CHICKEN SOUP

🕐 ♥ *Serves 6 - 10*

1	whole chicken
2	onions
2	large stalks celery with leaves
2	carrots
2	large stems parsley
2	quarts water
1	teaspoon salt
1	teaspoon freshly ground pepper
➤	pasta noodles or rice
1	cup sliced fresh mushrooms
➤	chopped fresh parsley for garnish

- Cook chicken and vegetables in large heavy pot (5 quart) with water to almost cover. Salt and pepper.
- Bring to boil over medium heat. Reduce heat. Simmer 1 hour until chicken is tender. Turn off heat.
- Remove chicken from pot. Strain liquid and refrigerate. Several hours later remove excess fat from stock. Stock is now ready to use.
- Discard chicken skin and bones, onion and celery. Reserve meat for other use. For a hearty chicken soup, part of chicken meat may be cut up and added along with carrots.
- Return stock to a boil for clear broth. Add noodles or rice, mushrooms and a shake of salt and pepper and soup will be ready in just a few minutes.
- If soup lacks strength, an additional chicken bouillon cube or two will work magic.

Add a parsnip and a turnip for additional nutrients and flavor.

CHEF'S NOTE

A large whole fryer chicken is about 2½ pounds. Some cooks may prefer the stronger, heartier taste of a stewing hen, which is larger.

LEMON CHICKEN SOUP

Easy *Serves 4 - 6*

4	(14 ounce) cans chicken broth
1	small onion, chopped
½	cup uncooked rice
2	egg yolks, beaten
¼	cup lemon juice
1	cup half and half or whole milk
2	tablespoons grated lemon peel
1	tablespoon grated Parmesan cheese

- Heat broth with onion and rice until boiling. Cover. Reduce heat and simmer 15 minutes. Rice should be tender. Remove from heat.
- Combine egg yolks and lemon juice. Mix well.
- Pour 1 cup broth into egg mixture. Whisk and add to remaining hot mixture. Add half and half.
- Serve at once, topped with lemon peel and Parmesan cheese.

PEASANT SOUP

Serves 8 - 10

6	large potatoes, peeled, chopped
4	stalks celery, chopped
2	bunches leeks, cleaned, chopped
2	large onions, chopped
2	carrots, chopped
2	teaspoons salt
1	teaspoon pepper
½	pound frozen butter
5	ounces (½ box) frozen chopped spinach

- Put potato, celery, leek, onion and carrot in cooking pot. Cover with water. Add salt and pepper. Bring to a boil.
- Add frozen butter. Cook covered until vegetables are soft.
- Add spinach and simmer additional 15 minutes. Purée soup.
- *Variation:* To reduce fat, chicken bouillon granules or cubes may be substituted for part of butter.

This is best if made 1 day ahead. It is very hearty and can be a dinner with crusty bread.

ITALIAN SAUSAGE SOUP

Serves 6 - 10

1½   pounds mild Italian sausage, cut in ½-inch rounds
2   cloves garlic, minced
2   large onions, chopped
28   ounce can Italian-style tomatoes, undrained
3   (14 ounce) cans beef broth
1½   cups dry red wine or water
½   teaspoon dried basil
3   tablespoons chopped fresh parsley
1   medium green bell pepper, chopped (optional)
2   medium zucchini, thinly sliced
2   cups uncooked pasta such as bow-ties, shells or ziti for a hearty soup
➤   grated Parmesan cheese

- In 5-quart pot, cook sausage over medium heat until lightly browned. Drain.
- Add garlic and onion. Sauté lightly.
- Stir in tomatoes, crushing with spoon.
- Add broth, wine and basil. Simmer 45 minutes or more.
- About 20 minutes before serving add parsley, green pepper, zucchini and pasta. Cook until tender.
- Sprinkle Parmesan cheese on soup to serve.

CREAM OF PEANUT SOUP

Easy   Serves 6 - 10

¼   cup vegetable oil
1   cup thinly sliced celery
1   medium onion, finely chopped
2   tablespoons all-purpose flour
8   cups chicken broth (fresh or canned)
1¼   cups creamy style peanut butter
1½   cups half and half
½   teaspoon white pepper
½   cup finely chopped fresh parsley
➢   coarsely ground peanuts for garnish

- In large heavy pot, sauté celery and onion in oil until tender.
- Stir in flour. Blend.
- Add broth. Stir and simmer 15 - 20 minutes.
- Using a whisk, stir in peanut butter. Mix well.
- Add half and half, pepper and parsley. Soup is ready to serve.
- Peanuts may be added to individual bowls.

This Southern recipe is adapted from an earlier Emory Woman's Club cookbook.

Serve in demitasse cups as an appetizer on a cold evening. This is guaranteed to start conversation while people move around getting acquainted.

HISTORY NOTE

A printed pamphlet of President Haygood's Thanksgiving sermon attracted the attention of New York banker, Methodist and philanthropist George I. Seney, who visited Emory College and donated $130,000.

Vegetable Beef Barley Soup

♥ *Serves 6 - 8*

4	cups beef broth (fresh, canned or bouillon cubes and water)
1	cup pearl barley and water to cook
4	ounces fresh mushrooms
2	carrots
1	large onion
2-3	stalks celery
½	cup chopped fresh parsley
2	bay leaves
½	teaspoon freshly ground pepper
1	teaspoon seasoning salt or No-Salt Herb Seasoning (page 69)

- Beef broth should be prepared ahead to remove fat and bones.
- Wash barley and cook over medium heat with 6 cups of water (see note).
- Chop vegetables and add to barley as it cooks.
- Add seasoning and broth. Simmer at least 1 hour longer.
- If desired adjust strength and seasoning with additional bouillon cubes and water.
- Beef stew meat can be used for a heartier soup.

The type of barley used will determine length of cooking time and amount of liquid needed. Using quick barley will shorten time.

Apple-Acorn Squash Soup

Wonderful aroma!   *Serves 6 - 8*

1	medium or 2 small acorn squash
3-4	carrots, chopped
2-3	parsnips, chopped
1	cup chopped yellow onion
4-5	cups apple juice or cider
1	teaspoon white pepper
2-3	chicken bouillon cubes
1	teaspoon grated fresh ginger (optional)
½	teaspoon ground nutmeg (optional)

- Halve acorn squash. Place (cut side down) in 2 inches of water in baking pan. Bake 1 hour at 350°F. Remove seeds and skin.
- While squash is cooking simmer carrot, parsnip and onion until tender.
- Purée vegetables with squash. Retain cooking water to use as needed in puréeing.
- Transfer vegetables to cooking pot. Add remaining ingredients.
- Simmer gently about 30 minutes. For thinner consistency add more apple juice.

This is lovely served in cups or mugs.

Mexican Corn and Cilantro Soup

Easy   *Serves 4 - 6*

➤ **corn cut from 3 fresh ears (or 2½ cups frozen)**
3 **tablespoons butter or margarine**
1 **medium onion, chopped**
2-3 **cloves garlic, minced or crushed**
1 **red bell pepper, chopped**
1 **green bell pepper, chopped**
1-2 **small jalapeño or banana peppers, chopped**
1 **large ripe tomato, roughly chopped**
2 **(14 ounce) cans chicken broth**
1 **chicken bouillon cube**
2-3 **tablespoons chopped fresh cilantro**
1 **teaspoon ground cumin**
➤ **salt and pepper to taste**

- Remove corn kernels with sharp knife. With knife, press down along ear to remove pulp.
- Sauté corn and pulp in butter or margarine in heavy pan.
- Add onion, garlic, peppers and tomato.
- Sauté 10 minutes. Add broth, bouillon cube and cilantro.
- Simmer 20 minutes. Add cumin, salt and pepper.

In a big hurry? Substitute commercial chunky salsa for tomato, peppers and onion.

Adding a small amount of chopped cooked chicken will enhance the soup.

Great served with cornbread or quick cheese quesadillas.

FRENCH MARKET BEAN SOUP À LA NEW ORLEANS

🕐 *Serves 8 - 10*

Wonderfully hearty soup, great with hot cornbread or crusty bread.

1	pound dried bean mix
➤	ham bone or ham hocks
2	onions, chopped
16	ounce can whole or crushed tomatoes
1-2	cloves garlic, chopped
2-3	stalks celery, chopped
➤	seasoning options:

> bay leaf, thyme, black pepper, several chopped sprigs parsley, 2 or 3 drops hot pepper sauce, other chopped vegetables such as bell pepper or carrot, second can of tomatoes

• Wash dried beans in cold water. Remove grit.
• Place beans in large pot with 2 quarts of water and a ham bone or ham hocks. Cover. Bring to boil.
• Reduce heat and simmer until tender, about 2 hours. Add remaining ingredients.
• Simmer 1 hour, adjusting seasoning and liquid to taste.

DRIED BEAN MIX

black beans
red beans
kidney beans
pinto beans
white great northern beans
navy (pea) beans
garbanzo beans
baby lima beans
large lima beans
black-eyed peas
yellow split peas
green split peas
lentils
pearl barley

• Buy 1 pound of at least 12 of these bean varieties and divide into equal amounts in 12 heavy-duty plastic bags. These may be stored for use or put into a more attractive container decorated with a bright bow for gift giving.
• With each bag of beans enclose the recipe above.
• Make a gift basket with a bag or jar of bean mix along with other ingredients. Add a loaf of French bread and a soup mug. A small container of seasonings could also be enclosed.

TORTILLA SOUP

Cook in one pot   *Serves 6 - 8*

4	corn tortillas, cut in strips
½	cup vegetable oil
1	medium onion, chopped
1	clove garlic, chopped
3	large ripe tomatoes, peeled, chopped
3	tomatillos, chopped
2	quarts water, divided
3	chicken bouillon cubes
➤	salt and pepper to taste
3	tablespoons chopped fresh cilantro, divided
➤	chopped ripe avocado (optional)
➤	grated Monterey Jack cheese

- Fry tortilla strips in hot oil. Remove to paper towels when crisp and golden. Drain excess oil from pan.
- Reduce heat. Add onion to oil. Add garlic, tomato and tomatillo. Stir gently while cooking.
- Add 2 cups water, bouillon cubes, seasoning and 2 tablespoons cilantro. Simmer 15 minutes. (May be refrigerated at this point for later use.)
- To proceed, add remainder of water.
- 15 minutes before serving, add crisp tortilla strips to pot. Prepare individual bowls with a tablespoon of avocado and a pinch of fresh cilantro.
- Ladle soup over this. Top each bowl with a heaping tablespoon of cheese. Serve.

This is actually a mild soup with a pleasant flavor. Fresh chicken stock would enhance it. Sometimes a few crisp tortilla strips are broken up on top.

This is fast — 20 - 25 minutes to table.

HISTORY NOTE

President Haygood's daughter, Mamie Haygood Ardis, 1862-1952, was the first woman to attend Emory College.

Zucchini Vegetable Soup

Serves 8 - 10

¼-½	pound bacon, cut in ½-inch pieces
⅔	cup each chopped green bell pepper and onion
3	cups chopped celery
8	ounce can tomato sauce
32	ounces canned tomato wedges or crushed tomatoes, undrained
8	ounces fresh mushrooms, chopped
1½	pounds zucchini, chopped
3-4	cups water
1	clove garlic, minced
½	teaspoon each oregano, paprika, garlic powder, onion powder, salt and pepper
1½	teaspoons basil
1	teaspoon sugar

- Brown bacon in large heavy pot.
- Add green pepper, onion and celery. Sauté.
- Add remaining ingredients.
- Simmer at least 1 hour until tender.

This is a great crock pot recipe, 8 - 10 hours on low.

History Note

Warren Akin Candler became president of Emory College in 1888 at the age of 31. He remained as president 10 years, resigning when he was elected bishop in the Methodist Church. He stayed on the board of trustees.

BRUNSWICK STEW

🕐 *Traditional Southern stew*   *Serves 10 - 12*

1	**whole fryer chicken (2½ - 3 pounds)**
➤	**several bay leaves**
➤	**celery salt to taste**
2	**pounds beef stew meat**
3	**(16 ounce) cans whole tomatoes**
3	**large onions, chopped**
2-3	**stalks celery, chopped**
2	**(16 ounce) cans creamed corn**
1⅓	**cups ketchup**
¼	**cup sweet pickle juice**
➤	**salt and pepper to taste**
➤	**dash of hot pepper sauce or bit of brown sugar (optional)**

- Stew chicken with bay leaves, celery salt and water in large heavy pot until tender, about 1 hour.
- Save all broth and remove meat from bones.
- Add chicken and broth to beef, tomato, onion and celery.
- Cook on low 3 - 4 hours until beef falls apart. Stir often to keep from sticking on bottom.
- Toward end of cooking add corn, ketchup, pickle juice, salt and pepper.
- Add hot pepper sauce or brown sugar if desired.

Serve with cornbread, coleslaw, barbecue and iced tea — another Southern classic!

HISTORY NOTE

This recipe came to us from Emory University President James T. Laney. He credits it to a friend from Macon, Georgia.

SPANISH GAZPACHO

Easy　　*No cooking*　　*Serves 6 - 8*

32	ounce bottle or can of vegetable juice
4	medium tomatoes, skinned, quartered
1	medium onion, quartered
2	small cucumbers, ends removed, roughly peeled
➤	juice of 2 lemons
¼	cup balsamic or red wine vinegar
⅓	cup olive oil
1	green bell pepper, finely chopped
2	stalks celery, finely chopped
¼	cup finely chopped fresh parsley
1	cup croutons
➤	hot pepper sauce (optional)

• Pour 2 cups vegetable juice into blender.
• Add tomato, onion and cucumber. Blend finely; do not purée.
• Add lemon juice, vinegar and olive oil. Blend briefly.
• Transfer to storage container. Whisk in remaining vegetable juice, green pepper, celery and parsley.
• To serve, ladle soup in each bowl. Top with croutons. Add an ice cube on a hot day and offer hot pepper sauce for those who prefer spicy taste.

Additional bowls of chopped tomato, celery and onion may be placed on serving table.

STRAWBERRY SOUP

🕐　♥　　*Serves 6 - 8*

2	pints strawberries (ripe, not hard)
¾	cup orange juice
¼	cup sugar
4½	cups low fat buttermilk or plain low fat yogurt
➤	mint sprigs or sliced strawberry for garnish

• Rinse and hull strawberries. Purée in blender until smooth.
• Transfer to large bowl or container.
• Add orange juice and sugar. Stir until sugar dissolves.
• Stir in buttermilk.
• Refrigerate several hours or overnight.
• To serve, spoon into dessert bowls. Garnish with mint sprigs or sliced strawberry.

Georgia Peach Soup

🕐 *Serves 6 - 8*

1½	**cups water**
¾	**cup rosé wine**
½	**cup sugar**
2	**tablespoons fresh lemon juice**
1	**stick cinnamon**
½	**teaspoon whole allspice**
2	**cloves**
1	**quart peach purée (see note)**
½	**cup each heavy cream and sour cream**
➤	**fresh mint and dollop of whipped cream for garnish (optional)**

- In saucepan combine water, wine, sugar and lemon juice.
- Add spices (tied in cheesecloth or put in tea ball).
- Bring to boil.
- Simmer uncovered 15 minutes, stirring occasionally.
- Add peach purée and simmer, stirring, 10 minutes longer.
- Discard spices. Cool.
- Whip cream and combine with sour cream.
- Fold into fruit mixture and refrigerate.
- Let stand at room temperature 15 minutes before serving.
- *Strawberry variation*: Use 1 quart strawberries in place of peaches.

Chef's Note

Fresh or frozen fruit may be used for purée. Remove skin and pit fresh ripe peaches. Purée in blender or food processor.

ZUCCHINI SOUP

Easy   Serves 6 - 8   Your choice — hot or cold

1½	pounds (5 - 6 medium) zucchini squash, chopped
1	large onion, chopped
3	cups chicken broth or 2 (14 ounce) cans
1½	teaspoons curry powder
1	cup half and half
➤	salt and pepper to taste

- Cook zucchini and onion in broth over low heat until tender.
- Purée in blender when vegetables cool slightly.
- Add curry powder and half and half, mixing well.
- May be refrigerated at this point until serving time.
- Heat very gently if serving hot.
- *Variations*: ½ teaspoon ground nutmeg may be used in place of curry.
- Plain nonfat yogurt may be substituted for half and half but decrease the amount slightly.
- Substitute yellow crookneck squash for zucchini.
- For summertime garnish add slice of lime.

RED PEPPER SOUP

An elegant first course soup or appetizer   Serves 6

6-8	red bell peppers
5	tablespoons olive oil
1	cup chicken broth
➤	salt and pepper to taste
½	cup half and half
➤	French bread, olive oil and 1 clove garlic, minced or
➤	dollop of yogurt or sour cream

- Roast peppers and remove skin and seeds. (Bake in 450°F oven 12 minutes. Turn off heat. Remove after additional 15 minutes. Place in paper or plastic bag. Close bag and allow to sit additional 15 minutes. Skin will easily peel off. Gently rinse peppers to remove seeds.)
- Purée in blender or food processor. Add olive oil, broth, salt and pepper. Whisk in half and half.
- *If serving hot*: Gently warm. Slice bread; brush with olive oil and garlic. Toast under broiler.
- Place toasted bread on top of soup and serve.
- *If serving cold*: Serve with dollop of yogurt or sour cream.

NORWEGIAN FRUIT SOUP (SOTSUPPE)

Looks beautiful served in an elegant glass bowl

Serves 12

16	ounce can pitted tart red cherries, undrained
2	cups pitted prunes
1	cup dried apricots
1	cup dried peaches
1	cup raisins
2	cups cranberry-grape juice
3	tablespoons lemon juice
1	stick cinnamon
2	tablespoons tapioca
2	cups water
➢	whipped cream or sour cream for garnish

- Combine all ingredients in heavy nonreactive saucepan.
- Bring to boil. Reduce heat.
- Cover and simmer 30 - 45 minutes until fruits are tender.
- Serve warm as soup or side dish. Serve cold for dessert.
- May be topped with whipped cream or sour cream.
- *Variation*: Other dried fruit may be substituted. Some add fresh rhubarb.

Old Norwegian recipe used for strengthening new mothers after a baby's birth.

EPICUREAN FALL SEATED DINNER FOR 12

YELLOW SQUASH BISQUE

Serves 12

⅔	pound onion
3	pounds yellow crookneck squash
6	cups chicken broth
¾-1	cup heavy cream
➤	salt and white pepper to taste

- Cut onion and squash in 1-inch cubes. Simmer in broth until soft.
- Strain vegetables and reserve liquid.
- Purée vegetables in food processor.
- Combine vegetables, broth and cream. Salt and pepper.
- If soup is prepared in advance, add cream when reheating.

EPICUREAN SUMMER DINNER FOR 25

CHILLED CUCUMBER VICHYSSOISE

Serves 25

9	pounds seeded, cubed cucumbers, unpeeled
3	pounds peeled, cubed Idaho potatoes
1½	pounds cubed onion
16	cups chicken broth
4	cups heavy cream
➤	salt and white pepper to taste

- Place vegetables in large stockpot.
- Add chicken broth and bring to a boil. Reduce heat and simmer until tender, about 45 minutes.
- Strain and reserve liquid.
- Purée solids in food processor. Add liquid to purée.
- Add cream, salt and pepper.
- Chill overnight or at least 4 hours before serving.

Weigh all vegetables after cubing to insure proper proportions.

Breads

Quick Breads

Yeast Breads and Rolls

Special Extras

*A*n Italian proverb holds that "without bread, everyone is an orphan." We agree wholeheartedly! Bread is the ultimate comfort food. There is nothing so inviting as the lovely, warm, yeasty aroma of freshly baked bread, and no other food says "home" quite as emphatically.

We feel fortunate that in the last decade there has grown a strong interest in crusty, flavorful and mouth filling — yes, even chewy — bread, so that real honest-to-goodness bread is now widely available from bakeries, specialty shops and supermarkets. Still, there is something uniquely satisfying about baking one's own bread. Bringing a loaf of bread to a friend is a wonderful gift of self.

Atlanta, along with much of the South, has a wonderful reputation for biscuits, hot rolls and quick breads like our Angel Biscuits and Lemon Tea Bread. These are much-loved recipes that go anywhere in the world a Southern cook may go.

We hope you will find these recipes an exciting addition to your table, whether you are a beginning baker or an experienced one. The given proportions of flour and liquid have worked well for us in Atlanta. Please keep in mind they may need small adjustments elsewhere.

We offer the following bread-making hints:

FLOUR: Feeling confused about which flour to use? There are two basic types. Soft wheat flour is lower in protein, lower in gluten and best used for quick breads, biscuits and muffins.

Hard wheat or winter wheat is the flour of choice for making yeast breads. It is higher in protein and gluten and responds best when making breads that require kneading and more than one rising. Hard wheat durum flour is generally used in making pasta.

All-purpose flour is a blend of hard and soft wheat flour and may be used in most baking. Self-rising flour is soft wheat flour with leavening (baking soda or baking powder) added.

Look for the nutritional information printed on the flour package to quickly determine which is high- or low-protein. Low-protein flour has 9 to 10 grams of protein per cup, while high-protein flour has 14 to 15 grams.

To further confuse the beginning baker, flours are made from different grains and combinations: wheat, whole wheat, rye, soy, brans, unbleached and enriched. Don't despair; try to follow a recipe exactly until you feel familiar with it.

Sifting flour, baking powder, salt and/or baking soda together is often not necessary but is an effective method of mixing those dry ingredients.

YEAST: Read instructions on the package. A thermometer is a practical investment for checking water temperature. If water is too cool, it will not activate the yeast. If it is too hot, the yeast will be killed. Between 105°F and 115°F is best. It takes a little practice to know when you have the right temperature. Warm your mixing bowl with a cup or more of hot water for a few minutes if your kitchen temperature is cool.

For those cooks who purchase dry granular yeast in bulk: 2 teaspoons active dry yeast is equal to 1 package.

Quick-rise yeast is best used for specific recipes until the cook is familiar with baking. Generally it is best used with yeast breads that require only one rising.

PROOFING YEAST: To ensure good results, always check the water temperature. Add 1 teaspoon of sugar. Mix and set aside. Mixture will swell and bubble within 5 minutes. Then proceed with recipe.

KNEADING: Test to see if you have finished kneading by making a two-finger indentation. Dough should spring back if you have kneaded adequately.

RISING: Time may vary greatly depending on several things — the amount of yeast, the chemical interaction of yeast, gluten, sugar and salt and the room temperature. Test to see if your rising is complete with a two-finger indentation. Dough will not spring back if it has adequately risen.

If you run into a time problem while dough is rising, punch dough down, cover and refrigerate 30 - 60 minutes or even overnight. This will not harm dough. Cover bowl lightly with plastic wrap.

Pan sizes and types may change the outcome of a recipe slightly. When using glass, you should generally lower the baking temperature 25°.

WHAT TO USE? Butter, margarine, oil, lard, cooking spray, vegetable shortening? Sometimes a particular fat is called for because of the texture desired. Sometimes it is designated for flavor. We have tried to reduce calories and fat content in these recipes in keeping with current nutritional guidelines. Recipes that specify shortening are referring to solid vegetable shortening sold in cans by the pound. We recommend greasing a baking pan with vegetable cooking spray.

When water is used in a bread recipe, the bread generally will be crusty and coarse. Milk will make a finer and, generally, a softer texture.

To cut fresh bread without crushing it, run your knife under hot water to warm. Wipe dry and then use. A knife with a serrated edge is best to use for cutting bread.

MICROWAVE DIRECTIONS FOR RISING: Begin by testing microwave capability. If your microwave melts 2 tablespoons cold stick margarine in less than 4 minutes on the lowest power setting (10% power), there is too much power and that power would kill the yeast before the dough could rise.

If your microwave passes this power test, proceed by kneading dough as directed and shaping it for rising. Place in a lightly greased microwave-safe mixing bowl. Turn dough to grease entire surface. Pour 3 cups water into a 4-cup measure. Heat, uncovered, at highest power 6½ - 8½ minutes or until boiling. Move measuring cup to back of oven. Cover the dough with wax paper. Place in oven. Heat dough and water side by side at LOW (10% power) 13 - 15 minutes or until dough has almost doubled. Punch down; cover and let rest 10 minutes. Grease two 8x4-inch microwave-safe glass loaf pans. Divide dough in half. Shape each half into a loaf and place in pan. Cover with wax paper. Heat dough and water at LOW 6 - 8 minutes or until almost doubled. Bake, as recipe directs, in conventional oven.

FRESH APPLE BREAD

1	cup sugar
½	cup shortening
2	eggs
2	cups all-purpose flour
1	teaspoon baking soda
½	teaspoon salt
1½	tablespoons buttermilk
½	teaspoon vanilla
1	tablespoon flour
1	cup chopped pecans
1	cup peeled, grated apple (Granny Smith or Rome)
1½	tablespoons sugar
½	teaspoon ground cinnamon

- Heat oven to 350°F and grease and flour 9x5-inch loaf pan.
- Cream sugar and shortening until light and fluffy.
- Add eggs one at a time, beating well after each.
- Combine 2 cups flour, baking soda and salt.
- Combine buttermilk and vanilla.
- Add dry ingredients to creamed mixture alternately with buttermilk mixture. Beat well after each addition.
- Mix 1 tablespoon flour with pecans. Stir pecans and apple into batter.
- Scrape batter into pan.
- Mix 1½ tablespoons sugar with cinnamon. Sprinkle over batter before baking.
- Bake 1 hour or until tests done.

BLUEBERRY COFFEE CAKE

♥　*Easy*

1½	cups all-purpose flour
2	teaspoons baking powder
½	teaspoon salt
½	cup sugar
2	tablespoons vegetable oil
1	egg white
¾	cup skim milk
1	heaping cup fresh or frozen blueberries

Topping:

⅓	cup firmly packed brown sugar
½	cup chopped nuts
2	tablespoons flour
2	tablespoons vegetable oil
2	teaspoons ground cinnamon

- Heat oven to 350°F and grease 8x8-inch pan.
- Mix first 4 (dry) ingredients.
- Add liquid ingredients. Mix. Stir in blueberries.
- Pour into pan.
- Mix topping ingredients and sprinkle over batter.
- Bake 35 - 40 minutes or until tests done.

Sour Cream Banana Bread

3	large ripe bananas (1 cup mashed)
1	teaspoon grated orange peel (optional)
½	cup (1 stick) butter or margarine
2	eggs
1	cup sugar
1	teaspoon baking soda
2	tablespoons sour cream
2	cups all-purpose flour
½	teaspoon baking powder
½-1	cup chopped pecans or walnuts (optional)

- Heat oven to 350°F and grease 9x5-inch loaf pan or two 7x3-inch pans.
- Mash bananas in large bowl. Add orange peel if desired.
- Add butter, eggs, sugar, baking soda and sour cream. Combine with electric mixer.
- Add dry ingredients and nuts. Mix well.
- Put batter in pan(s).
- Bake 45 minutes for small pans or 1 hour for large. Bread is done when it pulls away from sides of pan.
- Cool on rack 20 minutes before removing from pan.

Carrot Banana Bread

♥ *A healthy choice variation*

3	large ripe bananas (1 cup mashed)
1	medium carrot, grated (⅔ cup)
1	teaspoon grated orange peel or ¼ fresh orange
⅓	cup vegetable oil
2	eggs or egg substitute
2	tablespoons plain nonfat yogurt
¾	cup firmly packed brown sugar
1	teaspoon baking soda
½	teaspoon baking powder
1½	cups all-purpose flour
½	cup plus 2 tablespoons oat bran or toasted wheat germ
½-1	cup chopped pecans or walnuts

- Follow directions as for Sour Cream Banana Bread.

Carrot and ¼ orange may be put through food processor. (Remove seeds!)

This recipe is wonderful to double. Put one in your freezer or share with a friend. It is best the next day.

Chef's Note

Black bananas make flavorful banana bread. Freeze and save for baking when convenient.

CRANBERRY ORANGE BREAD

♥

2	cups all-purpose flour
¾	cup sugar
1½	teaspoons baking powder
1	teaspoon salt
½	teaspoon baking soda
1	cup coarsely chopped cranberries
½	cup chopped pecans or walnuts
1	teaspoon grated orange peel
1	egg, beaten
¾	cup orange juice
2	tablespoons vegetable oil

- Heat oven to 350°F and grease 9x5-inch pan.
- Mix flour, sugar, baking powder, salt and baking soda.
- Stir in cranberries, nuts and orange peel.
- Combine egg, orange juice and oil. Add to dry ingredients.
- Stir until just moistened. Do not overbeat.
- Pour batter into pan. Bake 50 - 60 minutes.
- Cool on rack about 30 minutes before removing from pan.

Great for gifts during the holidays!

LEMON NUT BREAD

2	cups all-purpose flour
2½	teaspoons baking powder
1	teaspoon salt
¼	cup butter or margarine, softened
¾	cup sugar
2	eggs
1	tablespoon grated lemon peel
¾	cup buttermilk
1	cup chopped pecans or walnuts

Glaze:

3	tablespoons sugar
3	tablespoons lemon juice
1	tablespoon butter or margarine

- Heat oven to 350°F and grease 9x5-inch pan or two 7x3-inch pans.
- Mix flour, baking powder and salt. Set aside.
- In large bowl, cream butter and sugar until light.
- Beat in eggs and lemon peel.
- Add dry ingredients alternately with buttermilk, beating well. Stir in nuts.
- Pour into pan(s). Bake 40 - 50 minutes depending on pan size. Bread is done when it pulls away slightly from sides of pan.
- While bread bakes, mix glaze ingredients and heat gently.
- Spoon glaze over top of bread in pan.
- Cool about 10 minutes.
- Loosen sides with spatula and remove to rack.

Delicious sliced very thinly and served with coffee, tea or lemonade.

SOUR CREAM COFFEE CAKE

1	cup (2 sticks) butter, softened to room temperature
2	cups plus 2 tablespoons sugar, divided
2	eggs, room temperature
2	cups all-purpose flour
1	teaspoon baking powder
½	teaspoon baking soda
¼	teaspoon salt
1¼	cups light sour cream
1	teaspoon vanilla
1	teaspoon ground cinnamon
1½	cups chopped pecans or walnuts

- Heat oven to 350°F and grease 1 bundt or 2 large loaf pans.
- Cream butter; add 2 cups sugar gradually. Beat until light and fluffy.
- Beat in eggs one at a time, beating well after each.
- Combine flour, baking powder, baking soda and salt.
- Fold in sour cream and vanilla alternately with flour mixture.
- Combine 2 tablespoons sugar, cinnamon and pecans. Sprinkle half on bottom of pan.
- Spoon half of batter into pan. Sprinkle remaining pecan sugar mixture over and swirl with knife.
- Add remaining batter.
- Bake 60 minutes or until done.
- Cool on rack.

This is easy and very special when served with fruit for coffee or brunch.

HISTORY NOTE

Under the leadership of Bishop Warren Candler, Emory University was established in Atlanta. The Atlanta Chamber of Commerce pledged $500,000 if the proposed school were located in Atlanta. Bishop Candler was aided by his brother, Asa G. Candler, the founder of Coca-Cola, with 75 acres of land and $1 million for the endowment of this new institution.

IRISH SODA BREAD

2	cups all-purpose flour
2	cups whole wheat flour
2½	teaspoons baking soda
2	teaspoons salt
1	tablespoon sugar
¼	cup butter or margarine
1	egg
1½	cups buttermilk
1	cup seedless raisins or currants (optional)

- Heat oven to 425°F and grease 8-inch circle on baking sheet.
- Mix flour, baking soda, salt and sugar in large bowl.
- Use fingers or pastry blender to crumble butter and mix in.
- Make a depression in center of ingredients and stir in buttermilk and egg with large spoon. Mix well. Add raisins or currants.
- Scrape out onto lightly floured surface and knead. Form into ball.
- Flatten to about 8 inches in diameter and place on baking sheet.
- Using sharp knife, draw a large X on top. Place in oven.
- Bake 20 minutes. Reduce temperature to 350°F and bake additional 20 minutes.
- Loaf will sound slightly hollow when tapped if done.

This is a sturdy bread that demands butter and jam or a bowl of hearty soup. With raisins, it is wonderful for teatime or breakfast.

MOTHER'S SPOON BREAD

3	cups milk, divided
1	cup white cornmeal
1	teaspoon salt
1	teaspoon baking powder
2	tablespoons butter or margarine
2	teaspoons sugar
3	eggs, separated

- Heat oven to 325°F and grease 2-quart casserole (soufflé dish works well).
- Cook 2 cups milk with cornmeal until mushy.
- Remove from heat. Add salt, baking powder, butter, sugar and remaining 1 cup milk. Mix.
- Beat egg yolks and stir in.
- Beat egg whites until stiff and fold into mixture.
- Gently spoon into casserole.
- Bake 1 hour. Serve immediately.

There are many variations on Southern spoon bread. This one is very attractive to serve and very light.

Best Cornbread You Ever Ate

Easy

1½	cups light mayonnaise
2	eggs or egg substitute
15-16	ounce can cream-style corn
12	ounce package (1½ cups) corn muffin mix

- Heat oven to 400°F and grease 13x9x2-inch pan.
- Beat eggs and mayonnaise together.
- Stir in other ingredients with a fork. Pour into pan.
- Bake 30 minutes. Cut in squares and serve hot.

Vegetable Cornbread

Easy

2	cups finely chopped vegetables: 10-ounce box frozen chopped broccoli, thawed, drained; or yellow squash and fresh corn cut from ear; or yellow squash and zucchini; or canned corn, drained, and bell pepper or chilies
1	onion, finely chopped (⅔ cup)
3	tablespoons butter or margarine
10	ounces low fat small-curd cottage cheese
2	eggs and 2 egg whites or egg substitute
13	ounces cornbread mix
1	teaspoon No-Salt Herb Seasoning (page 69)

- Heat oven to 350°F and grease 13x9x2-inch pan.
- Sauté vegetables in butter.
- Mix all ingredients and pour immediately into pan.
- Bake 30 - 45 minutes. Serve immediately.
- *Variation:* Instead of cornbread mix, use 1½ cups cornmeal, ½ cup all-purpose flour, 1½ tablespoons baking powder and additional 1 teaspoon No-Salt Herb Seasoning.

We offer a number of alternatives because cooks from all over suggested various vegetable combinations and all were good!

BEATEN BISCUITS VIA FOOD PROCESSOR

2   cups all-purpose flour
1   teaspoon salt
½   cup (1 stick) cold butter, cut in small pieces
⅓-½   cup ice water

- Heat oven to 400°F.
- Put flour and salt in food processor. Turn on/off twice.
- Add butter and process until mixture resembles cornmeal.
- With machine running pour ice water slowly into tube until dough forms a ball. Process briefly.
- Remove dough and roll on lightly floured surface to ⅛-inch-thick rectangle. Fold in half and over on itself. Press lightly with rolling pin. Cut in tiny rounds.
- Place on ungreased baking sheet.
- Pierce tops with tines of fork three times.
- Bake 20 minutes or until lightly browned.

'Tis a wonderful Southern custom to serve these with thinly sliced ham at breakfast, brunch or tea.

1-2-3 SUPER SUPPER BISCUITS

Easy

1   cup light sour cream
1   egg
2   cups buttermilk biscuit mix
➤   melted butter or margarine
➤   sesame or poppy seed (optional)

- Heat oven to 375°F and grease muffin pan.
- Beat sour cream and egg together.
- Add biscuit mix and stir until moistened, scraping bowl.
- Drop by spoonful into muffin pan cups.
- Lightly brush with butter and sprinkle seeds over top.
- Bake immediately 12 - 15 minutes. Serve hot.
- Recipe will make 6 - 8 large drop-style biscuits in a muffin pan.
- *Variation*: For Cheese Biscuits, make slight depression in top and place 1 teaspoon grated cheese (medium or sharp Cheddar). Eliminate brushing with butter and seeds.

BRAN MUFFIN MIX TO YOUR TASTE

♥   *Makes a light nutritious bran muffin*

2	cups 100% bran flakes
4	cups All Bran or Bran Buds
2½	cups whole wheat flour
2½	cups all-purpose flour
2	teaspoons salt
5	teaspoons baking soda
1	cup honey or molasses or 1½ - 2 cups white or brown sugar
2	cups boiling water
1	quart buttermilk
4	eggs or egg substitute
1	cup vegetable or canola oil
1	or more cups raisins, dates, dried apricots or chopped apple and nuts (optional)
2	tablespoons ground cinnamon or nutmeg (optional)

- Combine first 6 ingredients in very large bowl.
- Stir thoroughly with large spoon.
- Add sugar, water and buttermilk. Mix.
- Add eggs and oil. Stir vigorously until well mixed before adding any optional ingredients.
- Cover and refrigerate until ready to bake.
- Heat oven to 375°F and grease muffin pan.
- Bake 20 minutes (about 15 minutes for mini-muffin pan).
- *Variations*: All white flour may be used.
- Raisin bran may be substituted to save time.

This will keep 1 month in refrigerator. After 2 weeks lightly stir pinch of baking powder into batter before using.

Oatmeal Whole Wheat Muffins

♥ *A breakfast treat for yourself or friends*

½	cup whole wheat flour
½	cup all-purpose flour
¼	cup sugar
3	teaspoons baking powder
½	teaspoon salt
1	teaspoon ground cinnamon
1	cup quick or old-fashioned oats
3	tablespoons vegetable oil
1	egg, beaten, or egg substitute
1	cup skim milk
4	ounces (½ cup) applesauce

- Heat oven to 400°F and grease muffin pan.
- In large bowl, whisk dry ingredients, mixing well.
- Make depression in center and add remaining ingredients. Mix until moistened.
- Fill muffin pan cups ⅔ full and immediately bake 15 minutes. (A mini-muffin pan will make 24 tiny but plump muffins.)
- *Variations*: Shake cinnamon sugar over each muffin before baking.
- In place of applesauce, substitute ½ cup pumpkin, raisins, blueberries, crushed pineapple, apricot jam with citrus peel or chopped dried apricots.

Applesauce is handily packaged for sale in individual 4-ounce multi-packs.

Popovers

Makes 8 - 10

1	cup sifted all-purpose flour
¼	teaspoon salt
2	eggs
1	cup milk, warmed
1	tablespoon shortening, melted

- Heat oven to 450°F and liberally grease muffin pan or glass custard cups.
- Sift flour and salt together.
- Beat eggs. Add milk, shortening and then dry ingredients.
- Beat until batter is smooth.
- Fill well-greased muffin pan cups half full. Bake 20 minutes.
- Reduce temperature to 350°F and bake additional 15 minutes.
- DO NOT OPEN OVEN or popovers will fall.

If every other hole in muffin pan is used, popovers will rise higher. Use sharp knife to remove from pan.

The same batter is used in making English Yorkshire Pudding.

SCONES

½	cup currants
2	tablespoons brandy, dry sherry or Madeira wine
2	cups all-purpose flour
½	teaspoon baking soda
2	teaspoons baking powder
2	tablespoons vanilla sugar (see note)
½	cup (1 stick) unsalted butter or margarine, cut in pieces
1	egg
➤	buttermilk (about ½ cup)
1	egg white
1	tablespoon water
➤	vanilla sugar for glaze

- Plump currants several hours ahead by adding brandy or wine in small covered saucepan. Bring to boil; turn off heat immediately; keep covered until using.
- Heat oven to 425°F and grease baking sheet.
- Combine dry ingredients.
- Add butter. Using hands or pastry blender, blend until mixture resembles coarse oatmeal.
- Add buttermilk to egg to measure ⅔ cup. Mix into flour mixture.
- Scrape onto lightly floured surface and knead gently.
- Flatten ball of dough to about ¼ inch with hands.
- Place on baking sheet. Cut triangular or diamond shapes with sharp knife.
- Beat egg white with water. Brush over top of scones.
- Sprinkle with vanilla sugar.
- Bake 12 - 15 minutes or until lightly browned. Serve immediately.

Very special for brunch.

CHEF'S NOTE

Vanilla sugar is simply made by adding a whole vanilla bean to 1 - 2 cups white sugar in pint jar. Breaking the bean in half will give flavorful sugar for a long period of time. Add more sugar as mixture is used. For a quick trick, put ½ teaspoon vanilla in a cup of sugar. Secure the container lid and shake until vanilla is well distributed.

German Pancakes

Easy   *2 - 3 pancakes*

4	**eggs**
1	**cup milk**
½	**teaspoon salt**
3	**tablespoons powdered sugar**
1	**cup all-purpose flour**
➤	**dash of ground cinnamon or nutmeg**
2-3	**tablespoons butter or margarine**
➤	**lemon wedges and powdered sugar**

- Heat oven to 500°F.
- Beat eggs, milk, salt, sugar, flour and spice until frothy.
- Put 1 tablespoon butter in 7 - 9-inch cast-iron skillet (or any skillet with oven-proof handle). Heat to melting on stove top.
- Pour 1 cup batter into pan. Bake 7 minutes. NO Peeking!
- Serve immediately with powdered sugar and lemon wedges.
- Repeat process for second pancake.

This is done in the oven. It has a wonderful aroma that will permeate the house.

Yeast Waffles

🕐   *10 waffles*

1	**package active dry yeast**
¼	**cup warm water (105° - 115°F)**
2	**eggs**
1	**teaspoon salt**
1	**tablespoon sugar**
½	**cup vegetable oil**
3	**cups flour**
2	**cups warm milk**

- Dissolve yeast in warm water.
- Beat eggs well. Add salt, sugar, yeast mixture and oil. Mix.
- Add flour and milk alternately. Mix well. Batter is thin.
- Cover and refrigerate several hours or overnight.
- Stir batter down. When ready to cook, pour about ½ cup per waffle.
- Cook until golden brown.
- Serve with fresh berries, yogurt and dash of powdered sugar or maple syrup or brown sugar and sour cream.

This is a wonderful guest breakfast; batter can be made ahead and refrigerated.

Chef's Note

Check waffle iron instructions. Oiling may be needed.

Angel Biscuits

1	package active dry yeast
2	tablespoons warm water (105° - 115°F)
2½	cups all-purpose flour
2	tablespoons sugar
1½	teaspoons baking powder
½	teaspoon baking soda
½	teaspoon salt
½	cup shortening
1	cup buttermilk

- Dissolve yeast in warm water.
- Combine dry ingredients. Cut in shortening.
- Add buttermilk and yeast mixture. Mix with spoon.
- Scrape out on floured board or cloth. Knead until smooth.
- Refrigerate until 1 hour before meal. Dough will keep several days.
- Heat oven to 400°F and grease baking sheet.
- Punch dough down and roll to ½ inch with rolling pin. Cut with biscuit cutter and place on baking sheet.
- Bake 15 minutes or until lightly browned.

Freeze and bake later: Cut dough and freeze biscuits in foil pans. Place in a cold oven at night. Next morning, turn oven to 450°F when the coffee starts perking. Good morning! Hot biscuits for breakfast!

MARY LANEY'S ICE BOX ROLLS

🕐

3	packages active dry yeast
½	cup warm water (105° - 115°F)
2	cups milk, scalded
½	cup shortening
½	cup sugar
6	cups all-purpose flour, divided
1	teaspoon salt
½	teaspoon baking powder
½	teaspoon baking soda
➤	melted butter or margarine

- Dissolve yeast in warm water. Allow to sit. It should be bubbling within 5 minutes.
- Mix hot milk with shortening and sugar. Stir to dissolve. Cool slightly. Add 4 cups flour and dissolved yeast.
- Stir well and let rise 2 hours.
- Add salt, baking powder, baking soda and 2 cups flour. Beat well.
- Refrigerate dough, covered. This will keep several days.
- Take off desired amount of dough for baking. Roll ¼-inch thick on floured wax paper. Cut in circles and dip in melted butter.
- Fold about ⅓ of each circle over on itself to make a pocket roll.
- Place close together in shallow pan. Let rise until doubled.
- Heat oven to 375°F.
- Bake about 20 minutes until lightly browned. Serve immediately.

HISTORY NOTE

Mary Laney was given this recipe by an Arkansas friend long ago. A member of Emory University Woman's Club for many years, Mary is the mother of Emory President James T. Laney.

QUICK WHOLE GRAIN ROLLS

🕐

2	packages active dry yeast
1	cup warm water (105° - 115°F)
¼	cup honey
1	cup whole wheat flour
2¼	cups unbleached white flour, divided
1	egg
¼	cup vegetable oil
½	cup quick or old-fashioned oats
1	teaspoon salt

- In large bowl, sprinkle yeast over warm water.
- Pour honey over. Allow to sit about 5 minutes until bubbling.
- Add whole wheat flour and 1 cup white flour. Beat with electric mixer on low until well blended.
- Beat about 5 minutes on medium speed.
- Add egg, oil, oats, salt and as much of the remaining flour as mixer will easily handle. Stir in remaining flour with spoon. Scrape bowl, turning dough onto heavily floured surface to mix and knead.
- Add more flour if necessary to have ball of dough that is smooth and elastic. (At this point dough may be left a few minutes. Punch down and repeat kneading briefly.)
- Lightly grease 13x9x2-inch pan.
- Shape dough into 24 balls and place on pan. Cover and let rise about 1 hour or until doubled.
- Heat oven to 375°F.
- Bake 20 minutes or until lightly browned.
- *Variation:* ¼ - ½ cup cooked wild rice may be added to dough when kneading is nearly complete. It will give a wonderful nutty flavor and texture.

HISTORY NOTE

A charter was granted January 15, 1915, in DeKalb County. Emory University began with Bishop Candler as the chancellor.

Healthy Choice Rolls

🕐 ♥ *Makes 16*

1	**package active dry yeast**
1	**cup warm water (105° - 115°F), divided**
½	**cup sugar**
3¾-4	**cups sifted flour (see note)**
1	**egg**
1¼	**teaspoons salt**
5	**tablespoons vegetable oil**
➢	**melted butter or margarine (optional)**

- Dissolve yeast in ¼ cup warm water with 1 teaspoon of the sugar.
- Measure flour and set aside.
- Process egg, remaining water, salt and oil in blender or food processor (or use electric mixer).
- Add yeast mixture and then 1½ cups flour. Mix well about 2 minutes.
- If necessary, transfer dough to a bowl and stir in remaining flour. Mix until smooth.
- Refrigerate at least 1 hour. Dough will keep several days.
- Knead. Using a minimum of flour, roll into 16 - 18-inch circle.
- Cut into 16 wedges using sharp knife or pizza cutter. Roll up crescent style, starting at wide end going toward center. Place rolls well apart on large greased baking sheet. Cover loosely.
- Let rise until doubled, about 2 hours.
- Heat oven to 425°F.
- Bake 10 - 12 minutes or until lightly browned.
- If desired, brush with melted butter while hot.

Bread flour may be used alone or combined with whole wheat or rye flour. One cup of each of the latter makes an interesting and tasty bread!

To do ahead: Place formed rolls on greased baking pan. Cover tightly with plastic wrap and foil. Freeze up to 2 weeks. When ready to use, return to room temperature. Let rise and bake as above.

History Note

The area now known as Druid Hills was six miles from Atlanta and was a wilderness of undeveloped rolling countryside. Frederick Law Olmsted, who had designed New York City's grand Central Park, was brought to Atlanta to design Druid Hills. Architect Henry Hornbostel, influenced by the natural beauty, designed the first Emory buildings in the Italian Renaissance style.

MEXICAN ANISE BUNS

🕐 *Easy yeast bread   Makes 24*

2	packages active dry yeast
½	cup warm water (105° - 115°F)
½	cup sugar
½	teaspoon salt
1	tablespoon anise seed
½	cup (1 stick) butter or margarine, melted
3	eggs, room temperature (separate 1 for glaze)
4-4¾	cups flour
2	tablespoons light corn syrup

- In large warmed bowl, sprinkle yeast over warm water. Stir when dissolved.
- Add sugar, salt, anise, butter, 2 eggs, the egg white and 2 cups flour. Beat until smooth.
- Stir in additional flour to make soft dough.
- Turn out on lightly floured surface and knead 8 - 10 minutes.
- Place in greased bowl. Cover and let rise until doubled, about 1 hour.
- Grease jelly-roll pan.
- Punch dough down and knead lightly. Flatten to rectangle. Place on pan. Using fingers, press dough to fill pan.
- Cut in 6 large squares. Cut each square diagonally to form 4 triangles (24 total).
- Mix egg yolk with corn syrup to form glaze. Brush all of glaze over top of buns.
- Let rise 1 hour in warm place.
- Heat oven to 350°F.
- Bake 15 - 20 minutes until buns are golden brown.

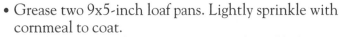
ENGLISH MUFFIN BREAD

No kneading required   Makes 2 loaves

6	**cups all-purpose flour, divided**
2	**packages active dry yeast**
1	**tablespoon sugar**
2	**teaspoons salt**
¼	**teaspoon baking soda**
2	**cups milk**
½	**cup water**
2	**tablespoons cornmeal**

- Grease two 9x5-inch loaf pans. Lightly sprinkle with cornmeal to coat.
- Combine 3 cups flour, yeast, sugar, salt and baking soda.
- Heat liquids to very warm (120° - 130°F). Add to dry mixture. Beat well.
- Stir in remaining flour. Pour batter into pans.
- Sprinkle tops with cornmeal. Cover lightly with plastic wrap and allow to rise in warm area about 45 minutes.
- Heat oven to 400°F.
- Bake 25 minutes until light golden.
- Remove from pan immediately. Cool on rack.

Delicious toasted.

FRENCH BREAD VIA FOOD PROCESSOR

1	**package active dry yeast**
⅓	**cup warm water (105° - 115°F)**
15	**ounces unbleached bread flour (about 4 cups)**
1	**teaspoon salt**
⅔	**cup ice water**
2	**tablespoons cornmeal**

- Dissolve yeast in warm water.
- Place flour and salt in food processor.
- Start processor and add yeast mixture.
- Add ice water as fast as flour will absorb it (about 20 - 25 seconds).
- When dough forms a ball, continue processing 60 seconds.
- Remove dough with floured hands. Shape into a smooth ball and place in lightly floured plastic bag.
- Squeeze air from bag. Close end with wire twist, allowing room for dough to expand (rise).
- Let rise until doubled.
- Grease large baking sheet and sprinkle with cornmeal.
- Remove twist and punch dough down in bag.
- Remove dough and shape into long (18 - 24 inch) loaf.
- Place on baking sheet. Make several diagonal slashes on top of loaf.
- Cover with oiled plastic wrap. Let rise until doubled.
- Heat oven to 400°F.
- Place shallow pan containing boiling water in bottom of oven.
- Place pan with loaf on middle shelf of oven. Bake 20 - 25 minutes or until nicely browned and hollow when tapped. Remove water pan after 10 minutes of baking time.
- Cool loaf on wire rack.

CHALLAH

Makes 1 large or 2 medium loaves

1	package active dry yeast
1¼	cups warm water (105° - 115°F)
¼	cup sugar
4½	cups all-purpose flour, divided
¼	cup vegetable oil
2	teaspoons salt
2	eggs (separate 1 for glaze)
2	tablespoons water
➤	poppy or sesame seed for sprinkling (optional)

- In large bowl, dissolve yeast in warm water with sugar. Whisk well.
- When sugar and yeast have dissolved, add 1 cup flour. Whisk until blended.
- Keep bowl in warm place 20 minutes. Mixture should be bubbly and frothy.
- Using electric mixer, add 2 cups flour, oil, salt, egg and egg white. Beat well 2 - 3 minutes, scraping sides of bowl.
- Use heavy spoon to mix in 1 cup flour.
- Turn dough out onto lightly floured surface. Knead until smooth and elastic, about 5 minutes. Add flour very lightly as needed to keep from sticking.
- Put ball of dough into clean greased bowl. Turn ball so that top is greased. Cover loosely with cloth or plastic. Let rise until doubled.
- Grease baking sheet.
- Work dough lightly. (Divide for 2 loaves.) To braid, divide dough into 3 cylinders and allow to rest a minute. Braiding seems easiest when beginning in the middle, loosely and quickly working to each end. Press each end together to hold. Transfer to baking sheet. Let rise until doubled. (Second rising time will be shorter.)
- Heat oven to 375°F.
- Mix egg yolk with water. Brush top of loaf with glaze.
- Sprinkle poppy or sesame seed if desired.
- Bake about 30 minutes until golden brown and hollow sounding when tapped.

One baking sheet will hold 1 large loaf crosswise or 2 smaller loaves lengthwise.

JULE KAGE

🕐 *Norwegian Christmas Bread*

2	packages active dry yeast
½	cup warm water (105° - 115°F)
1½	cups lukewarm milk
¾	cup sugar
1	teaspoon salt
2	teaspoons ground cardamom
2	eggs, beaten
½	cup shortening
7-7½	cups all-purpose flour
2	cups candied fruit
2	cups raisins
1	egg yolk mixed with 2 tablespoons water for glaze

- Dissolve yeast in warm water. Allow to sit until bubbling, about 5 minutes.
- Stir in milk, sugar, salt, cardamom, eggs, shortening and half of flour. Mix vigorously until smooth.
- Stir in remaining flour. Knead on floured board until dough is smooth and elastic, gradually adding fruit and raisins until evenly distributed.
- Place ball of dough in large greased bowl. Cover and allow to rise until doubled, about 1½ hours.
- Punch down in bowl. Let rise again about 45 minutes.
- Grease 2 round cake pans or a baking sheet.
- Shape dough into 2 round loaves and place on pans.
- Let rise until doubled, about 45 minutes.
- Heat oven to 350°F.
- Brush glaze over tops of loaves for a shiny golden-brown top.
- Bake 40 - 50 minutes until hollow sounding when tapped.

This recipe demands a long period of attention but is surprisingly easy! It is beautifully adapted for any special occasion by using dried apricots and golden raisins. Red and green candied cherries make a spectacular presentation for Christmas!

HISTORY NOTE

In 1920 Emory College was formally moved to Atlanta, and the old school was now a part of the new Emory University. It was not until 1929 that a new junior campus was established at Oxford.

Sprouted Wheat Bread

🕐 *A taste of the harvest*

⅓	**cup wheat kernels (also known as grains or berries)**
1	**package active dry yeast**
2	**cups warm water (105° - 115°F)**
1	**teaspoon sugar**
1½	**cups unbleached flour, preferably bread flour**
5	**ounce can evaporated milk**
⅓	**cup honey**
4¼	**cups stone-ground whole wheat flour**
3	**tablespoons vegetable oil**
2	**teaspoons salt**
➤	**melted butter or margarine for brushing top**

- *3 - 4 Days in advance*: Place wheat kernels in sprouting jar (a pint or quart jar with mesh lid).
- Run cool water through kernels, shaking gently and rinsing kernels 3 or 4 times per day. Drain each time. Keep jar out of direct sunlight in a slightly cool area. Sprouts will appear in about 3 days. If necessary, refrigerate to slow down growth.
- *Bread*: In large bowl, sprinkle yeast over warm water. When yeast dissolves, stir and whisk in sugar and 1 cup white flour. Mix well.
- Let stand 20 minutes. Yeast mixture should be quite active, bubbly and frothy.
- Add milk, honey, 2 cups whole wheat flour, oil and salt. Mix several minutes with electric mixer. Mixture will not be firm but should be gaining some elasticity.
- Use strong spoon to stir in remaining whole wheat flour, scraping sides of bowl and mixing well.
- Turn out onto floured cloth or board to knead. Add white flour as needed to work dough so it is not sticky.
- Drain sprouts and knead into dough. Sprouts are crisp and fold in easily.
- Knead until dough is smooth and elastic.
- Place ball of dough in large greased bowl, turning once. Cover and allow to rise until doubled.
- Briefly work dough, punching down and kneading. Divide into 2 loaves.
- Place bread in greased pans. Allow to double before baking.
- Heat oven to 375°F.
- Immediately before baking brush tops with melted butter. Make a sharp lengthwise slash in each top (or a cross for round loaf).
- Bake 30 minutes. Reduce temperature to 350°F and bake additional 10 minutes. Loaf should sound hollow when tapped.
- Remove from pan and cool on wire rack.
- *Variation*: Add 1 cup coarsely chopped pecans for a special "Georgia" taste.

FOCACCIA WITH CHERRIES

Makes 1 large loaf

1½	cups dried pitted sour cherries
1½	cups golden raisins
¾	teaspoon active dry yeast
¼	cup warm water (105° - 115°F)
1	cup plus 2 tablespoons water
1	cup starter (see below)
1	cup whole wheat flour
1¾	cups unbleached all-purpose flour
1½	teaspoons salt
➢	olive oil
➢	Turbinado or granulated sugar for sprinkling top

- Soak cherries and raisins in water to cover 30 minutes or more. Drain and pat dry on paper towel.
- In large bowl, dissolve yeast in warm water.
- Add remaining water and starter to yeast; mix with wooden spoon.
- Add flours and salt. Beat vigorously 4 - 5 minutes. Turn out on well-floured surface (dough will be sticky). Knead until smooth and elastic, adding up to ¼ cup more flour if necessary.
- Put in greased bowl. Cover with plastic wrap and let rise until doubled or tripled, 2 - 3 hours.
- Turn out dough onto floured surface. Flatten into an oval. Top with half of fruit and roll dough up. Rotate dough and flatten again. Top with remaining fruit and roll into a log. Form into a ball and allow to rest a few minutes.
- Lightly grease 12-inch pizza pan. Put dough in center. Pat or roll out to fill pan. Dimple all over with fingers.
- Brush lightly with olive oil. Cover loosely with plastic wrap and let rise until puffy, about 1 hour.
- Heat oven to 450°F. Sprinkle with Turbinado sugar.
- Bake 30 minutes or until golden brown on top and hollow sounding when tapped.

Starter (2 cups):

1	cup warm water, divided (105° - 115°F)
¼	teaspoon yeast
2½	cups unbleached flour

- Dissolve yeast in ¼ cup warm water.
- Add remaining water and flour. Mix 3 - 4 minutes.
- Cover with plastic wrap and let rise overnight in a cool place.

Focaccia freezes well, and don't worry about the shape.

VARIATION FOR ONION FOCACCIA

Instead of cherries, raisins and Turbinado sugar:

1   **large sweet onion, thinly sliced**
1   **tablespoon olive oil**
2   **teaspoons sugar**
➤   **coarse salt**
➤   **chopped fresh rosemary or thyme**
➤   **freshly ground pepper to taste**

- While dough is rising, sauté onion in olive oil over medium heat until tender, 15 - 20 minutes. Do not brown. Add sugar and continue cooking over low heat until mixture begins to caramelize. Turn off heat.
- When ready to bake, distribute onion over surface. Sprinkle with coarse salt, herb and pepper. Bake as above.
- *Variations*: Top with bell pepper (green, red or yellow) in combination with onion, sun-dried tomatoes, roughly cut, Parmesan cheese or black olives.

BISHOP'S BREAD

A very special fruitcake of German origin

2½	cups all-purpose flour
15	ounces dark raisins (about 2 cups)
15	ounces golden raisins (about 2 cups)
1	pound whole unblanched almonds
1	cup citron
½	cup candied lemon peel
1	teaspoon grated lemon peel
1½	teaspoons ground cinnamon
½	teaspoon ground cloves
6	eggs, separated
3¾	cups powdered sugar

- Heat oven to 325°F.
- Grease and flour 2 large loaf pans; line bottom with brown paper.
- In very large bowl, mix dry ingredients (except sugar). Set aside.
- Beat egg whites until stiff. Set aside.
- In large bowl, beat egg yolks with powdered sugar at low speed until well mixed.
- Add flour mixture. Mix with large spoon.
- Fold in beaten egg whites. Batter will be very stiff. Place in pans.
- Bake 1 hour or until done. Bread should be slightly chewy not hard.
- When cool, wrap tightly in heavy foil. Slice with very thin knife or serrated-edge bread knife.

MEUSLI

A low fat nutritious breakfast

2	cups quick or old-fashioned oats
16	ounces nonfat plain yogurt
2	cups skim milk
3	tablespoons honey
¼	teaspoon ground cinnamon
¼	cup each of any of the following: chopped walnuts, pecans, hazelnuts, almonds
¼	cup each of any of the following dried fruits: raisins, dates, apricots

- Mix desired ingredients together. Store covered in refrigerator. Mixture will be soupy at first.
- To serve add fresh fruit, such as cut-up banana, strawberries or apple, additional milk and sugar if desired.
- This should make enough for 10 or more servings. It will keep in refrigerator up to 2 weeks.

This recipe is easily changed using a fruit-flavored yogurt but the calories rise.

STRAWBERRY BUTTER

Easy

10	ounce package frozen strawberries with syrup
8	ounces soft butter or margarine
1	cup powdered sugar

- Place all ingredients in food processor or blender. Mix well.
- Store in refrigerator. Use within 2 weeks.

This is a surprise taste for breakfast, brunch or tea table. Lovely with biscuits, muffins or pancakes.

LULLWATER TEA SANDWICH SPREAD

Easy

2	cups seedless raisins (dark or golden)
1	egg
➤	juice and grated peel of large lemon
1	cup sugar
➤	dash of salt
1	tablespoon butter or margarine
1	teaspoon vanilla
1	cup mayonnaise
1	cup finely chopped nuts (pecans, hazelnuts or almonds)

- Grind raisins in food processor.
- Beat egg in double boiler.
- Add lemon juice, peel and sugar. Cook over hot water until mixture thickens. Stir constantly.
- Remove from heat. Add salt, butter and vanilla. Stir well.
- Blend in mayonnaise.
- Vigorously stir in raisins and nuts.
- Store in refrigerator, covered, until needed.
- Spread at room temperature.

Wonderful tea sandwiches. Lemon is a very important flavor; use 2 lemons if necessary.

HISTORY NOTE

Lullwater is "home" to Emory's president and family. It was built in 1925 for Walter T. Candler, son of the founder of Coca-Cola.

Vegetables

VEGETABLES AND SIDE DISHES

SALSAS

EPICUREAN

Vegetables are the magic in our menus. With a relatively small investment of time, money and calories we reap fantastic dividends of color, texture, taste and nutrition. Freshness is everything! Those of us lacking in time, space or will to cultivate a garden can certainly learn to choose vegetables from the market that are at their peak of color and flavor.

Rejoice at what is in season: asparagus in the spring, tomatoes and corn in the summer, a variety of squashes, cabbages and flavorful root vegetables in fall and winter. Cooking with the seasons gives us the opportunity for excellent produce that is not only cheaper but tastes and smells better. Like Pooh Bear before the first taste of honey, anticipation heightens our appreciation.

Simplicity is frequently the best approach to cooking fresh vegetables. They will shine with minimal enhancement. Steaming, grilling and microwaving preserve color, flavor and crispness. Try a drizzle of olive oil or butter with a sprinkling of chopped fresh herbs.

Herbs are easily grown on a sunny window sill. Begin with a pot of parsley and let yourself get hooked. Herbs enhance in many ways.

Be prepared to rescue the less-than-perfect vegetable — the corn that somehow stayed in the refrigerator a week or the monster zucchini found hiding in the garden. These, too, can be delicious when made into long simmered stews or puddings or stuffed with fragrant mixtures of herbs and bread crumbs or rice.

Southerners have always placed a high value on "greens," and the many varieties of beans and peas are a proud heritage! Sweet potatoes, too, have been a staple in the South. They are high in fiber and cholesterol-free. Southern restaurants and cafeterias are often famous for their hot vegetable plates; Southern cooks as well!

ROASTED ASPARAGUS

♥   *Easy   Serves 4*

1	**pound fresh asparagus**
1½-2	**tablespoons olive oil**
➤	**salt and pepper to taste**
➤	**wedge of lemon**

• Heat oven to 400°F.
• Cut off white tips of asparagus stalks.
• Peel tough green skin from lower stalks.
• Arrange spears in single layer in 13x9x2-inch baking dish or jelly-roll pan.
• Drizzle sparingly with oil.
• Roast 8 - 10 minutes or until just tender.
• Sprinkle with salt and pepper and drops of lemon juice to taste.

CHEF'S NOTE

Asparagus needs to be peeled for uniform cooking.

GREEN BEAN STIR-FRY

Easy   *Serves 2*

½	**pound green beans**
1	**tablespoon peanut oil**
1	**clove garlic, minced**
1	**teaspoon minced fresh ginger**
1	**tablespoon sesame oil**
2	**arrowroot bulbs or 4 water chestnuts, peeled, sliced**
2-4	**green onions, sliced, tops reserved for garnish (optional)**
1	**tablespoon soy sauce**

- Cut beans ¼-inch thick, slanted across grain (Chinese oblique style) for attractiveness and quick cooking.
- Heat wok over medium high heat. Add peanut oil and swirl around wok to coat.
- Add beans. Stir-fry 1 - 2 minutes. Stir in garlic and ginger.
- Cover. Lower heat and cook 2 - 3 minutes.
- Uncover and raise heat. Add sesame oil and vegetables.
- Stir-fry until crisp tender. Add soy sauce. Garnish with onion tops.

Carrots, snow peas, asparagus, mushrooms or onion may be added, as well as other Chinese sauces such as ground bean or salted black bean.

Classic Chinese cooking shows great deference to color presentation.

PURÉE OF WHITE BEANS TUSCAN

🕐 *Make ahead for appetizer   Serves 8 - 10*

1	**pound dried navy or great northern beans**
½	**cup olive oil, divided**
2	**large cloves garlic, chopped**
10-12	**leaves fresh sage or 3 - 4-inch sprig rosemary (not both)**
1½	**teaspoons salt or to taste**
➤	**sprig sage or rosemary for garnish**

- Soak beans overnight, covered by 2 - 3 inches of cold water.
- Drain. Put in large heavy pot and cover with fresh water.
- Add ¼ cup oil, garlic and herbs.
- Bring to boil. Reduce heat. Simmer until beans are tender, about 1 hour. Add water as necessary to keep from sticking.
- Add salt. Raise heat and boil briefly until excess liquid has thickened. Add remaining oil.
- Purée small amounts in food processor or blender until smooth.
- Garnish with additional fresh herbs.
- May be served either hot or cold as appetizer, first course or for Italian buffet.

Olive oil is used for flavor — use a very good quality oil.

Good served on Italian bread in lieu of butter.

HOPPIN' JOHN

🕐 *Serves 8 - 10*

1	pound dried black-eyed peas
3	quarts water for soaking peas
½	pound chunk salt pork or bacon, cubed
2	medium onions, finely chopped
2-3	celery ribs, peeled, finely chopped
2	cups water
2-4	cloves garlic, minced
½	teaspoon each rosemary, thyme and salt
⅛	teaspoon cayenne pepper
1	bay leaf
¼	teaspoon freshly ground pepper
➤	hot pepper sauce to taste
➤	salt to taste
1	cup rice, cooked

- Wash peas. Soak overnight (see note).
- In large pot, cook salt pork over low heat until crisp. Discard.
- Add onion and celery and sauté in fat.
- Add water, garlic and seasonings. Bring to boil.
- Add drained peas to boiling mixture.
- Lower heat to simmer. Partially cover and cook about 45 minutes until soft, adding water as needed. Do not allow to dry out.
- Add rice and mix gently.

Salt pork adds much more flavor than bacon to this dish. If using bacon, don't discard; add to peas.

CHEF'S NOTE

Drain black-eyed peas and dried beans after soaking. Refresh with cold water before continuing with recipe.

BRAISED CABBAGE

Serves 6

1	medium head red cabbage (2 - 2½ pounds)
4	tablespoons butter, cut in small pieces
1	tablespoon sugar
1	teaspoon salt
⅓	cup water
⅓	cup white vinegar
¼	cup red currant jelly
¼	cup grated apple

- Remove tough outer leaves and core of cabbage. Finely shred. If possible, use food processor (approximately 9 cups shredded cabbage).
- Heat oven to 325°F.
- In heavy stainless steel or enameled 4 - 5-quart casserole, combine butter, sugar, salt, water and vinegar. Heat to boiling.
- Add cabbage and toss.
- Cover tightly. Place in center of oven to braise 2 hours. Check occasionally and add water if needed.
- About 10 minutes before cabbage is done, stir in jelly and apple. Replace cover and complete cooking.

Tastes best if refrigerated overnight and reheated.

Serve with pork, roast chicken or goose.

BUTTERED CARROTS

Easy   *Serves 4 - 6*

8-10	fresh medium carrots, peeled
2-4	tablespoons butter
½-1	teaspoon sugar
➤	salt and freshly ground pepper to taste
➤	finely chopped fresh tarragon (optional)

- Cut carrots into equal lengths and thinly slice lengthwise or crosswise.
- In pan large enough to hold carrots in 1 layer, melt 2 tablespoons butter over medium-low heat.
- Add carrots. Sprinkle with sugar, salt and pepper.
- Cook, covered, stirring every 2 - 3 minutes until just tender and glazed. Add more butter as needed.
- Sprinkle with tarragon if desired.

CHEF'S NOTE

Very young fresh carrots are naturally sweet and need no sugar or salt. They will sweeten while cooking. Taste raw to test for sweetness. Two tablespoons orange-flavored liqueur and grated zest from fresh orange will make older carrots exceptional.

DILLY CARROTS

Easy   *Serves 4*

3	tablespoons butter or margarine
3	tablespoons vinegar
2	tablespoons light brown sugar
1	pound carrots, cut in 2-inch sticks
⅛	teaspoon dried dill weed (1 teaspoon fresh dill)

- In medium saucepan, mix butter, vinegar and sugar. Add carrots and dill. Bring to boil.
- Cover. Reduce heat; simmer 10 - 12 minutes until crisp tender.
- Serve.

BAKED SWISS CAULIFLOWER

Serves 6

1	head cauliflower, cleaned, cored
½	cup bread crumbs
2⅔	cups shredded Swiss cheese
1½	cups half and half
3	egg yolks, beaten
¼	teaspoon ground nutmeg (optional)
➤	salt and pepper to taste
2	tablespoons butter, melted

- Heat oven to 350°F.
- Break cauliflower apart if desired.
- Cook 10 minutes in salted boiling water. Drain well. (Or microwave 6 - 8 minutes at HIGH in covered dish with 3 tablespoons water.)
- Place in baking dish. (Use deep dish if keeping cauliflower whole.)
- Combine remaining ingredients. Pour over cauliflower.
- Drizzle butter over top. Bake 15 - 20 minutes.

SOUTHERN CORN PUDDING

Serves 4

4	**large ears of white or yellow corn**
2	**eggs, beaten**
1	**cup heavy cream**
➣	**salt and white pepper to taste**
1	**tablespoon sugar (optional)**

- Heat oven to 350°F and grease 1½-quart casserole dish.
- Cut kernels from corn using sharp knife (minimum 1 cup).
- Beat cream into eggs.
- Mix well with corn. Season. Pour into casserole dish.
- Place casserole in 2 - 3-inch-high pan half-filled with water.
- Bake 50 - 60 minutes.
- Insert knife in center to test for doneness.

CHEF'S NOTE

Soufflé: Change this recipe very slightly. Separate eggs and beat egg whites to soft peak stage for soufflé texture.

CRANBERRY APPLE CONSERVE

3	cups chopped apple
1	cup sugar
2	cups uncooked whole cranberries
½	cup (1 stick) butter or margarine, melted
½	cup firmly packed brown sugar
½	cup all-purpose flour
1	cup quick oats
½	cup chopped nuts

- Heat oven to 300°F.
- Combine apple, sugar and cranberries. Pour into 13x9x2-inch baking pan.
- Combine remaining ingredients and spread over fruit mixture.
- Bake 1 hour.

This may be served warm or cold as a side dish accompanying poultry, pork or ham. It may also be served warm with whipped cream or vanilla ice cream for dessert.

HISTORY NOTE

This was a favorite recipe of Mrs. William J. (Adelle) Dickey, former librarian at Oxford College. Adelle Dickey, who was 96 years old in December 1992, resides in Texas. Her husband, Professor Dickey, was associate professor of mathematics at Oxford College for 18 years, 1942-1960.

EGGPLANT PARMIGIANA CASSEROLE

Vegetarian entrée   Serves 6

2	tablespoons olive oil
2	medium onions, sliced
1	clove garlic, crushed
6	tomatoes, peeled, cored
2	tablespoons tomato paste
½	teaspoon thyme
¼	teaspoon sugar
½	teaspoon salt (optional)
½	cup dry bread crumbs
½	cup grated Parmesan cheese
1	tablespoon finely chopped fresh parsley
1½	pounds unpeeled eggplant, thinly sliced
2	eggs, lightly beaten
➤	vegetable oil
½	pound mozzarella cheese, thinly sliced

- Heat oven to 350°F and grease 13x9x2-inch pan.
- Heat olive oil in skillet. Sauté onion and garlic until tender.
- Add tomatoes, tomato paste, thyme, sugar and salt. Simmer 30 - 40 minutes.
- Mix bread crumbs, Parmesan cheese and parsley. Salt and pepper to taste. Set aside.
- Dip eggplant slices in beaten egg.
- In large skillet, sauté in 1-inch hot oil until tender and golden brown on both sides. Drain on paper towels.
- Place layer of eggplant on bottom of pan. Sprinkle with part of crumb mixture and part of tomato mixture. Repeat 2 - 3 times. End with eggplant.
- Cover with slices of mozzarella. Bake 30 minutes.

In winter, boxed or canned Italian plum tomatoes may be preferred to the fresh tomatoes at market.

CHEF'S NOTE

Vegetable cooking spray is a terrific way to grease a cooking pan or baking dish as you begin a recipe. It is a no-mess and low fat quick trick for cooks. Natural hydrocarbons, rather than the harmful chlorofluorocarbons, are used as propellant. Try to spray in such a way that your floor and counter top will not become slippery. Get in the vegetable cooking spray habit, and you may find you have lowered your fat consumption with ease!

AMARETTO HOT FRUIT COMPOTE

Easy   *Serves 12 - 20*

16	ounce can peach halves, drained
16	ounce can pear halves, drained
15	ounce can pineapple chunks, drained
17	ounce can apricot halves, drained
16	ounce can pitted tart pie cherries, drained
11	ounce can mandarin oranges, drained
2-3	bananas, sliced
2	teaspoons lemon juice
14	soft coconut macaroons, crumbled
2¼	ounces sliced almonds, toasted, divided
¼	cup butter or margarine
⅓	cup amaretto or other almond-flavored liqueur

- Heat oven to 350°F.
- Combine canned fruits in large bowl.
- Toss banana with lemon juice; add to fruit mixture.
- Set aside half of almonds for topping.
- In 2½-quart shallow baking dish, layer fruit mixture, crumbled macaroons and almonds. Dot with butter.
- Repeat until mixtures are used.
- Pour amaretto evenly over all.
- Bake 30 minutes.
- Sprinkle reserved almonds over top and serve.

Juices drained from fruit may be used in punch or gelatin salads.

SMOTHERED MUSHROOMS

Serves 4

1	ounce dried porcini mushrooms
1	cup warm water
¼	cup olive oil
1	large clove garlic, finely chopped
1	pound fresh mushrooms, halved or quartered if large
1	tablespoon freshly chopped Italian parsley
➤	salt and pepper to taste
➤	additional fresh parsley for garnish

• Soak dry mushrooms in water 20 - 30 minutes until soft.
• Lift from liquid. Filter liquid through dampened paper towel or cheesecloth. Save.
• Wash mushrooms in 2 changes of water. Squeeze dry. Chop finely.
• Sauté garlic in oil until just soft.
• Add fresh mushrooms. Sauté 5 minutes until lightly browned over medium to high heat, tossing gently.
• Add dry mushrooms and soaking liquid. Boil briefly until almost dry.
• Add parsley. Reduce heat to low. Cover. Cook 20 - 30 minutes.
• Remove cover. Raise heat to evaporate any liquid.
• Salt and pepper to taste. Toss with additional parsley and serve.

Leftovers may be coarsely chopped and spread on toasted slices of Italian or French bread. Top with grated Parmesan cheese. Broil briefly to melt cheese.

3-CHEESE ONION CASSEROLE

Serves 8 - 10

1	tablespoon unsalted butter
2	large yellow onions, thinly sliced
2	large red onions, thinly sliced
4	medium leeks, white part only, thinly sliced
➤	salt and freshly ground pepper to taste
4-5	ounces Havarti cheese, grated (1½ cups)
10	ounces Boursin cheese with herbs, crumbled
4-5	ounces Gruyère cheese, grated (1½ cups)
½	cup dry white wine

- Heat oven to 350°F and butter 2-quart baking dish.
- Layer ⅓ of onion and leek in dish. Lightly salt and pepper. Top with Havarti.
- Repeat for second layer. Top with Boursin.
- Top third layer with Gruyère.
- Pour wine over all.
- Bake 1 hour. Cover top with foil if browning too fast.
- Serve immediately.

This is an elegant, rich and wonderful dish for buffet table.

GRILLED VIDALIA ONIONS

♥   *Simply wonderful!*   *Serves 1 - 2*

1	large Vidalia onion, unpeeled, trimmed
1-3	teaspoons olive oil
➤	salt and pepper to taste
1	sprig fresh thyme or a pinch of dried thyme

- Slice onion in half, across grain.
- Brush with olive oil. Grill cut side down over brisk heat until grill marks appear.
- Turn skin side down. Brush with oil. Sprinkle with salt, pepper and thyme.
- Continue grilling until soft, 30 - 90 minutes. Time will depend on temperature and size of grill. Place onions on far sides or upper rack while other foods are cooking.
- Peel off outer burnt layer and enjoy!

Other onions may be used, such as Texas Sweet or Walla Walla.

Many fresh vegetables — tomatoes, eggplant, bell peppers, zucchini — are wonderful when grilled. Follow above recipe.

ONION PIE SUPREME

Serves 6 - 8

9	inch pie shell
3	cups thinly sliced onion (Vidalia if possible)
3	tablespoons butter or margarine, melted
½	cup half and half
½	cup sour cream
3	tablespoons flour
2	large eggs, well-beaten
1½	teaspoons No-Salt Herb Seasoning (page 69)
➤	pinch of ground cumin
¼	cup freshly grated Parmesan cheese
➤	chopped fresh parsley or crumbled bacon for garnish

- Prepare and bake pie shell (underbake slightly).
- Heat oven to 400°F.
- Sauté onion in butter until lightly browned.
- Blend half and half with sour cream and flour. Combine with eggs. Add seasonings. Pour over onion.
- Put mixture in pie shell. Sprinkle with Parmesan cheese.
- Bake 20 minutes. Reduce heat to 325°F. Bake additional 20 minutes.
- Top with parsley or bacon.

VIDALIA ONION PIE

Easy   Serves 6 - 8

1	heaping cup crushed crackers (mixed saltines and round buttery crackers)
⅓	cup butter or margarine, melted
3	cups thinly sliced onion (Vidalia if possible)
2	eggs, lightly beaten
½	teaspoon salt
1¼	cups milk, scalded
1½	cups grated medium or sharp Cheddar cheese

- Heat oven to 325°F.
- Mix crumbs with half of butter in 9-inch pie plate. Press onto sides and bottom to form crust.
- Sauté onion in remaining butter until soft.
- Mix remaining ingredients and lightly stir into onion.
- Pour mixture into crust and spread gently.
- Bake 30 - 40 minutes until lightly browned and center tests done.

This may look as if it is going to overflow, but that has not happened in our many testings.

HISTORY NOTE

This recipe was submitted by Sara Gregory, who served as librarian at Oxford College for many years. Her husband, Professor John W. Gregory, was associate professor of humanities for 32 years, 1947-1979.

SOUTHERN OYSTER DRESSING

🕐

½	cup butter, melted
3	green bell peppers, chopped
½	cup chopped fresh parsley
2	cups chopped celery
3	small bunches green onions, chopped
1	teaspoon thyme
1	bay leaf
➤	salt to taste
1	quart oysters, drained (save liquid)
6	cups crumbled cornbread
14-16	ounces soft French rolls or bread, crumbled
➤	bouillon (canned or cubes plus necessary water)

- Mix butter, vegetables and seasonings. Cook until soft. Remove bay leaf.
- Add oysters last 5 minutes and heat until edges curl.
- Toss with crumbled bread, oyster liquid and enough bouillon to make moist dressing.
- May be used to stuff turkey or bake in 2 (1½-quart) casseroles 45 minutes at 350°F.

2 (8 ounce) packages cornbread mix will make needed amount.

Recipe may be halved easily.

CHEF'S NOTE

Peeling celery removes bitterness.

Baked Pineapple Pudding

Easy　*Delicious hot or cold*　*Serves 6 - 8*

½	**cup butter**
¾	**cup sugar**
4	**eggs or egg substitute**
2½	**cups crushed pineapple (packed in own juice), drained**
5	**slices bread, cubed**

- Heat oven to 350°F and grease shallow baking dish.
- Cream butter and sugar. Add eggs and beat well.
- Stir in pineapple and bread.
- Bake, uncovered, 45 minutes until lightly browned. If needed, place under broiler to brown.

May be prepared ahead, baked later.

Baby Potatoes with Garlic and Thyme

Easy　*Serves 4*

16	**tiny new potatoes**
4	**cloves garlic, peeled, quartered**
➢	**several sprigs of thyme or ½ teaspoon dried thyme (or tarragon)**
2½	**tablespoons olive oil**
➢	**salt and pepper to taste**

- Heat oven to 375°F.
- Halve potatoes. Place in baking dish.
- Sprinkle garlic, thyme and then oil over potatoes.
- Salt and pepper.
- Bake, covered, 30 minutes. Uncover and bake 10 minutes. Serve.
- *Variation:* Substitute ½ teaspoon lemon-pepper seasoning and ½ teaspoon caraway seed for garlic and thyme.

GARLIC ROASTED NEW POTATOES

Easy   *Serves 10 - 12*

4	pounds small or medium new potatoes
⅓	cup olive oil
2	teaspoons minced or crushed garlic
½	teaspoon freshly ground pepper
➢	salt (coarse grind)

- In large saucepan, place potatoes in water to cover.
- Heat to boiling. Cook until tender, 10 - 15 minutes.
- Drain and cool. Cut in half or quarter.
- Heat oven to 350°F.
- Transfer to large bowl and toss with oil, garlic and pepper.
- Place in casserole dish. Sprinkle salt to taste. Bake, uncovered, 30 minutes until browned.

These potatoes are also a big hit when wrapped in foil and charcoal grilled.

MASHED POTATO CASSEROLE

Serves 8 - 10

Mashed Potatoes:

4	medium large baking potatoes, peeled, quartered
1	tablespoon chopped onion
½	teaspoon each salt and freshly ground pepper
2	tablespoons butter
½	cup milk

- *Mashed potatoes:* Boil potatoes, onion, salt and pepper 15 minutes, until just tender. Drain. Mash well. Add butter and milk. If too stiff add more milk. Set aside.

Casserole:

2	cups mashed potatoes
16	ounces cottage cheese
2	eggs
½	cup sour cream
¼	teaspoon cayenne pepper
½	cup chopped green onion
5	tablespoons grated Parmesan cheese

- *Casserole:* Heat oven to 425°F and grease 2-quart casserole dish.
- Mix cottage cheese and eggs in food processor or blender.
- Add other ingredients. Pulse several times. Beat mixture into potatoes.
- Pour into casserole. Bake about 40 minutes. Test for doneness by inserting knife in center.
- *Variation:* Substitute ½-pound medium or wide noodles, cooked, for potatoes.

Nice do-ahead dish to accompany fillet of beef, chicken, turkey or pork. Reheat in microwave.

Georgia Sweet Potato Soufflé

Easy   *Serves 8 - 10*

6	medium sweet potatoes, cooked, peeled, mashed (3 cups)
⅓	cup firmly packed brown sugar
2	eggs, beaten
½	teaspoon salt
2	tablespoons butter or margarine, melted
⅓	cup milk
1	teaspoon each vanilla and grated orange peel
1	tablespoon frozen orange juice concentrate

Topping:

2	tablespoons butter or margarine
¾	cup firmly packed brown sugar
¼	cup flour
½-¾	cup chopped pecans

- Heat oven to 350°F and grease shallow 2-quart baking or soufflé dish.
- Combine ingredients. Beat 3 - 5 minutes.
- Place in dish. Smooth top.
- *Topping*: Cut butter into flour with pastry blender or processor until texture is like cornmeal. Add sugar and pecans.
- Sprinkle topping over potatoes. Bake uncovered 35 - 45 minutes or until golden brown.

Use boiled or baked potatoes (or canned).

History Note

Haygood-Hopkins Memorial Gateway, which is pictured on the front cover, was given to the university in 1937.

ED'S SPINACH PIE

Serves 8

2	tablespoons olive oil
½	cup chopped onion
3	cloves garlic, minced
8	ounces fresh mushrooms, sliced
2	(10 ounce) packages frozen chopped spinach, thawed, drained
½	teaspoon each dried oregano and basil
¼	teaspoon each salt and pepper
½	pound feta cheese, crumbled
2	eggs, beaten
¾	cup grated Parmesan cheese

• Heat oven to 350°F and grease round, shallow casserole.
• In large pan, sauté onion, garlic and mushrooms in oil.
• When onion is transparent, add spinach and seasonings. Stir.
• Cook 5 minutes. Turn off heat.
• Stir in feta cheese.
• Add eggs. Stir until eggs begin to cook.
• Spoon into baking dish. Top with Parmesan cheese.
• Bake 30 - 40 minutes until cheese begins to brown.

SPINACH SANDWICH LOAF

Easy

➤	large fat loaf of French or Italian unsliced bread
2	(10 ounce) packages frozen chopped spinach, thawed, drained
4	cloves garlic, crushed or minced
½	cup (1 stick) butter or margarine
8-12	ounces mozzarella cheese, shredded

• Heat oven to 400°F.
• Split loaf lengthwise as if a large bun.
• Sauté spinach and garlic lightly in butter.
• Divide spinach mixture equally on two halves of bread. Sprinkle with cheese.
• Bake about 20 minutes, uncovered. For ease in cleanup, bake and serve on foil.
• Serve like pizza.

This may be put together earlier, wrapped in foil and refrigerated until baking.

HISTORY NOTE

Emory University officially became coeducational in 1953. However, Eleanore Raoul was the first woman to be admitted (in 1917 to the College of Law).

MICROWAVE SPINACH TORTA

Easy   *Serves 4 - 6*

10	ounce package frozen spinach, thawed, drained
4	eggs, lightly beaten, or egg substitute
2	cups cooked rice
1¼	cups freshly grated Parmesan cheese
1	cup whole-milk ricotta cheese
⅓	cup minced green onion
1	teaspoon No-Salt Herb Seasoning (page 69)
¼-½	teaspoon ground pepper

- Grease microwave dish (loaf pan, 6-cup ring mold or 8x8-inch).
- Mix ingredients in large bowl.
- Spoon into dish.
- Microwave at MEDIUM-HIGH 15 - 18 minutes until center is slightly firm to touch. Rotate every 3 minutes.
- Cool on wire rack at least 10 minutes.
- Prettiest if unmolded, thinly sliced and arranged on serving plate.

Nice luncheon or dinner dish with chicken. Can be topped with cheese or tomato-based sauce. Very versatile.

SPINACH CASSEROLE

♥   *Easy*   *Serves 4 - 6*

2	(10 ounce) packages frozen chopped spinach, thawed, drained
2	eggs, beaten, or egg substitute
8	ounces low fat Monterey Jack or Swiss cheese
8	ounces low fat cottage cheese
2	tablespoons flour
➤	salt, pepper, nutmeg and garlic powder to taste
➤	finely chopped Vidalia onion

- Heat oven to 350°F and grease 13x9x2-inch baking pan.
- Combine spinach, eggs, cheeses, flour and seasonings. Mix.
- Place in pan. Bake 30 - 40 minutes. Sprinkle onion over top after 20 minutes of baking.
- Cool 10 minutes and cut in squares.

CHEF'S NOTE

Microwaving spinach, if in box package, is simple and quick and less mess!

BAKED SQUASH CASSEROLE

Easy   *Serves 8*

1½   pounds yellow squash, sliced
1   medium onion, chopped
2   large carrots, grated
1   cup light sour cream
10   ounce can condensed cream of chicken soup
¼   cup (½ stick) butter or margarine, melted
2   cups herb-seasoned stuffing
➤   salt and pepper to taste

- Heat oven to 350°F and grease 2-quart casserole.
- In medium saucepan, cook squash and onion with small amount of water until tender. Drain.
- Add carrot, sour cream, soup and butter. Mix. Add stuffing and mix briefly.
- Bake 30 - 40 minutes.

Preparation time can be shortened by using a food processor; casserole will have a soufflé-like texture.

Recipe is easily divided and may be baked half at a time. (Save second half for next day or take to a friend!)

BAKED YELLOW SQUASH WITH FRESH TOMATOES

Easy   *Serves 8*

2   pounds yellow squash, sliced
3   medium tomatoes, peeled, sliced
2   small onions, sliced paper thin
1½   teaspoons salt
3½   tablespoons butter or margarine
1   cup round buttery cracker crumbs or fresh buttered breadcrumbs

- Heat oven to 350°F and grease shallow casserole.
- Place layer of squash in casserole.
- Add layer of tomato, then onion.
- Sprinkle with ½ teaspoon salt and 1½ tablespoons butter.
- Repeat layering until all vegetables are used.
- Sprinkle with remaining salt and butter.
- Cover and bake 45 minutes.
- Uncover. Top with crumbs. Bake 10 minutes.

This recipe has endless possibilities. Try adding Vidalia or red onion, zucchini or green bell pepper.

HISTORY NOTE

Emory became embroiled in the integration movement from 1958 to 1961, with Emory faculty publicly supporting the integration of Atlanta's public school system.

MICROWAVE SPAGHETTI SQUASH

♥   *Easy*   *Serves 2-4*

1	**small spaghetti squash (about 2 pounds)**
1	**tablespoon vegetable oil**
1	**cup sliced green or red bell pepper**
1	**cup sliced onion**
1	**cup sliced fresh mushrooms**
➤	**salt and pepper to taste**

- Prick squash skin all around with knife point.
- Place on paper towel and microwave at HIGH 5 minutes.
- Turn over and cook additional 5 minutes.
- Cut in half lengthwise and remove seeds.
- Place cut side down in glass baking dish. Microwave until done, about 10 - 15 minutes. Strands will separate easily when scraped out with fork.
- While squash is cooking, stir-fry other vegetables in oil.
- Scrape squash out of shells and toss with vegetables.
- Salt and pepper.

OTTAVIO MISSONI'S VEGETABLE CASSEROLE

Serves 6 - 8

4	potatoes, peeled, thinly sliced
½	cup olive oil, divided
➢	salt and pepper to taste
1	large unpeeled eggplant, thinly sliced
3-4	small zucchini, cut in ½-inch rounds
1	each red, green and yellow bell pepper, cut in strips
1	large onion, cut in half, sliced
1-2	ripe tomatoes, chopped
½	cup pitted Moroccan olives
1	teaspoon dried thyme (2 tablespoons fresh thyme)

- Heat oven to 350°F and grease large casserole.
- Layer potatoes in casserole. Sprinkle lightly with olive oil, salt and pepper.
- Layer other vegetables in attractive rows of color, alternating flavors.
- Scatter olives on top.
- Add remaining olive oil, salt and pepper.
- Cover with foil. Bake 45 - 60 minutes until tender.

Serve slices as in lasagna — looks very colorful.

HISTORY NOTE

The Missoni name is world-famous for colorful designs in fabric and knitwear.

Fried Green Tomatoes

Easy   *Serves 1-2*

1	large green tomato
3	tablespoons each flour and cornmeal
➤	salt and pepper to taste
➤	milk (optional)
➤	vegetable oil

- Slice tomato ¼ - ½ inch thick.
- Mix flour, cornmeal, salt and pepper.
- Dredge tomato slices with flour-cornmeal mixture.
- If desired, dip in milk and dredge again.
- Fry in ½-inch hot oil until golden brown.

Scalloped Fresh Tomatoes

Serves 4

3-4	tablespoons butter or margarine
½	cup finely chopped onion
1	clove garlic, minced
1	cup soft bread crumbs
1	teaspoon sugar
2	teaspoons chopped fresh basil
⅛	teaspoon pepper
¼	teaspoon salt
3	tablespoons grated Parmesan cheese
3-4	tomatoes, sliced

- Heat oven to 350°F and grease 1-quart casserole.
- Briefly sauté onion and garlic in butter.
- Add bread crumbs, sugar, basil, pepper, salt and cheese.
- Mix well. Cook 2 - 3 minutes.
- Place ⅓ of tomatoes in casserole. Add ⅓ of crumb mixture. Repeat layers twice more.
- Bake 20 - 30 minutes.

Fabulous with Vidalia onion, freshly grated Parmesan cheese and fresh basil and tomatoes.

Chef's Note

For sensitive palates, core garlic and onions before mincing.

Taste of Italy Tomato Sorbet

★   *Serves a "bunch"*

6	**large ripe tomatoes (3½ - 4 cups) or 28 ounces crushed, canned tomatoes**
⅓-½	**cup arugula, finely chopped**
⅓-½	**cup fresh basil, finely chopped**
1	**stalk tender celery, finely chopped**
3	**cloves garlic, crushed**
2	**tablespoons extra virgin olive oil**
1	**tablespoon sugar**
➤	**salt and freshly ground pepper to taste**
1	**egg white**

- Peel tomatoes and put through food mill or strainer to remove seeds.
- Combine all but egg white and freeze in ice cream machine to stiff slush stage.
- Beat egg white until stiff and stir into tomato mixture.
- Continue freezing sorbet until it holds shape.
- Serve a scoop in a champagne or sherbet glass garnished with a fresh basil leaf.
- This is best made at the last minute so that sorbet is not totally frozen.

Saltiness is sometimes masked by freezing. An extra pinch of salt may be needed for this recipe.

Canned tomatoes may be used in off-season. Crushed tomatoes will not need to be strained.

HOT PEPPER JELLY

Easy

½	cup chopped jalapeño pepper
¾	cup chopped green bell pepper
5	cups sugar
1½	cups white or cider vinegar
➤	green food color
1	container Certo

- Bring to boil peppers, sugar and vinegar. Simmer 10 minutes.
- Strain if desired. Add green coloring.
- Stir in Certo while hot but not boiling.
- Pour into jelly glasses and let set.
- Excellent served over cream cheese as an appetizer or as an accompaniment to meats.

Use red peppers and food color for red jelly.

CARROT AND SWEET PEPPER SALSA

3 cups

2	medium carrots, peeled, finely shredded
½	each red and green bell pepper, seeded, diced
½	cup minced shallot or red onion or white part of green onion
6	tablespoons white or rice vinegar
2	tablespoons brown sugar
1	tablespoon minced or grated fresh ginger
2	large cloves garlic, minced or crushed
➤	salt to taste

- Mix all ingredients.
- Stir until sugar is dissolved. Adjust seasoning.
- Cover and refrigerate at least 1 hour (up to 2 days).

CHEF'S NOTE

To keep fresh ginger, peel, put in jar and cover with sherry. Refrigerate.

CREOLE SALSA

Easy   *Serves 10 - 12*

1-2	tablespoons olive oil
1	small onion, chopped (Vidalia onion if possible)
⅓	cup minced green or red bell pepper or both
⅓	cup peeled, diced celery
4	tomatoes, peeled, chopped
½	cup sliced fresh mushrooms
1	teaspoon Creole seasoning
¼	cup chopped fresh cilantro (optional)
2-4	tablespoons Italian dressing (optional)

• Slightly cook onion in oil to remove sharpness unless Vidalias are available.
• Add remaining ingredients. Mix well.

Makes a wonderful sauce for grilled hamburgers or meats.

PINEAPPLE SALSA

3 cups

1	small pineapple (3 pounds)
1	medium red onion, minced
¾	cup chopped fresh cilantro
1	tablespoon white or rice vinegar
½	teaspoon hot pepper sauce

• Remove pineapple from shell; core and coarsely chop fruit. Drain.
• Mix with remaining ingredients.
• Serve in pineapple shell or bowl.

Goes well with grilled chicken.

HISTORY NOTE

Under Georgia law, private institutions had to remain segregated or risk losing tax-exempt status. The board of trustees passed a resolution in 1961 urging the admission of students without regard to race, creed or color as soon as tax laws would permit. After extensive court proceedings, this policy was confirmed.

Epicurean Fall Seated Dinner for 12

Broccoli and Baked Tomatoes

Serves 12

3	bunches broccoli, stems cut 3 inches below flower
4-6	tablespoons unsalted butter, divided
6	large tomatocs, cored, cut in half
1	teaspoon salt
➢	white pepper to taste
4	tablespoons grated Parmesan cheese
2	tablespoons chopped fresh parsley
2	tablespoons bread crumbs

- Heat oven to 350°F and grease baking dish.
- Broccoli: Cut larger pieces in half lengthwise to uniform size. Blanch 3 minutes. Drain and refresh in cold water. Drain. Place in baking dish. Dot with 3 - 5 tablespoons butter.
- Tomatoes: Place in baking dish. Sprinkle lightly with salt and white pepper. Sprinkle 1 teaspoon Parmesan cheese on each tomato then dot with ¼ teaspoon butter, ½ teaspoon parsley and ½ teaspoon bread crumbs.
- Bake, covered, 15 minutes.

Broccoli and tomatoes may be baked and served separately. Cover each dish and bake 15 minutes.

Epicurean Spring Cookout for 30

Papaya Salsa

Serves 30

12	cups (peeled, seeded) cubed ripe papaya (1-inch cubes)
12	cups seeded, cubed vine-ripened tomato (1-inch cubes)
2	cups cubed red onion (½-inch cubes)
1½	cups chopped green onion
¾	cup coarsely chopped cilantro
½	cup lime juice

- Combine all ingredients and toss.
- Chill 2 hours or more. (Best if prepared same day as served.)

Epicurean Summer Dinner for 25

Blanched Vegetables and Bibb Lettuce

Serves 25

2	tablespoons salt
3	heads of cauliflower, florets only
4	bunches of broccoli, florets only
2	pounds medium carrots, peeled, cut in 3-inch sticks
50	slices of tomato
50	slices of cucumber
50	slices of yellow squash
50	jumbo black olives
6	heads of Bibb lettuce
25	slices of lemon
➢	**Herb Vinaigrette (page 71)**

- In 10-quart pot, add salt to boiling water. Blanch cauliflower, a third at a time, for 3 minutes. Use wire basket or remove with slotted spoon and plunge into ice water to cool. Drain.
- Bring water back to boiling and repeat procedure.
- When finished with cauliflower, blanch broccoli and then carrots.
- Arrange on serving platter or individual plates on Bibb lettuce with sliced raw vegetables and 6 ounces of Poached Fresh Salmon (page 215).
- Spoon Herb Vinaigrette over vegetables just before serving.

Cheese,
Eggs, Pasta,
Grains

Cheese, Eggs, Pasta, Grains

CHEESE AND EGGS

PASTA

GRAINS

*P*asta and grains are superb sources of complex carbohydrates and fiber and would deserve a prominent place in our daily diet even if they were not so delicious. Cheese and eggs are excellent and economical sources of protein. We are indebted to cheeses for their flavors. A small amount can make something ordinary quite delicious, as, for example, cheese grits. True, many cheeses are high in fat, but there are more and more low fat varieties available. Be aware that grating your own cheese will give you a much more flavorful fresh taste.

There are literally hundreds of kinds of rice in this world, and not all may be used interchangeably. Long-grain rice is best for dishes in which a fluffy texture is desired. Short grains, especially the Italian ones, stick together and have a creamy consistency. Brown rice has a nutty flavor that marries well with poultry, herbs and nuts. Wild rice, which is not truly rice, adds a crunchy, nutty texture — perfect with poultry and game.

Pasta has become the food of the 90's, with a great explosion of variety available in both color and shape. If you have a source of fresh egg pasta, by all means use it, but we recommend the packaged, dried variety, which is so easy to keep and to use. It is also fun to make your own! One cookbook committee member enjoys family pasta parties, with everyone pitching in and producing a grand dinner.

We offer you advice on cooking pasta. It is most important not to overcook whatever variety you might use. Rely on a personal bite test for timing — not on the clock.

COOKING PASTA: It is important to use a large pot when cooking pasta and best to cook no more than a pound at a time. Bring 4 quarts of water to boil over high heat. Salting the water in which pasta is cooked is traditional. Salt is flavorful but is not necessary if you must reduce or omit for health reasons. Some pasta recipes call for a tablespoon of oil in the cooking water. This is not "the Italian way," but adding oil might help to reduce stickiness when cooking large-size pasta. Oil should not be needed if you cook pasta in adequate water.

Do not put pasta into pot until water is at full boil. If pasta is long spaghetti or fettucini, give it a minute or two to soften and fully submerge. Stir gently to ensure pasta is separated. Do not cover. Continue cooking until pasta is al dente, firm to the bite but no longer crunchy. Pasta will rise to the surface. When pasta tests done, immediately drain into colander. Be prepared to serve at once.

When cooking pasta for a cold salad, toss drained pasta with a tablespoon of oil. (You may need to rinse the pasta under cold running water before adding oil.)

EMORY'S CHEESE SOUFFLÉ

Serves 4 - 6

2½	tablespoons butter or margarine
2	tablespoons flour
¾	cup milk
5	eggs, separated
½	cup grated Parmesan cheese
¼	cup grated sharp Cheddar cheese
➢	dash of hot pepper sauce
¼	teaspoon cream of tartar

- Heat oven to 300°F and grease 2-quart casserole.
- In small saucepan, make white sauce: Melt butter. Add flour and stir until smooth. Do not allow to brown. Continue stirring (or whisk) while adding milk. Continue cooking until thickened.
- Beat egg yolks. Add to white sauce. Add cheeses and hot pepper sauce.
- Cool to lukewarm.
- Beat egg whites with cream of tartar until stiff. Fold into yolk mixture.
- Place in casserole.
- Bake 1 hour or until set.

Serve with asparagus, tossed salad and French bread.

HISTORY NOTE

Recipe comes (with minor changes) from Emory Cooks, the first Emory University Woman's Club cookbook. It was served for years at Emory's old Cox Hall cafeteria.

EASY CHEESY BAKED GRITS

Serves 4 - 6

1	cup uncooked grits (regular or quick, not instant)
¼	cup butter or margarine
½-1	cup grated Cheddar cheese
1	clove garlic, crushed (optional)
2	eggs, beaten
½	cup milk
➤	optional topping: 1 cup cornflakes 2 tablespoons butter or margarine, melted

- Heat oven to 350°F and grease 2-quart casserole.
- Cook grits according to package directions.
- Stir butter, cheese and garlic into hot grits.
- Beat eggs and milk and gradually add to grits.
- Pour into casserole. Top with cornflakes tossed with butter.
- Bake uncovered about 45 minutes.

This basic recipe appears in both previous Emory cookbooks, Emory Cooks and Emory Cooks Again. Certainly no self-respecting cookbook originating in the South could be without a good grits recipe!

HEARTY ARTICHOKE TART

Serves 8 - 10

9	ounce package frozen artichoke hearts or 14-ounce can, drained, rinsed
➤	juice of 1 lemon
1	tablespoon red wine vinegar
5	peppercorns
1	tablespoon butter or margarine
1	green onion, minced
½	cup finely diced ham
2	teaspoons Madeira wine
10	inch unbaked pie shell
4	ounces Monterey Jack cheese, diced
4	ounces mozzarella cheese, diced
½	cup heavy cream
➤	pepper to taste

- In saucepan, combine artichoke hearts, lemon juice, vinegar and peppercorns. Add water to cover, about ¼ cup.
- Bring to boil. Reduce heat. Cover and simmer 10 minutes.
- Lightly sauté green onion in butter.
- Stir in ham and Madeira.
- Cook over medium heat until ham is lightly browned and all liquid is absorbed. Cool.
- Heat oven to 375°F.
- Sprinkle ham mixture over bottom of pie shell.
- Drain artichokes and remove peppercorns. Arrange artichokes over ham.
- Add cheeses. Pour cream over top. Season.
- Bake 40 minutes.

This may be "finger food" for buffet.

SMOKED SALMON CHEESECAKE

Serves 10 - 12

¼	cup bread crumbs
3	tablespoons grated Parmesan cheese
3½	8-ounce packages cream cheese
4	large eggs
⅓	cup heavy cream
3	tablespoons butter
1	medium onion, finely chopped
1	green bell pepper, finely chopped
⅓-½	pound smoked salmon, finely diced
½	cup grated Gruyère cheese
¼	cup grated Parmesan cheese
➤	salt and pepper to taste

- Heat oven to 300°F and grease 8x3-inch cheesecake pan. Do not use pan with removable bottom. A second slightly larger pan also is needed. (See below.)
- Mix bread crumbs and 3 tablespoons Parmesan cheese. Sprinkle in pan. Coat bottom and sides evenly. Shake out excess.
- Cream, until smooth, cream cheese, eggs and cream.
- Sauté onion and green pepper in butter. Add to cheese mixture.
- Add salmon and cheeses. Salt and pepper.
- Pour into pan. Set pan in larger pan containing 2 inches boiling water. Sides of pans should not be touching.
- Bake 1 hour 40 minutes. Turn off oven. Leave cake in oven 1 additional hour.
- Remove from oven and from water bath. Cool on rack before turning out. Refrigerate. Serve cold.

Recipe may be made a day ahead. Serve as luncheon main course with fruit, green salad and crusty bread.

CRUSTLESS QUICHE

Serves a "bunch"

¼	cup butter
½	cup flour
1	cup milk, warmed
6	eggs, beaten, or egg substitute
1	pound Monterey Jack cheese, cubed
3	ounces cream cheese, cubed
2	cups small curd cottage cheese
1	teaspoon each sugar and salt

- Heat oven to 350°F and grease 6-cup rectangular baking dish.
- In small saucepan, make white sauce: Melt butter. Add flour and stir until smooth. Do not allow to brown. Continue stirring (or whisk) while adding milk. Bring just to boil over low heat.
- Remove from heat and whisk in beaten eggs.
- Stir in cheeses and seasoning. Pour into dish.
- Bake 45 minutes.
- Cut in bite-size squares to serve.

Taste may be changed by substituting Swiss, Gruyère or Cheddar cheese.

CHILE RELLEÑOS EGG CASSEROLE

Serves 10 - 12

10	eggs or egg substitute
½	cup unsifted flour
1	teaspoon baking powder
¼	teaspoon salt
¼	cup butter or margarine, melted
16	ounces low fat small curd cottage cheese
1	pound Monterey Jack cheese, shredded
¼	teaspoon ground cumin
2	(4 ounce) cans chopped green chilies

- Heat oven to 350°F and grease 13x9x2-inch baking pan.
- In large bowl, beat eggs until light and lemon colored. Add all ingredients except chilies. Mix.
- Pour half of mixture into pan. Sprinkle with chilies.
- Top with remaining mixture.
- Bake 35 minutes or until browned and center firm. Serve hot.

Casserole may be made in advance and refrigerated until baking.

This is a great dish for a special family brunch. Serve with warm tortillas, tostada chips, shredded lettuce with tomato salad and fresh fruit.

CHEESE-EGG BRUNCH STRATA

🕐 *Make ahead — Bake later   Serves 10 - 12*

4	**cups cubed dry bread**
2	**cups grated Cheddar cheese**
10	**eggs, beaten, or egg substitute**
4	**cups milk**
1½	**teaspoons dry mustard**
¼	**teaspoon onion powder**
➤	**dash of freshly ground pepper**
8-10	**slices bacon, cooked, crumbled**
½	**cup sliced fresh mushrooms**
½	**cup chopped tomato**

- Grease 13x9x2-inch baking pan.
- Arrange bread cubes in pan and sprinkle with cheese.
- Beat eggs, milk, mustard, onion powder and pepper.
- Pour egg mixture evenly over bread and cheese layer.
- Sprinkle with bacon, mushrooms and tomato. Cover with foil. Refrigerate overnight.
- Heat oven to 325°F.
- Bake uncovered until set, about 1 hour. Cover loosely with foil if top browns too quickly.
- *Variations:* Instead of bacon, use 4 cups cubed ham or 1 pound sausage, cooked, drained and cooled.
- Instead of black pepper, use ¼ teaspoon cayenne pepper.

BAKED EGGS IN TOMATO SHELLS

Easy   Serves 8

4	**large firm tomatoes, halved**
1	**teaspoon each salt, pepper, basil (mix)**
8	**eggs**
8	**teaspoons grated Parmesan cheese**
2	**teaspoons chopped fresh parsley**
8	**teaspoons butter or margarine, melted**

- Heat oven to 350°F and grease 13x9x2-inch pan.
- Carefully scoop pulp from each tomato half; drain on paper towel.
- Place tomato shells hollow side up in pan.
- Sprinkle each with seasoning mixture.
- Carefully break 1 egg into each tomato shell.
- Top with 1 teaspoon cheese and ¼ teaspoon parsley.
- Drizzle 1 teaspoon melted butter on each.
- Bake 20 - 25 minutes until egg is set.

Serve with muffins, sausage links and fresh cold fruit juice.

NOODLES ROMANOFF

Easy   *Serves 6 - 8*

1	cup small curd cottage cheese
1	cup sour cream
½	small onion, minced
1	clove garlic, crushed
➤	dash of Worcestershire sauce
➤	dash of hot pepper sauce
½	teaspoon salt
3	cups cooked medium noodles
½	cup grated Cheddar cheese
➤	paprika

- Heat oven to 350°F and grease 1½-quart casserole.
- Mix all ingredients except noodles, Cheddar cheese and paprika.
- Add noodles. Toss lightly.
- Turn into casserole.
- Sprinkle with Cheddar cheese and paprika.
- Bake 40 minutes.

NOODLE PUDDING (KUGEL)

Serves 10 - 12

8	ounces fine egg noodles
½	cup (1 stick) butter
1	cup sugar
1	cup small curd cottage cheese
16	ounces cream cheese
1	cup sour cream
2	cups milk
1	tablespoon vanilla
5	eggs
½	cup raisins (optional)
➤	ground cinnamon

- Have ingredients at room temperature.
- Heat oven to 350°F and grease 13x9x2-inch pan.
- Cook noodles according to package directions. Drain.
- In large bowl, cream butter and sugar.
- Add cottage cheese, cream cheese, sour cream, milk and vanilla.
- Add eggs one at a time, beating well after each.
- Stir in raisins and cooked noodles. Pour into pan. Sprinkle with cinnamon.
- Bake 1 hour. Let stand 5 minutes before cutting into squares.

QUICK LASAGNA

No pre-cooking needed   *Serves 6 - 8*

2	**cups ricotta cheese**
¼	**cup grated Parmesan cheese**
1	**egg, beaten**
3	**tablespoons chopped fresh parsley**
26	**ounce jar spaghetti sauce (or 3½ cups homemade spaghetti sauce)**
8	**lasagna noodles, uncooked**
2	**cups shredded mozzarella cheese**

- Mix ricotta, Parmesan, egg and parsley. Set aside.
- Spread 1½ cups spaghetti sauce in 11x7-inch glass baking dish.
- Layer with 4 noodles, half of ricotta mixture, half of mozzarella and 1 cup spaghetti sauce.
- Repeat with remaining noodles, ricotta, mozzarella and sauce.
- Cover tightly with plastic wrap.
- Microwave at HIGH 10 minutes.
- Meanwhile, heat oven to 350°F.
- Remove lasagna from microwave. Replace plastic wrap with aluminum foil, shiny side down.
- Bake 30 minutes.
- Let stand 10 minutes before cutting into squares for serving.

PESTO GENOVESE

2	cups fresh basil leaves
¼	cup pine nuts
2	cloves garlic
¼	teaspoon salt
½	cup extra virgin olive oil
½	cup freshly grated Parmesan cheese

- In blender or food processor, process basil, parsley, pine nuts, garlic and salt until mixture forms paste consistency.
- With motor running, gradually add oil until somewhat smooth. Do not overprocess; sauce should have some texture.
- Stir in grated cheese.
- To serve over pasta, stir about 2 tablespoons hot cooking water from pasta into sauce in a large bowl. Add cooked pasta and mix thoroughly. Serve hot.
- *Other uses for pesto*: Put a dollop in a bowl of vegetable soup.
- Brush on grilled chicken near the end of cooking.
- Spread on top of flattened pizza dough for a green focaccia.

Freezes well. Thaw at room temperature 2 - 3 hours.

CHICKEN PESTO PASTA

Easy   Serves 2-4

8	ounces spinach pasta
1	onion
1	red bell pepper
1	yellow bell pepper
2	tablespoons olive oil
1½	cups cubed cooked chicken
8	ounces pesto sauce (preceding recipe)
1	teaspoon salt

- Begin sauce before cooking pasta.
- Cook pasta according to package directions.
- Cut onion and peppers into thin, short strips.
- In medium skillet, lightly sauté onion and peppers in olive oil.
- Add chicken and pesto sauce. Heat thoroughly.
- Toss with drained pasta. Serve immediately.

CHEF'S NOTE

The word "pesto" derives from the Italian for pestle; traditionally this sauce is ground by hand in a mortar and pestle. If prepared ahead, the fresh green color will darken, but the taste will still be great.

LINGUINI AND CLAM SAUCE

Easy   *Serves 4*

8-12	ounces whole wheat linguini pasta
2	cloves garlic, minced
¼	cup extra virgin olive oil
2	(7 ounce) cans clams, drained, broth reserved
½	cup dry white wine
½	cup reserved clam broth
⅓	cup chopped fresh parsley
¼	teaspoon each basil, oregano and black pepper
¼	cup grated Parmesan cheese

- Begin sauce before cooking pasta.
- Cook linguini according to package directions.
- Sauté garlic in olive oil. Add clams.
- Stir in wine, clam broth and seasonings. Simmer 10 minutes.
- Toss with drained linguini.
- Sprinkle with Parmesan cheese and grind of fresh black pepper before serving.

May add ¼ cup sliced black olives and ½ cup crumbled feta cheese.

PASTA WITH TOMATO VODKA SAUCE

Easy   *Serves 4*

⅓	cup unsalted butter
¾	cup vodka
½	teaspoon hot red pepper flakes
16	ounces Italian plum tomatoes (canned or fresh), drained, seeded, puréed
1	cup heavy cream
¼	teaspoon salt
1	cup freshly grated Parmesan cheese, divided
16	ounces penne or ziti pasta

- Melt butter in large skillet.
- Add vodka and pepper flakes. Simmer 2-3 minutes.
- Add tomato, cream and salt. Simmer 5 minutes.
- Stir in ¼ cup Parmesan cheese.
- Cook pasta until al dente, following package directions.
- Add drained pasta to tomato mixture. Stir in remaining Parmesan.
- Serve immediately with additional Parmesan if desired.

PENNE PASTA WITH PEPPER TOMATO SAUCE

Easy   *Serves 4*

⅓	cup extra virgin olive oil
2	teaspoons chopped garlic
3-4	large bell peppers (red, yellow, green, orange), roasted, peeled, cut in strips
4	fresh tomatoes, chopped
16	ounces penne or ziti pasta
3	tablespoons chopped fresh basil
½	cup chopped fresh parsley
¼	cup grated Romano cheese (Pecorino)

- In large skillet, sauté garlic in oil.
- Add prepared peppers. Cook briefly. Add tomatoes.
- Cook pasta until al dente, following package directions.
- Stir vegetables and heat through before adding drained pasta and herbs.
- Sprinkle with cheese and serve.

Peppers may be used unroasted for a slightly different flavor.

CHEF'S NOTE

To roast peppers, bake in 450°F oven 12 minutes. Turn off heat. Remove after additional 15 minutes. Place in paper or plastic bag. Close bag and allow to sit additional 15 minutes. Skin will easily peel off. Gently rinse peppers to remove seeds.

SHRIMP EN PASTA

Easy   *Serves 4*

8	ounces spaghetti or fettucini
3	tablespoons butter or margarine
3	tablespoons flour
½	teaspoon dill weed or dill seed
1	clove garlic, minced
½	teaspoon tarragon
1½	cups milk
½	cup white wine
½	pound fresh shrimp, peeled, cleaned
¼	cup sliced black olives
2	tablespoons lemon juice
1	tablespoon chopped fresh parsley

- Begin sauce before cooking pasta.
- Cook pasta according to package directions.
- In medium skillet, melt butter. Add flour, dill, garlic and tarragon.
- Slowly add milk. Stir constantly until smooth.
- Add wine. Cook and stir until slightly thickened and bubbly.
- Add shrimp, olives, lemon juice and parsley.
- Cook just until shrimp are pink. Serve over hot pasta.

CHEF'S NOTE

Time pasta cooking to your guests. The water needs to be boiling and the sauce should be readied before the pasta is dropped into its pot. Last-minute attention to the final stages of cooking the sauce and the pasta will enable you to bring the dish to the table in grand style.

30-Minute Spinach Pasta

Easy   *Serves 4*

8	ounces spinach linguini or fettucini
¼	cup olive oil
2-4	cloves garlic, finely chopped
1	carrot, finely chopped
½	red or yellow bell pepper, chopped
½	teaspoon hot red pepper flakes or cayenne pepper to taste
½	pound small shrimp or 1 can anchovy fillets, drained, chopped (optional)
1	pound fresh spinach, cleaned, chopped, or 10-ounce package frozen spinach, thawed, drained
8	ripe plum tomatoes or 16 cherry tomatoes, chopped
¾	cup grated Parmesan cheese

- Prepare sauce before cooking pasta.
- Cook pasta according to package instructions.
- In large skillet, heat olive oil. Sauté garlic, carrot and peppers about 5 minutes.
- Add shrimp or chopped anchovy.
- Cook 1 - 2 minutes. Add other vegetables. Stir until spinach is wilted.
- Toss drained pasta with sauce.
- Stir in Parmesan and serve immediately.

CHEF'S NOTE

Ready-to-use shrimp can be found packaged in plastic bags in frozen food section of grocery store. They can be easily added to a recipe such as the one above.

Pasta Salad for a Crowd

Serves 25 - 30

16	ounces Italian reduced-calorie dressing
16	ounces regular Italian dressing
¼	cup red wine vinegar
2	tablespoons each garlic powder, onion powder, basil and parsley flakes
1	teaspoon sugar
½	cup water
16	ounces mixed pasta shells (spinach, regular, tomato)
16	ounces curly ruffles pasta
16	ounces fresh cheese tortellini pasta
3	cups broccoli florets
2	cups each thinly sliced carrot, celery and green bell pepper
12	green onions and tops, sliced
12	ounces fresh mushrooms, sliced
½	pound hard salami, sliced, julienne cut
½	pound turkey ham, sliced, julienne cut
½	pound crab meat, separated
1½	pounds small shrimp, cooked, peeled, cleaned
8	ounces diced pimiento, drained
½	cup sliced black olives
¾	pound dry feta cheese, crumbled
12	ounces fresh Parmesan cheese, grated
6	ounces Cheddar cheese, shredded
➢	fresh parsley for garnish

- Mix salad dressings, vinegar and seasonings in blender.
- Rinse dressing bottles with ½ cup water and add.
- Prepare pasta according to package directions. Chill under running water. Drain.
- In large bowl, toss pasta with half of dressing.
- Blanch broccoli 60 - 90 seconds. Chill in ice cubes. Drain.
- Add to pasta. Stir.
- Add other vegetables to pasta gently.
- Add meats and seafood.
- Add remaining dressing, pimiento, olives and cheeses.
- Toss lightly and cover. Chill 6 hours or longer.
- Garnish with fresh parsley.

Requires large utensils: bowl and spoon.

Recipe will feed many hungry teenagers or a picnic crowd after the Peachtree Road Race!

SAVANNAH RED RICE

Serves 4 - 6

4	slices bacon, cooked, crumbled
2	medium onions, chopped
1	medium green bell pepper, chopped (optional)
6	ounce can tomato paste
1½-2	cans water (9 - 12 ounces)
➤	dash or more of hot pepper sauce
2	teaspoons salt
2-3	teaspoons sugar
➤	black pepper to taste
1½	cups uncooked long-grain white rice

- Sauté onion in bacon grease.
- Add other ingredients except bacon and rice. Cook 10 minutes.
- Add rice. Cover and simmer 30 minutes.
- Add crumbled bacon and cook, covered, 30 minutes longer.

This recipe is a Georgia low-country specialty. It is good served with smoked ham.

HERBED LENTILS, RICE AND VEGETABLES

♥   *Excellent vegetarian main dish   Serves 4-6*

2	teaspoons olive or vegetable oil
¾	cup chopped onion
½	cup each thinly sliced red and yellow bell pepper
1	clove garlic, minced or crushed
2⅔	cups chicken broth
¾	cup dry lentils, washed
½	cup uncooked brown rice
½	cup dry white wine
1	bay leaf
¼	teaspoon each oregano and thyme
⅛	teaspoon freshly ground pepper
4	ounces low fat Swiss cheese, shredded

- Sauté onion, peppers and garlic in oil until tender, about 10 minutes.
- Heat oven to 350°F.
- Combine broth, lentils, rice, wine and seasonings. Add vegetables.
- Stir half of cheese into lentil mixture.
- Turn into ungreased 1½-quart casserole.
- Bake, covered, 1½ hours or until lentils and rice are done. Stir twice.
- Remove bay leaf.
- Sprinkle remaining cheese over top of casserole.
- Continue baking uncovered until cheese is melted.

FRUITED CURRIED RICE

Easy   *Serves 4*

2½	**cups water**
2	**tablespoons butter or margarine**

RICE MIX

1	**cup uncooked long-grain white rice**
1	**tablespoon instant minced onion**
2	**teaspoons curry powder**
4	**teaspoons chicken or beef bouillon granules**
½	**teaspoon salt**
⅓	**cup chopped dried fruit mixture (such as apples, apricots, peaches)**
2	**tablespoons golden raisins**
⅓	**cup blanched slivered almonds**

- In heavy saucepan, combine rice mix with water and butter.
- Cover tightly and bring to boil. Reduce heat to low and simmer 20 minutes. Do not remove cover.

Wonderful with baked or broiled meats.

CHEF'S NOTE

Gift Idea: Combine rice mix ingredients and package in airtight container. A glass freezer jar is perfect. Makes a thoughtful gift; tie with a ribbon and include recipe.

BARLEY CASSEROLE

Easy   Serves 8

1	cup fine or medium pearl barley
6	tablespoons butter or margarine
¼-½	cup slivered almonds
1	medium onion, chopped
½	cup minced fresh parsley
¼	cup chopped chives or green onion
¼	teaspoon each salt and pepper
2	(10 ounce) cans beef or chicken broth

- Heat oven to 375°F.
- Rinse barley in sieve with cold water. Drain.
- In heavy skillet, lightly sauté nuts in butter.
- Add barley and onion. Cook until lightly browned. Stir often.
- Put in 2-quart casserole. Add parsley, chives, salt and pepper.
- Heat broth to boiling. Pour over mixture. Stir.
- Bake uncovered 1 hour or until liquid is absorbed.

Using quick barley will speed cooking.

BARLEY PILAF

♥   *Easy   Serves 6 - 8*

1½	tablespoons vegetable oil
1	cup quick-cooking barley
1	medium onion, chopped
2	cups broth (chicken, turkey or beef)
➢	salt and freshly ground pepper to taste
2	stalks celery, peeled, finely chopped
¼	cup chopped fresh parsley
1	cup sliced fresh mushrooms

- Sauté onion and barley in oil until lightly browned.
- Add broth, salt and pepper.
- Bring to a boil and simmer 30 minutes until tender.
- Toss with celery, parsley and mushrooms while hot.
- Cover until serving.

HISTORY NOTE

In 1979 Emory University received $105 million from the Emily and Ernest Woodruff Foundation, the largest single educational gift in the history of the United States at that time.

Entrées

*E*ntrées in the 90's can be meat, poultry, fish or vegetarian. Frequently our menus are eclectic combinations adapted from several cuisines. The speed and efficiency of modern transportation bring us fresh produce daily from all parts of the world. We have become familiar with cooking techniques, attitudes and styles from countries we have never been to and may only dream of visiting!

These recipes come from traditions as diverse as our Emory/Oxford faculty and student population. They vary widely, from a casserole utilizing a can of condensed soup to a marinated beef tenderloin. In a number of these recipes vegetables play an important role, reflecting changing attitudes toward personal health and nutrition.

Of course some dishes are inescapably linked in our memories to festive holiday occasions, and we share with you some favorites that have been tested many times with family and friends. We have selected some real "showstoppers" for parties and special occasions — poached salmon and roasted stuffed quail. For the grill there are tantalizing recipes for smoked turkey, pork tenderloin and shish kabob.

In Georgia we have many months of wonderful weather to enjoy the outdoors. Whether it be in our own backyard, in the mountains, at the beach or at one of our many parks, we like to gather our friends around us and enjoy food and fun. We hope these recipes will help you enjoy those special times.

Bon Appétit!

Chicken Roll-ups

♥   *Easy*   *Grill or broil*   *Serves 4*

2	whole chicken breasts, halved, skinned, boned
8	slices bacon (can be turkey bacon)
¼	cup unsweetened pineapple juice
¼	cup Dijon mustard
1	tablespoon brown sugar

- Cut chicken pieces in half crosswise. Roll up lengthwise.
- Wrap each with slice of bacon. Secure with toothpick.
- Mix pineapple juice, mustard and brown sugar. Marinate prepared chicken at least 1 hour.
- Grill chicken over medium heat 20 - 25 minutes or until done.
- Baste with sauce and turn occasionally.

This may be prepared the day before and marinated in refrigerator until cooking time.

Indonesian Spicy Peanut Chicken

Serves 6

¼	cup chopped onion
1	clove garlic, minced
¼	teaspoon cayenne pepper
¼	cup crunchy peanut butter
½	teaspoon salt
1	teaspoon vegetable oil
1	tablespoon soy sauce
½	cup water
1	tablespoon lime or lemon juice
1	chicken, cut up, or 3 whole chicken breasts, halved, skinned, boned

- Sauté first 5 ingredients 3 minutes in oil.
- Add soy sauce, water and lime juice. Cook over low heat 5 minutes.
- Cool 10 - 15 minutes.
- Pour over chicken and marinate about 1 hour.
- Heat oven to 350°F.
- Bake 15 minutes.
- Broil or grill 6 inches from heat 15 minutes.
- Turn several times and brush with marinade.

Easy Chicken Surprise

♥ *Serves 4*

½	cup plain nonfat yogurt
½	cup low fat sour cream
1	tablespoon lemon juice
1	teaspoon celery salt
¼	teaspoon black pepper
1	clove garlic, minced
1	teaspoon paprika
1	teaspoon Worcestershire sauce
4	boneless, skinless chicken breast halves
1	cup fine bread crumbs

- Combine first 8 ingredients and marinate chicken 1 hour or overnight in refrigerator.
- Heat oven to 350°F and grease shallow baking pan.
- Remove chicken, shaking off excess marinade.
- Roll in bread crumbs and arrange in pan.
- Bake, uncovered, 30 - 40 minutes. Do not overbake.

1-2-3 Chicken and Artichokes

Easy   *Serves 3 - 4*

2	whole chicken breasts, skinned, boned
➤	flour for dredging
4	tablespoons butter or margarine
1	tablespoon olive oil
1	clove garlic, minced
14	ounce can water-packed artichoke hearts, halved or quartered
➤	juice of ½ lemon
¾	cup chicken stock
➤	salt and pepper to taste
➤	additional lemon juice, lemon slices and fresh parsley for garnish

- Cut chicken in chunks. Dredge with flour.
- In large skillet, heat butter and oil. Sauté garlic briefly.
- Add chicken. Cook over medium heat about 10 minutes.
- Add artichokes, lemon juice, stock, salt and pepper. Cook briefly to thicken.
- Place on serving plate. Sprinkle with additional lemon juice.
- Garnish with lemon slices and parsley.
- Serve with pasta or rice.

SHERRIED CHICKEN CASSEROLE

♥   *Easy*   *Serves 8*

4	whole chicken breasts, halved, skinned, boned
½	teaspoon salt
¼	teaspoon pepper
½	teaspoon paprika
3	tablespoons vegetable oil, divided
½	pound fresh mushrooms, sliced
⅔	cup chicken broth
2	tablespoons flour
¼	cup dry sherry or white wine or vermouth
9	ounce package frozen artichoke hearts, thawed

- Season chicken with salt, pepper and paprika.
- Brown in 2 tablespoons oil; place in 2-quart casserole.
- Add remaining oil to pan. Sauté mushrooms. Add a little broth if necessary.
- Sprinkle flour over mushrooms. Stir in remaining broth.
- Simmer 5 minutes. Add sherry.
- Place artichoke hearts on chicken. Pour sauce over all.
- Bake, covered, 30 minutes at 375°F. Remove cover and bake additional 10 minutes.

CHICKEN AND WILD RICE CASSEROLE

Serves 6

4	tablespoons butter or margarine
6	ounce package wild and white rice mix
8	ounces fresh mushrooms, sliced
10	ounce can condensed cream of celery soup
10	ounce can condensed cream of mushroom soup
1	soup can white wine
1	chicken, cut up

- Heat oven to 350°F and melt butter in casserole dish.
- Stir in rice. Sauté until lightly browned.
- Add mushrooms and sauté 5 minutes.
- Mix soups, wine and seasoning packet from rice mix. Add ⅓ to rice mixture.
- Place chicken pieces on rice. Top with remaining soup mixture.
- Cover and bake 1 hour. Remove cover. Bake additional 30 minutes.

Skinned, boned chicken pieces may be used but shorten baking time.

CHICKEN-ARTICHOKE PIE

Serves 4 - 6

10	ounce package frozen spinach, thawed, drained
2	cups cooked long-grain rice
4	tablespoons butter or margarine, melted
9	ounce package frozen artichoke hearts, thawed, or 14-ounce can, drained, quartered
1½	cups diced cooked chicken or turkey
1	cup shredded Monterey Jack cheese
¼	pound fresh mushrooms, sliced
1	clove garlic, minced
2	tablespoons flour
¼	teaspoon curry powder
1	teaspoon Dijon mustard
1	cup milk
➢	salt and pepper to taste

- Heat oven to 350°F and grease 9-inch pie pan.
- Combine spinach, rice and 2 tablespoons melted butter. Press evenly into pan. Cover and refrigerate 30 - 60 minutes.
- Arrange artichoke hearts over rice and spinach. Top with chicken; sprinkle with cheese.
- Sauté mushrooms and garlic in remaining 2 tablespoons butter.
- Stir in flour and curry powder. Cook until bubbly. Add mustard.
- Gradually add milk and stir until thickened. Salt and pepper.
- Pour sauce over pie. May refrigerate at this point.
- Bake 45 minutes (1 hour if chilled).

AUSTRIAN CHICKEN PAPRIKA

Serves 4

2-3	pound chicken, cut in pieces
➤	salt and pepper to taste
½	teaspoon tarragon or sage
2	tablespoons vegetable oil
1	medium onion, chopped
1	tablespoon paprika
1	medium tomato, chopped
¾	cup chicken broth, divided
1	tablespoon flour
1	cup sour cream
2	tablespoons sherry

- Wash chicken and pat dry. Season with salt, pepper and tarragon or sage.
- Heat oil. Brown chicken on both sides until golden. Remove from pan. Drain excess fat and keep warm.
- Add onion to drippings. Sauté until tender. Add paprika and cook 1 minute.
- Add tomato and ½ cup broth. Top with chicken pieces. Cover and cook slowly 15 - 20 minutes until chicken is tender. Add more broth if necessary.
- Remove chicken to platter. Stir flour into remaining ¼ cup broth. Add to mixture in pan.
- Stir in sherry and cook until thickened. Spoon over chicken.
- Serve with cooked noodles or other pasta.
- *Variation*: Substitute nonfat plain yogurt for sour cream and increase flour to 2 tablespoons.

HISTORY NOTE

Emory University has a special endowment to provide for the preservation and maintenance of campus holly bushes.

GUATEMALAN BAKED CHICKEN

🕐 *Serves 6 - 8*

2	small chickens (2 - 3 pounds each)
4-6	cups bread crumbs
½	cup raisins or currants
3	large onions, thinly sliced
1	bell pepper, finely chopped
➤	freshly ground pepper to taste
➤	juice of 1 lime
➤	salt and pepper to taste
2-4	tablespoons butter, margarine or vegetable oil
2	limes, thinly sliced
➤	dash of Angostura bitters (optional)
⅓	cup chopped nuts
12	large stuffed olives or black olives, sliced
3	inch cinnamon stick, broken
2	bay leaves
½	cup sherry or Madeira wine

- Heat oven to 325°F and grease large baking dish.
- Wash and dry chickens inside and out.
- Mix bread crumbs, raisins, onion and chopped pepper. Season highly with freshly ground pepper. Stuff chickens.
- Sew up tightly and brush with lime juice. Salt and pepper.
- Brown chickens lightly in butter.
- Cover bottom of baking dish with sliced limes, bitters, nuts, olives, cinnamon and bay leaves.
- Lay chicken on top and sprinkle with remaining frying butter.
- Cover tightly. Roast 2 hours or until tender.
- Remove bay leaves and cinnamon.
- Put lime mixture on platter. Top with chicken and sprinkle sherry over all.

MEDITERRANEAN CHICKEN

Serves 4 - 6

1	chicken, cut up, or 2 - 3 whole chicken breasts, halved
1	teaspoon paprika
1¼	teaspoons salt
⅛	teaspoon pepper
2	tablespoons vegetable oil or margarine
10	small white onions, peeled
½	pound fresh mushrooms, sliced
1	small eggplant, cubed
1	green bell pepper, thinly sliced
1	teaspoon seasoned salt
⅛	teaspoon thyme
1	teaspoon crushed basil
½	teaspoon garlic powder
2	bay leaves
½	cup sherry
4	tomatoes, chopped, or 16-ounce can whole tomatoes

- Sprinkle chicken with paprika, salt and pepper.
- In large skillet, heat oil. Sauté chicken until golden.
- Place in large casserole.
- Add onions to skillet. Sauté until golden.
- Add mushrooms, eggplant and green pepper. Sauté 3 - 5 minutes.
- Sprinkle with seasoned salt, thyme, basil and garlic powder.
- Pour over chicken. Add bay leaves and sherry.
- Bake, covered, 30 - 40 minutes at 350°F.
- Add tomato and bake, uncovered, 30 - 40 minutes longer.
- Serve with rice or pasta.

For added flavor, use sherry to deglaze the drippings in skillet. Add to casserole.

Mexican Chicken Quesadilla Casserole

Serves 8

10	ounce can condensed cream of chicken soup
⅔	cup finely chopped onion
2	(4 ounce) cans chopped green chilies
16	ounces sour cream
8-10	corn tortillas, quartered
4	cooked whole chicken breasts, skinned, boned, chopped
8	ounces Monterey Jack cheese, shredded
8	ounces sharp Cheddar cheese, shredded

Topping:

16	ounce can black beans, drained
2-3	tomatillos, chopped, drained
2	tablespoons chopped fresh cilantro
¼	teaspoon ground cumin
2-3	tablespoons chunky salsa (optional)

- Heat oven to 350°F and grease 13x9x2-inch baking dish.
- Spread soup on bottom. Sprinkle with part of onion and ½ can chilies; dot with sour cream.
- Layer tortillas, chicken, onion, chilies, sour cream and cheeses until ingredients are used. End with sour cream and cheese.
- Cover with foil and bake 35 minutes.
- Mix topping ingredients and distribute around inside edge of casserole to frame chicken mixture.
- Return to oven for 10 - 12 minutes. Serve hot.

This is a wonderful party entrée served with salad, fresh fruit and special dessert.

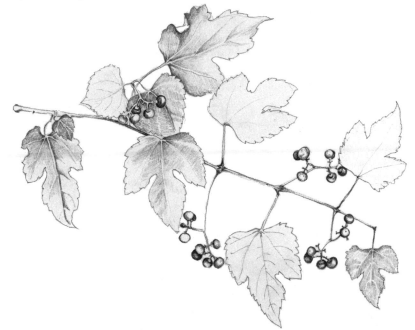

Chicken Salad Mousse

🕐 ♥ *Serves 16 - 18*

1	large (4-5 pound) chicken
½	teaspoon each salt and pepper
10	ounce package frozen peas, thawed, drained
¾	cup sweet pickle relish
1	teaspoon lemon juice
¼-½	teaspoon curry powder
4	hard-cooked eggs, diced
1½	cups finely chopped celery
1	cup light mayonnaise
1	cup light sour cream
3	envelopes gelatin
½	cup cold water
1½	cups broth reserved from cooking chicken

- Cook chicken in water to cover until tender. Salt and pepper.
- When cool, discard skin and bones. Cut chicken meat in ½-inch pieces (should be about 4 cups).
- Reserve 1½ cups chicken broth (remove fat).
- Mix chicken, peas, relish, lemon juice, curry powder, eggs, celery, mayonnaise and sour cream.
- Dissolve gelatin in water. Stir into broth. Heat to boiling.
- Combine with chicken mixture.
- Pour into 10-cup mold or two 9x5-inch loaf pans prepared with vegetable cooking spray.
- Refrigerate until firm. Unmold and slice.

This is elegant as a luncheon entrée and can also be served as an appetizer with large crackers.

History Note

This recipe was submitted by Marian Richardson, president of Emory University Woman's Club in 1957-58. Her husband, Dr. Arthur Richardson (d. January 1993) was dean of Emory Medical School. Marian served this at a welcoming party for Betty and Sanford Atwood (Emory president, 1963-1977).

Oyster Sauce Chicken Legs

Serves 6 or more

6	chicken leg quarters
2	tablespoons peanut oil

Braising liquid:

3	tablespoons thin soy sauce
6	tablespoons sherry
½	teaspoon sugar
2	cloves garlic, crushed or minced
¼	teaspoon white pepper
➢	slice of fresh ginger, grated or minced
3	tablespoons oyster sauce
¼	cup chicken broth

Binder and final seasoning:

1	tablespoon cornstarch
1	tablespoon cold water
½	teaspoon sesame oil
2	whole green onions, cut in ¼-inch rounds

- Separate legs and thighs.
- Heat oil in wok. Swirl to coat pan.
- Brown chicken on all sides, about 10 minutes. Do in 2 batches if necessary.
- Mix braising ingredients in 4-quart pot. Bring to boil.
- Transfer chicken to pot with slotted spoon, draining excess oil. Turn each piece until coated with liquid.
- Cover and reduce heat to low. Simmer 45 - 50 minutes, or until done.
- Mix cornstarch and water. Stir into braising liquid.
- Cook a few minutes to thicken slightly.
- Add sesame oil and onion. Stir. Serve hot.
- *Variation*: Use skinned chicken. Do not brown; put directly into boiling braising liquid.

This recipe can be prepared ahead of time, always a plus when serving a Chinese dinner.

History Note

The historic railroad depot was first a passenger stop named Emory, Georgia, then a freight depot, a lunch cafe and many times a meeting place.

Sesame Chicken and Sauces

Easy   *Serves 6*

4	eggs or egg substitute
¼	cup soy sauce
¼	cup water
2	cups fine bread crumbs
2	teaspoons paprika
½	teaspoon pepper
½	cup sesame seed
1	teaspoon garlic powder
3	pounds boneless, skinless chicken breast (3 whole breasts)
➤	flour for dredging (about ⅓ cup)
➤	vegetable oil (or half oil and half butter)

- Combine eggs, soy sauce and water.
- In separate bowl, mix bread crumbs, paprika, pepper, sesame seed and garlic powder.
- Dip chicken in flour, then in egg mixture, then in crumb mixture.
- Sauté in oil 7 - 8 minutes per side.
- Pass warm sauce of choice to pour on chicken.

Sesame Chicken is wonderful for buffet entrée or appetizer. All ages love it!

SAUCES

Apricot:

10-12	ounce jar apricot preserves
2	teaspoons soy sauce
1	clove garlic, minced
¼	cup water

- Simmer all ingredients 15 minutes.

Madeira:

2	cups chicken stock
2	chicken bouillon cubes
½	cup Madeira wine
➤	salt and pepper to taste
1	tablespoon cornstarch
1	tablespoon cold water

- Simmer first 3 ingredients 15 minutes. Salt and pepper to taste.
- Mix cornstarch with water. Stir into sauce until slightly thickened.

ASIAN CHICKEN

Easy   *Serves 4 - 6*

3-4	pounds chicken pieces, skin on
1	cup dry sherry
½	cup fresh lemon or lime juice
1	clove garlic, minced
½	cup soy sauce (may use low-salt)

- Heat oven to 500°F.
- Wash and dry chicken pieces.
- Place in baking dish. (Do not skin or brown chicken.)
- Mix remaining ingredients and pour over chicken.
- Bake 15 minutes. Turn and baste chicken.
- Lower temperature to 350°F. Bake additional 30 minutes. Turn and baste every 15 minutes.

CHICKEN BOMBAY

♥   *Serves 8 - 10*

4	whole chicken breasts, skinned, boned
3	tablespoons vegetable oil
1	large onion, thinly sliced
28	ounce can crushed tomatoes
1	cup sliced fresh mushrooms or 2 (4 ounce) cans chopped mushrooms
1	green bell pepper, chopped in large pieces
1	clove garlic, minced
2	teaspoons salt
1	tablespoon chopped fresh parsley
1	teaspoon black pepper
¾	teaspoon curry powder
¼	teaspoon oregano
¼	teaspoon hot pepper sauce
➤	Walnut Rice

- Cut chicken in bite-size chunks.
- Sauté in oil over medium heat.
- Remove chicken. Add onion and cook until tender.
- Add remaining ingredients and then chicken.
- Simmer, uncovered, 20 - 30 minutes, or until chicken is tender.
- Serve with Walnut Rice: Cook rice according to directions for 8 servings. Before serving toss with ¼ cup melted butter or margarine and ½ cup chopped walnuts.

SAUTÉ OF CHICKEN BREASTS CILANTRO

Serves 5 - 6

3	whole chicken breasts, halved, skinned, boned
2	tablespoons flour
➤	salt and pepper to taste
4	tablespoons butter, margarine or olive oil, divided
2	tablespoons chicken stock
¾	pound egg noodles or other pasta
2	tablespoons fresh cilantro
➤	grated Parmesan cheese for garnish

CILANTRO SAUCE:

1	cup packed fresh cilantro
1	cup pine nuts (or half pine nuts and half almonds)
¾	cup grated Parmesan cheese
1	clove garlic
½	cup plus 1 tablespoon olive oil
½	teaspoon salt

- Dredge chicken with mixture of flour, salt and pepper. Shake off excess.
- In heavy skillet, heat 2 tablespoons butter. Add chicken and brown lightly on all sides.
- Add stock. Cover and simmer 10 minutes.
- While chicken is simmering, cook pasta according to package directions.

- *Cilantro sauce:* In food processor, process cilantro, nuts, cheese and garlic to a paste. Slowly add olive oil.
- Place drained pasta on large platter. Toss with 2 tablespoons butter and cilantro sauce, reserving some of sauce.
- Place chicken on a second platter and sprinkle with cilantro.
- Pass remaining sauce and additional Parmesan cheese.

HISTORY NOTE

The chapel in the church school building of Glenn Memorial Church is an exact replica of a Sir Christopher Wren church in London, England.

GRILLED STUFFED CHICKEN BREASTS

♥ *Serves 8 - 12*

4-6	whole chicken breasts, halved, skinned, boned
➤	juice of 3 limes
1	medium onion, finely chopped
1	large carrot, finely chopped
6	fresh mushrooms, chopped
2	tablespoons chopped fresh parsley
1½	cups grated low fat mozzarella cheese
➤	melted margarine for grilling

- Pound chicken between wax paper with flat side of mallet.
- Place in pan with lime juice, turning to coat. Marinate briefly.
- Mix chopped vegetables and cheese. Put a small handful on each chicken piece. Use a skewer to pull sides of chicken around filling to hold in place.
- Brush with melted margarine.
- Grill over low heat about 20 minutes. Turn and brush as needed.

May be prepared for grilling several hours in advance. Refrigerate.

CHICKEN CURRY

Serves 4

2	whole chicken breasts, skinned, boned
1	small onion, thinly sliced
2	tablespoons vegetable oil or chicken broth
2	tablespoons curry paste (see note)
1	tart apple, peeled, sliced
2	cups chicken broth
1	tablespoon cornstarch
➤	condiments: chutney, coconut, peanuts, almonds, chopped green onion, raisins, diced hard-cooked egg, bacon

- Cut chicken in bite-size pieces.
- Sauté onion in oil or broth 2 - 3 minutes. Add curry paste.
- Stir in apple and chicken.
- Add broth and simmer 5 minutes.
- Make a paste of cornstarch and a little hot broth. Add to pot. Simmer 1 hour.
- Serve over rice and pass condiments.

CHEF'S NOTE

Curry paste may be purchased or made by cooking 1 tablespoon curry powder in 1 tablespoon olive oil 3 - 5 minutes.

GRILLED SMOKED TURKEY

¼	cup vegetable oil
½	cup salt
10-12	pound turkey
1	cup cider vinegar
¼	cup freshly ground pepper

- Prepare grill for cooking turkey.
- Mix oil and salt. Rub on turkey inside and out.
- Add vinegar and pepper to remaining salt mixture.
- When coals are white, pile charcoal on one side of barbecue. Place turkey on grill, breast side down, on opposite side.
- Cook 20 minutes per pound. Baste every 30 minutes with mixture. Turn after first hour.
- *Variation:* Use a turkey breast instead of whole turkey. Cut other ingredients in half. Turkey breast takes about 2 hours to cook.

You must try it to believe it!

Plan on 3 servings per pound of turkey.

CHEF'S NOTE

A disposable aluminum roasting pan eliminates flare-ups and works very well with a gas grill.

Chicken Marinades

TOMATO MARINADE

8	ounce can tomato sauce
½	cup olive oil
½	cup orange juice
¼	cup vinegar
1½	teaspoons oregano, crushed
1	teaspoon each salt and pepper
2	cloves garlic, minced

GINGER MARINADE

¾	cup white zinfandel or rosé wine
¼	cup soy sauce
¼	cup olive oil
1	clove garlic, minced
1	tablespoon ground ginger
¼	teaspoon oregano, crushed
1	tablespoon brown sugar

- Combine marinade ingredients.
- Marinate chicken or turkey at least 1 hour or overnight.
- Broil or grill over medium-low heat. Turn and baste frequently with marinade.

CHEF'S NOTE

Chicken and turkey are delicious when marinated in a flavorful sauce and then broiled or grilled. To shorten cooking time, meat may be heated first in the microwave 10 - 15 minutes. Poultry may also be baked in the marinade and if desired removed from the liquid and broiled until brown.

In addition, a glaze of ¼ cup honey mixed with ½ teaspoon dry mustard may be brushed on for the last 10 minutes of grilling.

Epicurean Fall Seated Dinner for 12

Roasted Quail with Cornbread Stuffing and Watercress Salad

Serves 12

24	**(4 ounce) quail, cleaned, dried**
½	**pound ground pork sausage (hot or mild)**
⅓	**cup unsalted butter**
⅓	**cup finely chopped onion**
¼	**cup finely chopped green bell pepper**
¼	**cup finely chopped celery**
1½	**teaspoons chopped garlic**
1	**bay leaf**
½	**cup chicken broth**
2	**eggs**
2½	**cups crumbled cornbread**
1	**teaspoon each salt and pepper**
½	**teaspoon dried oregano**
¼	**teaspoon dried thyme**

WATERCRESS SALAD:

6	**bunches watercress, cleaned, trimmed, dried**
➤	**vegetable oil and vinegar to taste**

- Salt and pepper quail cavities. Set aside.
- Brown sausage. Drain excess oil and set aside.
- In large skillet, sauté onion, green pepper, celery, garlic and bay leaf in butter over medium-high heat about 2 minutes. Stir occasionally.
- Thoroughly mix seasonings in small bowl and add.
- Continue cooking about 5 minutes until vegetables are just softened.
- Stir in sausage and broth. Turn off heat.
- Add eggs and cornbread. Stir well.
- Spoon stuffing into quail. Tuck wings under quail. Cross legs and secure with toothpick. Place breast side up in baking pan. Do not crowd. Refrigerate, covered with foil, until roasting.
- Heat oven to 400°F.
- Roast quail, uncovered, about 30 minutes. Test for doneness.

- *Watercress salad*: Divide watercress among 12 plates.
- Sprinkle with oil and vinegar. Top with 2 quail.

If using larger size Bob White quail, increase roasting time.

EPICUREAN SPRING COOKOUT FOR 30

GRILLED BONELESS CHICKEN BREASTS

Serves 30

15	whole chicken breasts, halved, boned
2	cups Herb Vinaigrette (page 71)

- Trim any excess fat from chicken pieces.
- Marinate chicken in vinaigrette. Turn to coat well. Refrigerate overnight.
- Heat grill to ensure even temperature. Drain chicken pieces of excess marinade to prevent flaming.
- Place chicken, skin side down, on grill. Grill about 5 minutes per side or to desired doneness. Halfway through cooking on each side, turn each piece ¼ turn to make a cross pattern.

SCALLOPED OYSTERS

Serves 8

⅓	cup butter, melted
3	cups saltine and/or round buttery cracker crumbs
2	pints fresh oysters, drained, liquid reserved
⅓	cup finely chopped green bell pepper
⅓	cup finely chopped onion
1	tablespoon prepared horseradish
➢	salt and freshly ground pepper to taste
1	cup heavy cream
½	cup reserved oyster liquid
½-1	cup grated sharp Cheddar cheese

- Heat oven to 350°F and grease large pie plate or shallow casserole.
- Pour melted butter over cracker crumbs.
- Place layer of crumbs in baking dish. Layer oysters.
- Sprinkle green pepper, onion, horseradish, salt and pepper.
- Repeat layering until all is used. End with crumbs.
- Pour cream and oyster liquid evenly over top.
- Sprinkle with cheese.
- Bake 40 - 50 minutes.

HISTORY NOTE

This recipe was a favorite of Jack Boozer, according to his wife, Ruth. Jack Boozer, 1918-1989, Emory graduate and faculty member for 38 years, left Emory with a legacy of love for people, for music and for truth and justice.

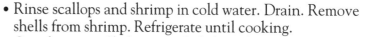
BROILED SCALLOPS AND SHRIMP

Easy   *Serves 6 - 8*

1	pound large fresh scallops
½	pound large fresh shrimp
4	tablespoons olive oil, butter or margarine, divided
1	clove garlic, finely chopped
1	small onion, chopped
1	each green, yellow and red bell pepper, seeded, cut in strips or chopped
3	Italian plum tomatoes, chopped or quartered
➤	ground Italian seasoning to taste (or fresh basil, thyme, oregano)
1	pound feta cheese, cubed
¼	cup chopped fresh parsley
½	cup dry white wine or juice of 1 lemon

- Rinse scallops and shrimp in cold water. Drain. Remove shells from shrimp. Refrigerate until cooking.
- Coat bottom of baking pan lightly with oil. Place scallops in single layer and drizzle 1 tablespoon oil over top.
- With oven rack at highest level, broil scallops about 2 minutes.
- Stir. Return to broiler. When scallops begin to turn white, stir in shrimp. Drizzle 2 tablespoons oil over top. Broil about 3 minutes. Stir well. Sprinkle with onion and garlic. Broil 1 minute.
- When all shrimp begin to turn pink, distribute remaining vegetables and seasonings over shrimp and scallops.
- With broiler still on, place pan on middle rack of oven 4 - 5 minutes, until vegetables are steaming and shrimp are pink all over. Stir and turn. Check scallops and shrimp for doneness.
- Sprinkle feta cheese over top. Broil 2 minutes until cheese is lightly browned. Remove from oven.
- Sprinkle parsley and wine. Serve with hot rice. (Cook 2 cups.)

Colorful enameled steel cook-and-serve ware is ideal for this recipe.

SHRIMP CACCIATORE

Easy *Serves 4 - 6*

1	tablespoon olive oil
½	cup chopped onion
1	clove garlic, crushed
1	small green bell pepper, chopped
16	ounce can stewed tomatoes
8	ounce can tomato sauce
½	teaspoon each basil, oregano and salt
¼	teaspoon sugar
¼	cup chopped fresh parsley
¼	cup red wine (optional)
½	pound fresh shrimp, peeled, cleaned

- Sauté onion, garlic and green pepper in olive oil.
- Stir in tomatoes, tomato sauce, seasonings and wine.
- Simmer about 10 minutes. Add shrimp. Cook until pink (3-4 minutes). Do not overcook shrimp.
- Serve with hot rice. (Cook 1½ cups.)

ASIAN STYLE BROILED SHRIMP

  Serves 6 - 8

Marinade:

⅓	cup vegetable oil
1	tablespoon sesame oil (optional)
¼	cup fresh lemon juice
⅓	cup soy sauce
1	tablespoon rice vinegar
1	teaspoon fresh parsley
2	cloves garlic, crushed
¼	teaspoon freshly ground pepper
2	green onions, finely chopped
➤	dash of hot pepper sauce
2	pounds large shrimp in shell, rinsed, drained

- Combine marinade ingredients. Cover shrimp with marinade.
- Refrigerate minimum 2 hours. Drain.
- Place drained shrimp in shallow pan.
- Broil 3 - 5 minutes until shrimp are pink all over. Use tongs to turn. Do not overcook.

Great served with beer. Have lots of paper napkins handy!

SIMPLY GOOD GARLIC SHRIMP MICROWAVE

Serves 4

¼	cup butter or margarine
¼	cup olive oil
2	tablespoons chopped fresh parsley
1	tablespoon fresh lemon juice
1	tablespoon chopped onion
2	large cloves garlic, crushed
➤	salt and freshly ground pepper to taste
1	pound large fresh shrimp, peeled, cleaned
8	ounces linguini pasta

- Begin sauce before cooking pasta.
- Melt butter in microwave-safe dish; stir in olive oil, parsley, lemon juice, onion and garlic.
- Add shrimp; stir gently to coat. Cover dish with plastic wrap and refrigerate at least 1 hour.
- Cook linguini according to package directions.
- To cook shrimp, loosen plastic wrap and microwave at HIGH 7 minutes or until shrimp are pink all over. Turn and rearrange every 2 minutes.
- Toss drained pasta with shrimp. Serve immediately.

IMPERIAL CRAB-SHRIMP CASSEROLE

Easy   Serves 8 - 10

1	pound fresh crab meat, special or back fin
1½	pounds medium-size fresh shrimp, peeled, cleaned
1	red bell pepper, chopped
⅓	cup chopped fresh parsley
16	ounce package frozen baby peas
1⅔	cups mayonnaise
3	teaspoons Dijon mustard
➤	salt and freshly ground pepper to taste
⅓	cup white wine

- Rinse crab and shrimp in cold water. Check for shell.
- Heat oven to 350°F and grease attractive baking dish.
- Mix all ingredients together lightly.
- Turn into casserole; cover with foil. (Refrigerate if not baking immediately.)
- Bake 30 - 40 minutes. Check for doneness. Shrimp should be pink all over.
- Add additional wine if casserole seems dry.
- Serve immediately over hot white rice. (Cook 3 cups.)

This is a handsome casserole for a party or luncheon. It may be readied several hours ahead to pop into the oven at just the right time.

OPEN FACE CRAB SANDWICH

Easy   *Serves 2-4*

6-8	ounce can quality crab meat
1	cup finely chopped celery
½	cup finely chopped onion
1	cup grated Cheddar cheese
2	tablespoons mayonnaise
➤	bread of choice: tiny biscuits, English muffin or soft baguettes
➤	paprika

- Heat oven to 350°F.
- Mix first 5 ingredients. Distribute on bread to cover.
- Sprinkle with paprika.
- Bake 15 - 20 minutes. Broil 1 - 2 minutes to brown.

SOLE FLORENTINE

Easy   *Serves 2*

1	cup light sour cream
1½	tablespoons flour
¼	cup finely chopped green onion
1	tablespoon lemon juice
½	teaspoon salt or to taste
10	ounce package frozen chopped spinach, thawed, drained
1	pound thin fillets of sole or flounder
1	tablespoon butter
➤	lemon slices for garnish

- Blend sour cream with flour, onion, lemon juice and salt.
- Mix half with spinach and spread over bottom of shallow baking dish.
- Arrange fillets. Overlap as needed.
- Dot with butter. Spread remaining sour cream mixture over top.
- May be refrigerated a few hours.
- Heat oven to 375°F.
- Bake 20 minutes or until fish flakes easily with fork.
- Garnish with lemon slices.

Sole (or Flounder) Amandine Microwave

Easy   Serves 4

⅓	cup sliced almonds
⅓	cup butter or margarine
1	pound sole or flounder fillets (thin for best results)
¼-½	teaspoon salt
¼	teaspoon dill weed
⅛	teaspoon pepper
1	tablespoon chopped fresh parsley
1	tablespoon lemon juice
➢	paprika
➢	lemon wedges and parsley sprigs for garnish

- Place almonds and butter in 10-inch glass pie plate (microwave-safe dish).
- Microwave, uncovered, at HIGH 4 - 5 minutes until golden brown.
- Remove almonds and set aside.
- Dip fillets in butter, turning to coat both sides.
- Sprinkle with salt, dill, pepper, parsley and lemon juice.
- Roll each fillet (leave in pie plate).
- Cover with wax paper and cook at HIGH 4 minutes. Uncover and sprinkle with almonds.
- Cover and cook at HIGH 2 minutes or until fish flakes easily.
- Let stand a minute before serving. Sprinkle with paprika.
- Garnish with lemon wedges and parsley sprigs.
- *Variation:* Stir 10-ounce package frozen chopped spinach, thawed and drained, and 1 clove crushed garlic into butter and seasonings. Place rolled fillets on top of spinach. Place tomato slices on fillets. Microwave 5 minutes. Continue to follow recipe as above.

This can be on the table within a half hour!

History Note

Antoinette Candler, the wife of Bishop Warren A. Candler, took such a strong personal interest in the gardens and landscaping surrounding the campus that an area between Glenn Memorial Church and the old Law Building was named "Antoinette Gardens."

LIME AND GINGER GRILLED SALMON

Serves 4

2	pounds salmon fillets, skinned
2	tablespoons grated fresh ginger
2	tablespoons grated lime peel
½	teaspoon sea salt
¼	teaspoon ground white pepper
¼	teaspoon freshly ground black pepper
2	tablespoons butter or margarine, melted
2	teaspoons lime juice
➤	fresh lime slices for garnish

- Rinse salmon in cold water and pat dry.
- Mix ginger, lime and seasonings. Press onto both sides of salmon fillets.
- Allow salmon to absorb flavors for 30 - 40 minutes before grilling.
- Brush grill or broiler pan with vegetable oil.
- Mix lime juice and melted butter.
- Gently remove ginger-lime marinade from fillets with back of knife.
- Grill salmon over medium-low heat, brushing with lime butter, until done (opaque in center), about 5 minutes per side.
- Garnish with fresh lime slices.

Fabulous way to cook salmon!

ZESTY SALMON MICROWAVE

♥   *Easy*   *Serves 4*

1½	pounds salmon fillets
½	cup dry vermouth or white wine
1	small onion, chopped
2	tablespoons chopped fresh parsley
➤	dash of cayenne pepper

Sauce:

1	cup plain yogurt
2-3	tablespoons prepared horseradish
2	teaspoons grated lemon peel

- Place fish and other ingredients in microwave-safe baking dish. Cover and microwave at HIGH 4 - 10 minutes depending on thickness of fish. Check after 4 minutes.
- To brown fish, place under broiler about 2 minutes.
- Blend sauce ingredients and heat gently.
- Serve fish with sauce.
- *Variation*: Sole, flounder or orange roughy may be used. If using a dry, non-oily fish, spread sauce on fish for cooking.

CHEF'S NOTE

Broiling, grilling or poaching are easy, fast methods for cooking fish. This recipe will work well with those methods.

1-2-3 SALMON CAKES

♥   *Easy*   *Serves 4*

1	large can pink or red salmon, undrained
1	large egg or 2 egg whites
½	cup fine cracker crumbs, dry bread crumbs or 2 slices bread, torn and crumbled
¼	cup each minced onion, celery, bell pepper and fresh parsley
➤	dash of hot pepper sauce
➤	dash of Worcestershire sauce
➤	salt and pepper to taste
2	tablespoons vegetable oil
➤	lemon slices for garnish

• Place salmon in glass or stainless steel bowl. Discard skin.
• Break up with fork. Add remaining ingredients. Mix well.
• Form into patties. If too moist, add additional crumbs.
• Cover with wax paper; refrigerate until ready to use.
• Sauté lightly in oil until golden brown on each side.
• Garnish with lemon slices.

Bones in canned salmon are fine to leave in and will not be noticeable if mashed with fork.

CHEF'S NOTE

Using a nonstick pan sprayed with vegetable cooking spray works great.

BAKED RED SNAPPER

♥   *Easy*   *Serves 2*

1½	pounds whole red snapper, backbone removed, ready for stuffing
1	cup crushed oyster or round buttery crackers
¼	cup chopped green bell pepper
½	cup chopped onion
1	tablespoon lemon juice or white wine to taste
2	tablespoons butter, melted
1	egg
¼	cup chopped fresh mushrooms
¼	pound crab meat (optional)

- Heat oven to 350°F.
- Lightly grease baking dish and line with foil.
- Place fish on foil.
- Mix stuffing ingredients lightly; carefully fit into fish.
- Cover with foil.
- Bake 30 minutes. Test for doneness.

This recipe can be made with larger size fish. Allow more stuffing and longer cooking time. It will make a very festive presentation whether for two or four! or more!

BAKED TILAPIA CASSEROLE

♥   *Easy*   *Serves 2 - 4*

1	pound tilapia fillets
¼	cup lemon juice
¼	cup white wine
½	teaspoon salt
¼	teaspoon pepper
1	small clove garlic, crushed
1	cup chopped tomato
1	cup chopped carrot
¼	cup chopped green onion
¼	cup chopped fresh parsley

- Heat oven to 350°F.
- Place fish in rectangular baking dish.
- Combine lemon juice and white wine. Pour over fish.
- Combine seasonings. Sprinkle half on fish.
- Mix vegetables. Sprinkle over fish.
- Sprinkle remaining seasoning over top.
- Bake, covered, 25 - 30 minutes until fish flakes easily.

Seasoning may be varied to taste with ¼ teaspoon dill weed or tarragon.

BAKED LEMON-STUFFED FISH

Easy   *Serves 4 - 6*

3	**tablespoons butter or margarine**
½	**cup finely chopped celery**
¼	**cup finely chopped onion**
4	**cups dry bread cubes (½ inch)**
1	**tablespoon chopped fresh parsley**
½	**teaspoon freshly grated lemon peel**
4	**teaspoons lemon juice**
½	**teaspoon salt**
➢	**dash of white pepper**
1½-2	**pounds fish fillets (such as flounder or orange roughy)**
➢	**paprika**
➢	**lemon slices and fresh parsley for garnish**

- Heat oven to 350°F and grease 13x9x2-inch pan.
- Sauté celery and onion in butter. Pour over cubed bread.
- Add other ingredients except fish. Toss together.
- Place half of fish in pan; cover with stuffing. Top with remaining fish.
- Drizzle additional butter if desired; sprinkle with paprika.
- Cover pan with foil.
- Bake 20 - 25 minutes or until fish tests done.
- Garnish with fresh lemon and additional parsley.

FISH IN WHITE WINE

Easy   *Serves 4*

2	**pounds fish fillets (6 - 8 pieces)**
2	**onions, thinly sliced**
¼-½	**cup butter or margarine**
1	**cup dry white wine or vermouth**
➢	**paprika**
➢	**fresh parsley for garnish**

- Heat oven to 350°F.
- Lightly rinse fish and pat dry.
- Melt butter in heat-proof baking dish.
- Sauté onion until opaque.
- Place fish, skin side up, over onion. Sprinkle with paprika.
- Add wine and bake 25 minutes. Garnish with parsley.

This recipe is very mild and works well with a variety of fish.

Baked Citrus Orange Roughy

♥   *Easy*   *Serves 2*

1	pound orange roughy (2 fillets)
➤	salt and pepper to taste
½	cup white wine
2	tablespoons frozen orange juice concentrate
1	tablespoon lemon juice
2	tablespoons cornstarch
½	teaspoon dried dill weed or 1 teaspoon dried parsley

- Heat oven to 325°F and grease baking pan.
- Place fish in pan. Salt and pepper.
- Mix liquid ingredients and cornstarch until smooth. Pour over fish.
- Sprinkle with dill or parsley. Cover with foil.
- Bake 20 minutes or until fish tests done.

Baked Orange Roughy

Easy   *Serves 2*

1	pound orange roughy (2 fillets)
½	cup fine dry bread crumbs
½	teaspoon each basil, paprika and salt
¼	cup grated Parmesan cheese
⅛	teaspoon curry powder
¼	teaspoon lemon pepper seasoning
4	tablespoons butter or margarine
2	tablespoons sliced almonds

- Heat oven to 375°F and grease baking pan.
- Arrange fish in pan.
- Mix remaining ingredients except butter and almonds.
- Lightly sprinkle over fish. Dot with butter.
- Bake 15 minutes.
- Sprinkle almonds over fish. Place under broiler 1 - 2 minutes. Watch to keep from burning.

Dry crumb mixture may be kept several weeks in refrigerator. Use airtight container.

Epicurean Spring Cookout for 30

Grilled Fish

Serves 30

1	cup olive oil
2	tablespoons lemon juice or to taste
30	(3 - 5 ounce) steaks of firm non-flaky fish (tuna, amberjack, swordfish, grouper)
➤	salt and white pepper to taste

- Mix olive oil and lemon juice. Brush on both sides of fish.
- Salt and pepper.
- Heat grill and wipe rack with oiled cloth.
- Grill fish approximately 5 minutes per side or to desired doneness. Halfway through cooking on each side, turn each steak ¼ turn to make a cross pattern on fish.

Epicurean Summer Dinner for 25

Poached Fresh Salmon

Serves 25

9	pounds salmon side fillets
6	cups chicken broth

- Heat oven to 350°F.
- Place salmon in single layer in baking pan, skin side down. (If too long, cut in half.)
- Add broth. Adjust amount to be ¾-inch deep.
- Cover and bake 15 minutes per inch of thickness of salmon fillet.
- Cool in liquid. Remove from pan. Carefully remove skin from salmon.
- Chill at least 1 hour before serving.
- Serve with Blanched Vegetables and Bibb Lettuce (page 161).

Korean Beef Stir-Fry (Bul-go-gi)

Serves 4

2   **pounds sirloin tip roast or steak, cut in ¼-inch slices**
2   **tablespoons sesame seed, roasted**
1   **teaspoon salt**

Marinade:
1   **teaspoon sesame seed powder (see directions)**
⅓-½   **cup soy sauce**
2   **tablespoons sugar**
1   **teaspoon crushed garlic**
1   **teaspoon grated fresh ginger**
1   **teaspoon sesame oil**
1   **teaspoon black pepper**
1   **tablespoon finely chopped green onion**

- Spread sliced meat in shallow pan.
- Prepare sesame seed powder: Heat skillet over high heat. When pan is hot, reduce heat to medium high. Put sesame seeds in pan. Stir constantly until seeds turn brown and crisp. Remove from heat. Pound hot seeds to crush. Mix 1 teaspoon salt with 1 teaspoon crushed sesame seed powder for marinade.
- Combine marinade ingredients and pour over meat.
- Refrigerate, covered, at least 1 hour. Turn meat once or twice. Drain before cooking.
- Stir-fry or grill meat. (If grilling, place on sheet of foil so that meat will not lose all juice.)

Served with rice traditionally. Koreans serve this with spicy vegetable salad as an accompaniment.

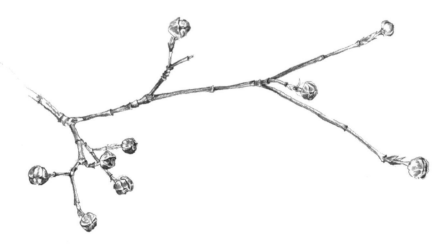

History Note

Emory President and Mrs. James T. Laney lived in Korea years ago. This is a favorite recipe.

Beef Tenderloin

🕐 *Serves 20*   *Superb buffet entrée*

5-6	**pound trimmed tenderloin**
10	**ounce bottle teriyaki marinade or sauce**
½	**pound bacon, sliced**
8	**ounce bottle no-oil Italian or vinaigrette dressing**

- Heat oven to 400°F.
- Rub meat generously with teriyaki sauce.
- Cover with bacon slices; hold in place with toothpicks.
- Bake 35 minutes (for rare meat).
- Allow to cool and remove bacon.
- Mix remaining teriyaki sauce with dressing. Put meat and marinade in plastic bag overnight, turning once.
- Remove meat from marinade and slice. Serve room temperature.

Good served with sour cream horseradish sauce and small biscuits or rolls.

Canadian Beef Stew

🕐 *Serves 8*

3	**pounds beef stew meat**
3	**large carrots, cut up**
6-10	**small white onions**
15	**ounce can tomatoes, undrained**
16	**ounce can peas, undrained, or 16 ounce package frozen peas**
½	**cup white or red wine**
10	**ounce can condensed beef consomme**
4	**tablespoons minute tapioca**
1	**tablespoon brown sugar**
½	**cup bread crumbs**
1	**teaspoon each salt and pepper**
1	**bay leaf**
1	**teaspoon Kitchen Bouquet**

- Heat oven to 300°F.
- Do not brown meat. Put all ingredients in dutch oven.
- Bake 4 - 5 hours.
- Serve to a crowd or divide and freeze.
- Serve over rice, noodles or potatoes.

Emory University Woman's Club is honored to have a number of active members who are Canadian.

GREEK STIFATHO (STEW)

🕐 *Serves 4 - 6*

2	pounds beef stew meat, fat removed, cubed
⅓	cup flour
2½-3	pounds small white onions or 5 large onions, cut in large chunks
½	cup olive oil
14-16	ounces canned crushed plum tomatoes, undrained
½	cup balsamic vinegar
5	cloves garlic, crushed
½	teaspoon pickling spice or ½ stick cinnamon, 2 cloves and 1 bay leaf
➤	salt and pepper to taste
½	cup red wine
1	tablespoon tomato paste (optional)

- Dredge meat with flour.
- In large dutch oven or stock pot, brown meat in olive oil. Remove.
- Add onions to pan and stir until translucent.
- Add tomato, vinegar, meat and spices (tied in cheesecloth or put in tea ball). Salt and pepper.
- Bake, covered, 2 hours at 325°F. Remove spices after 1 hour.
- Stir. Add wine and tomato paste to make sauce the right consistency. Stew should be thick.

Serve with parsleyed noodles, green beans and salad.

CHEF'S NOTE

Dredge meat by mixing meat with flour in self-sealing bag. Give a good shake or two. Remove floured meat. Repeat if necessary.

GROUND BEEF SUPREME CASSEROLE

Serves 8

1½	pounds ground round or ground sirloin
15	ounce can tomato sauce
16	ounce can chunky stewed tomatoes
1	teaspoon sugar
1	teaspoon basil
1	teaspoon No-Salt Herb Seasoning (page 69)
2-3	cloves garlic, crushed
12-16	ounce package pasta (Southern-style dumpling suggested)
6-8	green onions and tops, chopped
8	ounces low fat sour cream
4	ounces cream cheese, softened
1¾	cups shredded Cheddar, Monterey Jack or fontina cheese

- Heat oven to 350°F and grease large baking dish.
- Brown beef in skillet. Drain.
- Add tomato sauce, tomatoes, seasonings and garlic. Simmer.
- Cook pasta according to package directions. Undercook slightly.
- Drain pasta and return to pan but not heat.
- Stir in onion, sour cream and cream cheese. Mix to coat pasta.
- In large baking dish, layer beginning with half of meat sauce, then half of pasta, ½ cup cheese, remaining pasta and ½ cup cheese.
- Top with remaining meat sauce.
- Bake 35 minutes.
- Top with remaining cheese. Return to oven 10 minutes until cheese melts.
- Serve with green salad and crusty bread.

A family pleaser.

GRILLED TERIYAKI STEAK

Serves 4 - 6

1½	pounds steak (your favorite for grilling)

Marinade:

½	cup soy sauce
2	tablespoons honey
1	tablespoon ground ginger
2	cloves garlic, chopped
¼	cup vegetable oil
2	tablespoons cider vinegar

- Combine marinade ingredients and pour over steak.
- Refrigerate at least 6 hours. Turn meat once or twice.
- Grill 7-10 minutes for medium rare.

A good company recipe. Do ahead — cook later!

MEXICAN CORN AND BEEF CASSEROLE

Serves 6 - 8

1	pound lean ground beef
➢	salt and pepper to taste
1	cup yellow cornmeal
½	teaspoon salt
1	small onion, finely chopped
8	ounces Cheddar cheese, shreddcd
2-4	jalapeño peppers, chopped (optional)
1	cup milk
3	eggs, beaten
17	ounce can cream-style corn

- Heat oven to 350°F and grease 2-quart casserole.
- Salt and pepper beef and sauté in skillet. Drain and set aside.
- In large bowl, mix cornmeal, salt, onion, cheese and peppers.
- Stir eggs into milk. Add to cornmeal mixture, stirring just to moisten.
- Blend in corn.
- Spoon half of mixture into casserole. Distribute beef evenly.
- Top with remaining batter mixture.
- Bake 45 minutes or until done.

Serve with tossed salad.

AFRICAN JOLOFF RICE

🕐 *A celebration dinner*   *Serves 8 - 10*

1	**(3 pound) chicken, cut in pieces**
1	**pound beef stew meat, cubed**
2	**teaspoons each salt and black pepper**
5	**cloves garlic, crushed**
¼	**pound salt pork**
2	**small smoked ham hocks**
1	**cup peanut oil, divided**
3	**large onions, chopped (4 - 5 cups)**
4	**or more hot peppers (jalapeño, serrano and banana)**
3	**large ripe tomatoes, chopped (about 4 cups)**
10	**cups water, divided**
1	**teaspoon - 1 tablespoon cayenne pepper to taste**
2	**tablespoons thyme**
2	**each beef and chicken bouillon cubes**
2	**(12 ounce) cans tomato paste, divided**
3	**cups uncooked long-grain white rice**
½	**head cabbage or brussels sprouts**

- One hour before cooking, season chicken and beef with salt, black pepper and garlic.
- Use 2 large pots. In first pot, lightly brown salt pork over low heat. Remove and discard.
- Put ½ cup oil in each pot. In first pot, brown chicken and meats over medium-low heat. Remove.
- In second pot, sauté onion, peppers and tomato. Add 4 cups water, cayenne pepper, thyme and bouillon cubes. Bring to boil. Reduce heat and simmer 30 minutes. Add 1½ cans tomato paste and 2 cups water. Simmer additional 30 minutes.
- Transfer vegetable mixture to first pot. Stir.
- Return 3 cups vegetable mixture to second pot. Stir in 4 cups water and remaining tomato paste. Bring to boil.
- Return browned meat to vegetable mixture in first pot. Stew gently 1 - 2 hours.
- When second pot comes to boil, add rice and stir. Return to boil. Lower heat and cover. In 10 minutes check that rice is not sticking to bottom of pot. Stir well. Add small amount of liquid if needed. When most of water is absorbed, turn off heat. Let stand with tight cover to steam.
- Continue stirring meat in first pot as it simmers.
- Cut cabbage in chunks and put on top of meat to steam (about 1 hour before meal).
- Serve on large platter. Arrange pieces of meat and chunks of steamed vegetable attractively around rice.
- *West African variation*: Substitute couscous. Read instructions on package. Cooking time for couscous will be slightly shorter than for rice.

Joloff Rice is a traditional African dish that varies from region to region. This recipe came from a member of the medical school faculty who was originally from Sierra Leone.

CAMPFIRE BEAN CASSEROLE

Easy   *Serves 8*

1   **pound lean ground chuck**
1   **large onion, chopped**
¼   **cup brown sugar**
½-⅔ **cup ketchup**
1   **teaspoon dry mustard**
4   **(16 ounce) cans beans (a combination of pinto, kidney, great northern, black or other)**
1   **pound (cooked) smoked sausage, sliced like pennies**

- Brown meat (lean ground chuck should not need draining). Add onion and cook until soft.
- Stir in beans, ketchup, sugar and sausage.
- Heat over medium-low heat until bubbling. Stir occasionally.
- Serve with cornbread or crusty bread.

This is super easy to take to the mountains or the beach or for a quick family casserole on a busy day — 15 minutes to put together and ready in 30 minutes if necessary.

CHURCH SUPPER CHILI

🕐 *Serves 25 - 30*

8	pounds lean ground chuck
2	pounds sweet Italian sausage (remove from casing)
1½	tablespoons freshly ground black pepper
3	pounds onions, chopped
2	(12 ounce) cans tomato paste
3	tablespoons minced fresh garlic
3	tablespoons ground cumin
3	tablespoons chili powder
1½	teaspoons dry mustard
3	tablespoons salt
4	tablespoons each dried basil, dill and oregano
⅔	cup chopped fresh parsley
6	pounds canned crushed tomatoes, undrained
1	cup dry red wine
4	(16 ounce) cans kidney beans, undrained
3	(6 ounce) cans pitted black olives, drained
➤	sour cream, shredded Cheddar cheese and chopped green onion for garnish

- Using very large pot, sauté meat until browned.
- Add onion and garlic. Drain fat when onion is cooked.
- Reduce heat to low. Stir in other ingredients except beans and olives.
- Simmer minimum 30 minutes.
- Add beans. Simmer additional 20 minutes. Add olives.
- Serve garnished with sour cream or plain yogurt, Cheddar cheese and green onion.

DUTCH MEATLOAF NESTS (GEHAKTNESTJES)

Serves 6

½	pound ground beef
½	pound ground veal
½	pound ground pork
¼	teaspoon black pepper
1½	teaspoons salt
¼	teaspoon ground nutmeg
½	cup chopped onion
5	tablespoons butter or margarine, divided
½	cup soft bread crumbs
⅓	cup milk
6	hard-cooked eggs
½	cup dry bread crumbs
½	cup water

- Mix ground meats and seasonings.
- Brown onion in 2 tablespoons butter.
- Add soft bread crumbs to milk. Mix with meat and onion.
- Divide mixture into 6 equal portions; flatten each. Place an egg in center and cover with meat to form a ball.
- Roll balls in dry bread crumbs. Brown on all sides in remaining butter.
- Add water and simmer, covered, 25 - 30 minutes until meat is well-done.
- Cut each ball in half. Place cut side up on plates.
- Pour remaining sauce from pan over meatballs. Add a little water or milk to sauce if needed.

This recipe is quite imaginative and children find it a great surprise.

MEAT BALLS

4 - 6 dozen

A great time-saver to do ahead and freeze

3	**pounds ground chuck**
1	**pound ground pork**
1	**pound ground veal**
⅓	**cup chopped fresh parsley**
16	**ounce package crumbled herb-seasoned stuffing mix**
½	**bottle regular barbecue sauce (1¼ cups)**
➤	**salt and pepper to taste**

- Heat oven to 350°F.
- Mix all ingredients in large bowl.
- Form into balls. Ball should be solid but not hard. If more liquid is needed, add a small amount of water until ball holds.
- Place on jelly-roll pan, close but not touching.
- Bake 20 minutes until lightly browned.
- Cool 20 minutes. Freeze on flat surface. Store in heavy plastic bags.
- Meat balls may be used in many recipes for an easy, quick entrée.
- *Variation*: Change barbecue sauce to hot salsa or, for very mild flavor, to half and half.

To use as appetizer, form balls slightly smaller. Surround with heated chunky salsa and offer toothpicks.

Braised Lamb Shanks en Casserole

Serves 6

3	pounds lamb shanks (have butcher cut)
➤	flour for dredging
➤	salt and freshly ground pepper to taste
½	teaspoon oregano
⅓	cup vegetable oil
¾	cup chopped onion
¾	cup chopped celery
¾	cup chopped carrot
1-2	cloves garlic, crushed
➤	pinch of thyme
¾	cup dry red wine or dry sherry
1	cup beef bouillon or water and dried bouillon

- Heat oven to 350°F.
- Wipe lamb well with damp cloth.
- Combine flour, salt, pepper and oregano; dredge lamb shanks in flour mixture.
- In large skillet, brown meat in oil. Transfer to large ovenproof casserole or dutch oven.
- Add vegetables, garlic and thyme to skillet and sauté, stirring, 5 minutes.
- Pour vegetables over lamb and add liquids.
- Cover and bake 1½ - 2 hours or until meat is tender.
- If desired, thicken gravy with small amount of flour mixed with water.

Butterfly Leg of Lamb

Serves 6-8

5-6	pound leg of lamb, boned, excess fat removed
6	ounce jar Dijon mustard
1	teaspoon each rosemary and ground ginger
1	clove garlic, crushed
2	tablespoons soy sauce
1	tablespoon olive oil

- Have butcher bone leg of lamb.
- Mix all ingredients except lamb.
- Marinate meat 1 hour.
- Broil or grill 10 - 15 minutes on each side for medium-rare meat.

An easy and flavorful entrée for summertime grilling.

Roast Leg of Lamb

Serves 8-10

1	**whole leg of lamb**
1	**clove garlic**
1	**teaspoon salt**
¼	**teaspoon pepper**
½	**teaspoon ground ginger**
2	**cups strong coffee**

- Heat oven to 325°F.
- Rub lamb with cut clove of garlic. Slice garlic and insert pieces into meat. (Use sharp knife.)
- Mix salt, pepper and ginger. Rub lamb with mixture.
- Pour coffee over meat and bake 2½ - 3 hours, basting frequently. Meat thermometer should read 170°F. (Leave thermometer in meat.)
- Remove from oven and allow to sit 20 minutes before slicing.
- Check meat for desired doneness.

Elegant holiday entrée.

Rack of Lamb

Serves 4

2	**racks of lamb (7 - 8 ribs each)**
2	**cups fresh bread crumbs**
1	**cup chopped fresh parsley**
4	**cloves garlic, crushed**
2	**teaspoons salt**
1	**tablespoon fresh rosemary or 1 teaspoon dried rosemary**
½	**teaspoon pepper**
½	**cup olive oil**

- Have butcher trim fat and ends of bone from lamb and crack backbone.
- In medium bowl, combine bread crumbs and seasonings. Toss to mix well.
- Add oil and toss again.
- Place rack with ribs down. Press mixture onto meat to hold in place.
- Wrap tightly with plastic and refrigerate overnight.
- One hour before cooking, unwrap carefully and place on roaster pan rack.
- Heat oven to 400°F.
- Roast 45 minutes.

Party Shish Kabob

🕐 *Serves 8*

Marinade:

1	cup olive oil
½	cup vegetable oil
1½	teaspoons salt
1	tablespoon freshly ground pepper
1	cup light soy sauce
2	tablespoons dry mustard
2	teaspoons finely chopped fresh parsley
½	cup red wine vinegar
2	cloves garlic, crushed
⅓	cup fresh lemon juice

Shish Kabob:

2-2½	pounds lamb or beef sirloin, cut in 1½ - 2-inch cubes
10-12	ounces fresh small white onions or quartered medium onions
6	bell peppers (2 green, 2 yellow, 2 red), cut in 1½ - 2-inch squares
1-1½	pounds fresh mushrooms, stem on (medium size)
12	cherry tomatoes

- Mix marinade ingredients. Store tightly covered in refrigerator. Keeps several weeks.
- Cover meat with marinade and marinate 4 hours.
- Blanch peppers and onions 1½ minutes.
- Assemble meat, onions, peppers and mushrooms on skewers, alternating attractively for color.
- Baste with marinade. Refrigerate 1 hour, basting occasionally.
- Grill over medium heat 25 - 40 minutes, rotating kabobs for even cooking.
- Add tomatoes shortly before end of grilling or place on foil on grill about 10 minutes.
- Edges of meat and vegetables will be nicely browned when done.
- Gently remove meat and vegetables from skewer for ease of guests.
- Serve with wild or brown rice, a green salad and crusty bread.

The choicest lamb meat is from leg or shoulder; beef sirloin or tenderloin is great too. Color and flavor make a winning combination!

History Note

Alben W. Barkley, member of the class of 1900 and vice president under Harry Truman, said in his memoirs, "The year I spent there (Oxford) was a major factor in shaping my thinking."

DOOLEY'S BBQ PORK SPARE RIBS

Serves 2 - 3

2	pounds spare ribs or back ribs, cut in individual servings
1	medium onion, finely chopped
2	tablespoons vegetable oil
¼	cup lemon juice
1	tablespoon Worcestershire sauce
2	tablespoons brown sugar
½	cup water
1	cup chili sauce
➢	salt and pepper to taste

- Heat oven to 350°F.
- Place ribs in baking pan preferably on rack. Bake 30 minutes.
- Meanwhile, sauté onion in oil.
- Add remaining ingredients and cook slowly 20 minutes.
- Baste ribs with sauce and bake 1 hour.
- These may be grilled also (low heat)!

Recipe from Dooley's Delicacies, *published 1992, Oxford College.*

HISTORY NOTE

Dooley has become legendary. He originated as a skeleton in the Emory College biology lab in 1899, writing anonymous observations on campus events for the student newspaper. Dooley takes the first and second names of the current president, so that he is now known as "James T. Dooley." In October 1909 he wrote, "Presidents may come and presidents may go; professors may come and professors may go; students may come and students may go; but Dooley goes on forever." (H. M. Bullock, A History of Emory University.)

GRILLED PORK LOIN WITH 3 MARINADES

🕐 *Versatile buffet entrée*

1   **boneless rolled pork loin or boneless pork tenderloin**

Marinade #1:

½   **cup lemon juice**
½   **cup thawed frozen orange juice concentrate**
¼   **cup vegetable oil**
1   **teaspoon dried rosemary, crushed**
¼   **teaspoon each ground nutmeg and cloves**
½   **teaspoon each salt and freshly ground pepper**

Marinade #2:

10   **ounces beer**
¼   **cup honey**
2   **tablespoons chopped fresh sage or 1 teaspoon dried sage**
½-1   **teaspoon chili powder**

Marinade #3:

½   **cup light soy sauce**
6   **ounce can pineapple juice**
¼-½   **cup dry sherry or vermouth**
2   **tablespoons honey**
2   **cloves garlic, crushed**
½   **teaspoon ground ginger**
➢   **salt and pepper to taste**

- Choose 1 marinade. Marinate pork at least 2 hours or overnight in refrigerator.
- Grill over medium heat, basting often with marinade (about 20 minutes per pound).
- To oven roast, heat oven to 325°F. Bake, uncovered, about 45 minutes per pound.
- Use meat thermometer and remove roast when temperature reaches 160°F.

Pork loin roast is wonderful sliced when hot; great in sandwiches next day. Very little effort with big reward.

Marinades #1 and #3 are great for chicken; #3 is also especially good for teriyaki steak.

PORK CHOP DINNER

Serves 2 - 4

2-4	lean center-cut or loin pork chops, ¾ - 1-inch thick
2	tablespoons vegetable oil
1	cup uncooked white or brown rice
10	ounce can condensed cream of chicken or cream of celery or cream of mushroom soup
1	cup water
¼	cup chopped fresh parsley
1	cup sliced fresh mushrooms
½	medium onion, thinly sliced
➤	salt and pepper to taste
½	orange, including peel, sliced

- Heat oven to 350°F and grease casserole.
- Lightly brown chops on both sides in oil over medium-high heat.
- Mix rice, choice of soup and water in casserole. Stir in parsley.
- Top with mushrooms and onion.
- Salt and pepper pork chops and place in casserole. Deglaze pan with 2 tablespoons water. Pour over chops.
- Add orange slices and cover casserole with foil.
- Bake 45 - 50 minutes. Remove foil and check rice for doneness. If needed add 2 tablespoons water and bake additional 10 minutes.
- Use second half of orange as decorative accompaniment if desired.

ZINGY CHERRY SAUCE

Easy   Serves 8

1½	cups cherry preserves
¼	cup red wine vinegar
2	tablespoons light corn syrup
¼	teaspoon each ground cinnamon and cloves
➤	pinch of ground nutmeg

- In saucepan, combine all ingredients.
- Bring to boil over medium heat. Simmer 2 minutes.
- Serve warm as sauce for ham or pork roast.
- Cover and refrigerate.

Nice gift for a friend!

Veal à la Parma

Easy   *Serves 2*

4	**veal cutlets (about ½ pound)**
1	**egg**
1	**tablespoon water**
1	**teaspoon lemon juice**
⅓	**cup flour**
¼	**cup freshly grated Parmesan cheese**
¼	**teaspoon each salt and pepper**
1	**tablespoon chopped fresh basil**
1	**teaspoon chopped fresh parsley**
2	**tablespoons butter**
➢	**lemon slices for garnish**

- Gently pound veal cutlets flat with mallet.
- Mix egg, water and lemon juice.
- Mix flour, Parmesan cheese and seasonings.
- Moisten veal in egg mixture.
- Dredge with flour mixture.
- In nonstick pan over medium-high heat, sauté veal in butter about 2 minutes per side until delicately browned.
- Garnish with lemon slices.

Serve with sautéed mushrooms and sliced prosciutto over angel hair pasta. Pass additional Parmesan cheese.

Veal Scallopine for Two

Easy   *Serves 2*

½	**pound veal cutlets**
⅓	**cup Parmesan cheese**
3	**tablespoons butter**
½	**cup finely chopped onion**
¼	**cup grated carrot**
1	**cup thinly sliced fresh mushrooms**
➢	**salt and pepper to taste**
1	**tablespoon flour**
¾	**cup chicken stock**
¼	**cup Marsala wine**

- Cut veal in serving pieces. Gently pound veal flat.
- Dredge with Parmesan cheese.
- Lightly sauté veal 2 minutes each side in 3 tablespoons butter. Remove from pan.
- Sauté vegetables in remaining butter. Salt and pepper.
- Sprinkle with flour. Add stock and Marsala. Simmer 20 minutes or until tender.
- Add veal. Gently reheat and serve.

If there is too much liquid, thicken with cornstarch or manie butter. (Manie butter: Equal parts butter and flour blended. May be frozen.)

EPICUREAN WINTER BUFFET FOR 36

LAMB MOUSSAKA

Serves 36

9	pounds eggplant, cut in ½-inch slices
12	pounds lean ground lamb from leg or shoulder
8	(24 ounce) cans whole tomatoes, undrained
5	cups chopped onion
¼	cup chopped garlic
5	cups chopped fresh parsley
3	tablespoons salt or to taste
2½	teaspoons ground black pepper
5	teaspoons ground cinnamon
2½	teaspoons ground nutmeg
1	cup (2 sticks) unsalted butter
1⅓	cups all-purpose flour
4	teaspoons salt
2	quarts half and half, scalded
12	large eggs, lightly beaten
4	cups grated Parmesan cheese (about 2 pounds), divided

- Heat oven to 400°F and grease baking sheet.
- Place eggplant in single layer on baking sheet.
- Bake until golden brown. Set aside.
- Brown meat. Drain excess fat.
- Break up tomatoes. Add undrained tomatoes, onion, garlic, parsley and seasonings to meat. Simmer 45 minutes or until most of liquid is absorbed.
- Cover bottom of 4 (11x12x4-inch) baking dishes with eggplant.
- Top with even layer of meat mixture. Allow at least 1 inch for cheese topping.
- Heat oven to 350°F.
- In large saucepan, melt butter over medium heat. Stir in flour and whisk until blended. Add half and half, stirring constantly until thickened, about 5 minutes.
- Add 3 cups Parmesan cheese and stir until absorbed. Set aside.
- In large bowl, beat eggs lightly. Add ⅓ of cream sauce mixture to eggs while beating.
- Mix egg mixture into remaining ⅔ cream sauce. Pour over meat mixture in pans.
- Sprinkle with remaining Parmesan cheese.
- Bake 45 minutes. Cool 20 minutes before cutting. Each pan should be cut in 9 squares.

Lean ground beef may be substituted for lamb.

Desserts and Beverages

Desserts and Beverages

*D*essert, for many of us, is the most important part of the meal and the one most eagerly anticipated. As the grand finale to an elegant dinner, dessert can provide a lingering note of flavor to a memorable evening. Desserts can be a tour de force for the enthusiastic baker or a light mixture of seasonal fruits, artfully presented to please the eye as well as the palate. Dessert may be a special treat to be shared at tea time or enjoyed for coffee break at the office. Any celebration involving food must have dessert!

The classic Southern dessert for Christmas and New Year's is ambrosia, simply made with sliced oranges and grated coconut — always light and refreshing after a full-course meal. This section has luscious old-fashioned cobbler and peach pound cake, as well as feasts for the ardent chocolate lover. Many of the cookies and candies are perfect for holiday gift giving, presented in a gaily painted tin or a beribboned jar.

The following are quick dessert ideas to make your family and friends think you have spent hours in the kitchen:

POUND CAKE: Toast slices and serve with topping (such as puréed berries, liqueur sauce or toasted nuts).

APRICOT CREAM: Whip 1 cup heavy cream until stiff. Fold in ¼ cup softened apricot preserves and 1 teaspoon lemon juice. Serve over sliced strawberries sweetened with ¼ cup powdered sugar.

RASPBERRY WHIP: Beat 1 large egg white to soft peaks. Fold in ½ cup sugar and ½ cup raspberries. Beat on high 15 - 20 minutes until stiff and opaque. Serve in glass goblets.

RASPBERRIES: Thaw frozen berries packed in syrup. Purée. Strain to remove seeds. Serve over other fruit, ice cream or cake.

STRAWBERRIES: Sprinkle sugar and Grand Marnier or Kirsch over fresh berries. Serve in sherbet glasses with your favorite cookie.

COFFEE ICE CREAM: Top scoop with crushed toffee bar and jigger of coffee liqueur or chopped macadamia nuts, pineapple chunks and 2 tablespoons rum.

LEMON ICE CREAM, SORBET OR SHERBET: Serve in wide mouth champagne glass surrounded with 2 tablespoons champagne and garnished with mint leaves.

ICE CREAM: Roll ball of ice cream in chopped nuts or chocolate wafer crumbs and serve with chocolate fudge or caramel topping or roll ball of ice cream in shredded coconut; serve with mango and papaya.

ICE CREAM PIE: Crush package of Bordeaux cookies for crust. Drizzle 3 tablespoons melted butter over crumbs and mix. Press onto pan. Refrigerate 1 hour. Spread quart of softened butter almond ice cream. Drizzle with caramel topping. Serve with whipped cream and toasted sliced almonds.

CRANBERRY BOURBON SLUSH

🕐 *Serves 12 - 14*

1	quart (32 ounces) cranberry or cran-raspberry juice
1	liter (33 ounces) ginger ale
12	ounce can frozen lemonade concentrate, thawed
1½	cups bourbon whiskey

- In large container, mix all ingredients.
- Freeze in airtight containers.
- To serve, thaw 10 minutes; scoop into punchbowl or glasses.

The cookbook committee gave this recipe a perfect score of "10" on a scale of 1 - 5!

CHAMPAGNE PUNCH

Serves 25

1	cup sugar
¼	cup water
1	tablespoon lemon juice
½	cup brandy
½	cup orange liqueur
½	cup unsweetened lime juice
3-6	cups champagne, chilled
3	cups white zinfandel or sauterne, chilled
1	liter (33 ounces) soda water, chilled

- Boil sugar and water 5 minutes or until clear.
- Remove from heat. Stir in lemon juice. Refrigerate.
- Mix brandy, liqueur and lime juice. Refrigerate.
- In punch bowl, mix sugar syrup and brandy mixture.
- Stir in champagne, wine and soda water. Add ice. Serve.

CHEF'S NOTE

It is not necessary to use the best quality or most expensive wines or liqueurs when making a punch.

BUNNY'S COFFEE PUNCH

Serves 12 - 15

3	cups boiling water
¼	cup instant coffee granules
6	tablespoons chocolate syrup
½	cup sugar
1	quart milk
½	gallon vanilla ice cream
2	cups ginger ale or soda water

• In large container, mix water, coffee, chocolate syrup and sugar.
• Cool and refrigerate.
• To serve add milk, ice cream and ginger ale or soda water.

TROPICAL PUNCH

Serves 30 - 40

2	quarts apricot nectar, chilled
46	ounce can pineapple juice, chilled
2	liter bottle ginger ale or soda water, chilled

• Mix all ingredients and serve.

CHEF'S NOTE

For a large party, make up ½ recipe of punch and freeze in ring mold. Float frozen ring in punch when serving. Fruit may be added to mold before freezing.

ALMOND FRUIT PUNCH

Serves 25

18	ounces frozen lemonade concentrate
2	(46 ounce) cans pineapple juice
8	cups water
3	quarts orange juice
2	tablespoons vanilla
2	tablespoons almond extract
½	cup sugar

- Mix all ingredients.
- Refrigerate until serving.

  The almond flavor is unusual for punch.

HOT SPICED HOLIDAY PUNCH

Serves 25

2	quarts cranberry juice
2	quarts unsweetened pineapple juice
1	quart water
⅔	cup light brown sugar
1	tablespoon whole cloves
1	tablespoon whole allspice
4	cinnamon sticks
2	lemons, quartered

- In large pot, combine all ingredients and simmer 30 minutes.
  OR:
- Combine juices and water in bottom of 30-cup electric percolator.
- Place remaining ingredients in basket.
- Perk 30 minutes or until light signals done.

  This punch will fill your home with a wonderful aroma.

BAKED PEARS

Serves 6

6	**fresh ripe pears, unpeeled**
12	**whole cloves**
➤	**ground cinnamon to taste**
2	**cups firmly packed brown sugar**
1½	**cups water**
1	**cup heavy cream or crème fraîche**
⅓	**cup toasted sliced almonds**

- Heat oven to 350°F.
- Stick each pear with 2 cloves.
- Arrange pears on their sides in deep baking dish. Sprinkle with cinnamon.
- In saucepan, bring brown sugar and water to boil. Simmer 5 minutes. Pour over pears.
- Bake, uncovered, 1 hour. Baste occasionally. Cool and refrigerate.
- To serve, float cream on top of brown sugar syrup. Place pear on top and sprinkle with almonds.

BISHOP WHIPPLE

Easy   *Serves 8*

2	**eggs**
1	**cup plus 2 tablespoons sugar**
⅔	**cup all-purpose flour**
1	**teaspoon baking powder**
1	**cup chopped pecans**
1	**cup cut-up dates**
➤	**powdered sugar**

- Heat oven to 350°F and grease and flour 8x8x2-inch pan.
- Beat eggs. Add sugar, flour and baking powder. Mix.
- Stir in nuts and dates.
- Bake 30 minutes.
- While hot, break in small pieces and shake in bag of powdered sugar.
- Serve cold with whipped cream.

Do not use packaged chopped dates.

HISTORY NOTE

Mrs. H. B. Trimble, "Miss Mattie" as she is known and loved, contributed this recipe for the first Emory Woman's Club cookbook in the 1960's. She said it originated in Nashville, Tennessee, and called it a "40-year favorite." Miss Mattie, whose husband was Dean of the School of Theology, was Emory University Woman's Club president in 1933-1934. She celebrated her 100th birthday in April 1993.

CARAMEL CUSTARD

Serves 6

2	cups milk
2½	tablespoons sugar
3	eggs
1	teaspoon vanilla
6-9	tablespoons brown sugar for caramelizing

- Heat oven to 450°F.
- Bring milk to boil.
- Beat sugar and eggs 1 minute.
- Stir in hot milk. Beat until blended. Add vanilla.
- Put 1 - 1½ tablespoons brown sugar in bottom of each of 6 custard cups (or use soufflé dish).
- Gently fill with milk mixture. Place cups in pan of hot water.
- Bake 30 minutes. Custard is set when a knife inserted in center comes out clean. Cool.

RICE PUDDING

8 cups   Serves 12-16

1	cup uncooked white rice
½	teaspoon salt
2	quarts milk
¾	cup sugar
4	egg yolks
¼	teaspoon ground nutmeg
1	tablespoon vanilla
¾	cup raisins (optional)
➢	ground cinnamon

- Use a heavy saucepan or double boiler.
- Mix and cook rice, salt, milk and sugar over medium-low heat.
- Simmer, uncovered, 45 minutes, stirring occasionally.
- Beat egg yolks and slowly add 1 cup of hot rice mixture. Stir into rice mixture in saucepan. Add nutmeg.
- Heat gently additional 5 minutes.
- Remove from heat. Add vanilla and raisins.
- Pour into 2-quart serving dish. Sprinkle with cinnamon. Refrigerate.
- May be served warm or cold.

CLASSIC CHOCOLATE MOUSSE

🕐 ★   *Serves 6-8*

8	ounces semi-sweet chocolate
¼	cup plus 2 tablespoons boiling water
5	eggs, separated
2-3	tablespoons rum

- Process chocolate in blender or food processor on high 6 seconds.
- Turn off motor and scrape down sides of container with rubber spatula.
- Add water and blend 10 seconds.
- Add egg yolks and rum. Blend 3 seconds or until smooth.
- Beat egg whites until stiff. Fold chocolate mixture into egg whites.
- Spoon into individual serving dishes.
- Refrigerate at least 3 hours before serving.

CHOCOLATE MOUSSE MARNIER

★   *Serves 6-8*

1½	teaspoons unflavored gelatin
➤	juice of 1 medium orange (½ cup)
6	ounces semi-sweet chocolate bits
¼	cup water
3	eggs and 2 egg yolks
¼	cup sugar
1	teaspoon grated orange peel
1	cup heavy cream, softly whipped
1-1½	tablespoons Grand Marnier liqueur
➤	whipped cream, finely grated chocolate or crystallized violets for garnish

- In small saucepan, dissolve gelatin in orange juice (see note). Cool.
- Melt chocolate with water.
- In large bowl, beat eggs, yolks and sugar until very thick.
- Fold in chocolate.
- Add gelatin and orange peel. Add cream.
- Spoon into individual chocolate shells or small serving dishes.
- Decorate with dollop of whipped cream, finely grated chocolate or crystallized violets.

Serves 12 or more in demitasse cups.

CHEF'S NOTE

To dissolve gelatin, sprinkle on top of measured cold liquid. Allow to stand 5 minutes to soften before dissolving over low heat. Do not boil. Do not stir.

LEMON ICE

🕐 ★   *Serves 6-8*

4	eggs
1	cup sugar
1	cup light corn syrup
➤	grated peel of 2 lemons
½	cup lemon juice
3	cups milk

- Beat eggs until thick and lemon colored.
- Beat in other ingredients.
- Pour into bowl and freeze overnight.
- Remove from freezer and whip until light and creamy.
- Return quickly to freezer and freeze until firm.
- May be topped with whipped cream.

Mrs. Ruth Becker, chief cook at Lullwater for President and Mrs. Laney, contributed this favorite recipe.

CITRUS ICE CREAM

🕐   *3 cups*   *Serves 6-8*

2	cups heavy cream or half and half
1	cup sugar
1	tablespoon freshly grated orange or lemon peel
⅓	cup freshly squeezed orange or lemon juice
➤	strawberries and fresh mint for garnish

- In large bowl, combine cream and sugar. Stir until sugar dissolves.
- Blend in orange peel and juice.
- Pour in shallow glass pan; freeze until firm (4 hours or more).
- Serve in dessert glasses. Garnish with strawberries and fresh mint.

CHEF'S NOTE

These desserts are colorful and eye-catching served in lemon or orange shells.

OLD DOMINION COBBLER

Easy   *Serves 8 - 10*

3-4   **cups fresh fruit (peaches, apples or blueberries)**
3   **tablespoons sugar**
½   **teaspoon each ground nutmeg and cinnamon**
½   **cup (1 stick) butter or margarine**

Crust:
1   **cup all-purpose flour**
1   **cup sugar**
2   **teaspoons baking powder**
⅔   **cup milk**

- Heat oven to 350°F.
- Sprinkle fruit with sugar, nutmeg and cinnamon. Set aside.
- Melt butter in 9x9-inch baking pan.
- Mix flour, sugar and baking powder. Stir in milk.
- Spoon gently over melted butter in pan.
- Spoon fruit gently on top.
- Bake 45 minutes or until crust is lightly browned.
- Serve warm. Top with ice cream or whipped cream.

This is an old-fashioned, home-style Southern dessert, particularly delicious made with a mix of fruits. Always a hit!

EASY APPLE-PECAN CRISP

Easy   *Serves 6 - 8*

4½	**cups sliced tart apples, tossed with lemon juice**
¾	**cup firmly packed brown sugar**
½	**cup all-purpose flour**
½	**cup quick oats**
1	**teaspoon each ground cinnamon and nutmeg**
½	**cup (1 stick) butter or margarine, softened**
⅔	**cup chopped pecans**

• Heat oven to 350°F and grease 8x8-inch pan.
• Layer apples on bottom.
• Mix remaining ingredients until crumbly. Sprinkle over apples.
• Bake 30 - 45 minutes or until apples are tender and top is golden brown.
• Serve with whipped cream or ice cream.

BROWNIES

Easy

1⅓	cups sifted all-purpose flour
1	teaspoon baking powder
½	teaspoon salt
⅔	cup butter or margarine
4	ounces unsweetened chocolate
4	eggs, well beaten
2	cups sugar
2	teaspoons vanilla
1	cup chopped nuts

- Heat oven to 350°F and grease 13x9x2-inch pan.
- Sift flour, baking powder and salt.
- Melt butter with chocolate.
- Add sugar gradually to eggs. Beat thoroughly.
- Add chocolate mixture and then flour mixture. Mix well.
- Add vanilla and nuts. Spread in pan.
- Bake 30 minutes or until tests done. Cool.

CRÈME DE MENTHE BROWNIES

🕐

Brownie:

½	cup (1 stick) butter or margarine, softened
1	cup sugar
4	eggs, beaten until thick
1	cup all-purpose flour
½	teaspoon salt
16	ounce can chocolate syrup
1	teaspoon vanilla

- Heat oven to 350°F and grease 13x9x2-inch pan.
- Cream butter and sugar. Add eggs.
- Mix in flour, salt, chocolate syrup and vanilla.
- Pour into pan. Bake 20 - 25 minutes. Cool.

Middle Layer:

2	cups powdered sugar
½	cup (1 stick) butter or margarine
2	tablespoons green crème de menthe liqueur

- *Middle layer:* Mix powdered sugar, butter and crème de menthe until fluffy. Spread over cooled brownie.

Glaze:

1½	cups chocolate chips
6	tablespoons butter or margarine

- *Glaze:* Melt chocolate chips with butter. Cool until mixture spreads easily but does not melt middle layer.
- Spread over brownie. Refrigerate. Cut into small bars.

These are very rich. Small pieces are quite satisfying.

BUTTERSCOTCH BROWNIES

Easy

2	cups all-purpose flour
¾	teaspoon salt
1	tablespoon baking powder
¾	cup (1½ sticks) butter, melted
3	cups firmly packed brown sugar
3	eggs
1½	cups chopped pecans
1	tablespoon vanilla
¼	cup flaked coconut (optional)

- Heat oven to 350°F and grease and flour 13x9x2-inch pan.
- Sift flour, salt and baking powder.
- Mix butter with sugar, eggs, nuts and vanilla.
- Add to dry ingredients and mix. Spread in pan.
- Bake 20 - 30 minutes. Cut into squares when cool.

OATMEAL DATE BARS

1	pound dates, chopped
½	cup sugar
1½	cups water
¾	cup shortening
1	cup firmly packed brown sugar
1¾	cups flour
½	teaspoon salt
½	teaspoon baking soda
1½	cups quick oats
1	cup chopped walnuts

- Cook dates, sugar and water in saucepan over low heat.
- Stir constantly 10 - 15 minutes or until thickened. Cool.
- Heat oven to 400°F and grease 13x9x2-inch baking pan.
- Cream shortening and brown sugar.
- Add flour, salt, baking soda and oats. Mix.
- Press half of mixture evenly in bottom of pan.
- Cover with date mixture. Top with remaining crumbly mixture. Press lightly.
- Sprinkle nuts over top.
- Bake 25 - 30 minutes or until lightly browned. Cut into bars while warm.

PUMPKIN BARS

2	cups sugar
2	cups all-purpose flour
2	teaspoons baking powder
½	teaspoon salt
1	teaspoon baking soda
½	teaspoon each ground ginger, cloves and nutmeg
2	teaspoons ground cinnamon
4	eggs
1¾	cups canned pumpkin
1	cup vegetable oil
1	cup chopped nuts (optional)

- Heat oven to 350°F and grease 15x10x1-inch jelly-roll pan.
- Mix dry ingredients. Set aside.
- In large bowl, mix eggs, pumpkin and oil.
- Add dry ingredients. Beat until smooth. Stir in nuts.
- Pour into pan and bake 25 - 30 minutes. Cool completely before frosting.

Frosting:

3	ounces soft cream cheese
6	tablespoons butter or margarine, softened
1	teaspoon vanilla
1½	cups powdered sugar

- *Frosting:* Mix all ingredients until fluffy. Spread over top.
- Cut into bars. Store, covered, in cool place or refrigerator.

CHINESE WEDDING COOKIES

1	cup (2 sticks) butter
¼	cup sugar
2	cups all-purpose flour
½	teaspoon salt
2½	cups chopped nuts
➢	powdered sugar

- Heat oven to 350°F.
- Cream butter and sugar.
- Add flour and salt. Mix well. Add nuts.
- Form dough into small balls or crescents.
- Bake 15 minutes. Dust with powdered sugar while still hot.

CHEF'S NOTE

To coat cookies with powdered sugar, put a small amount of powdered sugar in bag. Drop in a few cookies at a time and shake to coat.

SURPRISE ALMOND COOKIES

Easy   2 - 3 dozen

1	cup (2 sticks) butter or margarine, softened
¾	cup sugar
½	teaspoon baking soda
½	teaspoon white vinegar
1	teaspoon each almond extract and vanilla
1½	cups all-purpose flour
½	cup chopped nuts (optional)

- Heat oven to 300°F and grease baking sheet.
- Beat butter and sugar until fluffy.
- Add baking soda, vinegar, almond extract and vanilla. Mix 4 - 5 minutes.
- Blend in flour and nuts.
- Drop by tablespoonful on baking sheet.
- Bake 30 minutes.

GINGERBREAD COOKIES

1	cup (2 sticks) butter or margarine
½	cup sugar
½	cup firmly packed light brown sugar
⅓	cup molasses
⅔	cup light corn syrup
4½	cups all-purpose flour
1	teaspoon each baking soda and salt
1	teaspoon each ground ginger and cinnamon
½	teaspoon ground cloves
➤	red cinnamon candies and raisins (optional for decoration)

- Cream butter and sugars until light.
- Add molasses and corn syrup. Mix well.
- Stir in dry ingredients with heavy spoon. Work until smooth. Use hands to knead if necessary.
- Cover dough and refrigerate until firm, 1 hour.
- Heat oven to 350°F.
- Remove portion of dough and roll on lightly floured board. Cut with desired cutters.
- Gingerbread men may be decorated with red candies and raisins.
- Bake until lightly browned at edge. Cool 30 seconds before transferring to rack.
- While warm make small hole at top of cookie. Thread with string or yarn for tree ornament or gift giving.

HISTORY NOTE

Betty Atwood made hundreds of these each year for Emory's Glee Club and Chorale when her husband was president of Emory.

SOFT GINGER COOKIES

Easy   *4 dozen*

¾	cup vegetable oil
1¼	cups sugar, divided
1	egg
¼	cup molasses
2	cups all-purpose flour
½	teaspoon salt
2	teaspoons baking soda
1	teaspoon each ground cinnamon and ginger

- Heat oven to 350°F and grease baking sheet.
- In large bowl, mix oil and 1 cup sugar. Add egg and beat well.
- Stir in molasses.
- Combine flour, salt, baking soda and spices. Stir into mixture.
- Form dough into 1-inch balls and roll in remaining sugar.
- Place balls on baking sheet 2 inches apart.
- Bake 8 - 10 minutes.

These cookies are soft and chewy. It's hard to stop eating them!

SWEDISH GINGERSNAPS

7 dozen

1½	cups all-purpose flour
1½	teaspoons ground ginger
1	teaspoon ground cinnamon
¼	teaspoon ground cloves
1	teaspoon baking soda
½	cup (1 stick) butter
¾	cup sugar
1	egg, beaten
1½	teaspoons dark corn syrup

- Sift first 5 ingredients together. Set aside.
- Cream butter. Add sugar gradually. Beat until fluffy.
- Add egg and corn syrup gradually. Beat well.
- Blend in dry ingredients, ¼ at a time. Mix.
- Refrigerate several hours.
- Heat oven to 375°F and grease baking sheet.
- Remove a portion of chilled dough and roll very thin on lightly floured surface. Cut with floured cookie cutters.
- Bake 6 - 8 minutes until golden brown.

These cookies are thin and crispy. Delicious with milk or apple juice!

RUGALACH

🕐 *Make in food processor*

Dough:

2½-3	cups all-purpose flour
¼	teaspoon salt
1	cup (2 sticks) cold butter, cut in chunks
8	ounces cream cheese, cut in chunks
2	eggs

Filling:

1	cup raisins
1	cup chopped walnuts
½	cup sugar
1	tablespoon ground cinnamon or to taste
➤	additional cinnamon sugar mix for rolling (1 part cinnamon and 8 parts sugar)
½	cup (1 stick) melted butter or apricot preserves

- Place flour and salt in food processor. Add butter and cream cheese.
- Pulse food processor until pea-size balls form.
- Add eggs. Process until ball forms. Refrigerate dough several hours.
- Heat oven to 375°F.
- Mix filling ingredients in food processor.
- Divide dough in 6 equal parts.
- Sprinkle rolling surface with additional cinnamon sugar mix.
- Roll each part into a thin circle. Brush lightly with melted butter or apricot preserves. Put ⅓ cup filling on each circle.
- Cut each circle into 16 wedges. Roll up starting at wide end.
- Place on ungreased baking sheet.
- Bake 10 - 15 minutes or until lightly browned.

SUGAR COOKIES

1	cup vegetable oil
1	cup (2 sticks) butter or margarine
1	cup powdered sugar
1	cup granulated sugar
2	eggs
2	teaspoons vanilla
4	cups all-purpose flour
1	teaspoon baking soda
1	teaspoon cream of tartar
➤	additional sugar for rolling

- Combine oil, butter, sugars and eggs. Beat well.
- Add vanilla and dry ingredients.
- Refrigerate dough at least 1 hour.
- Heat oven to 350°F.
- Form small balls and roll in additional sugar.
- Place on ungreased baking sheet. Press flat with bottom of glass.
- Dip glass in sugar after each cookie.
- Bake 10 - 12 minutes.

OATMEAL CHOCOLATE CHIP COOKIES

2½	cups quick or old-fashioned oats
1	cup (2 sticks) butter or margarine
1	cup sugar
1	cup firmly packed brown sugar
2	eggs
1	teaspoon vanilla
2	cups all-purpose flour
½	teaspoon salt
1	teaspoon baking powder (optional, makes cookie crunchy)
12	ounces chocolate chips
4	ounce plain chocolate bar, roughly chopped
1½	cups chopped pecans or walnuts

- Heat oven to 375°F.
- Process oats in blender or food processor until flour consistency.
- In large bowl, cream butter, sugar and brown sugar.
- Add eggs and vanilla. Mix well.
- In separate bowl, mix flour, oats, salt and baking powder.
- Add to creamed mixture. Mix. Add chocolate and nuts.
- Using spoon, place golf-ball-size drops about 2 inches apart on ungreased baking sheet.
- Bake 8 - 10 minutes until golden. Allow to set 1 minute before removing cookies to wire rack.
- *Variation*: Use white chocolate and macadamia nuts.

MISS DAISY'S NUT KISSES

2	egg whites, stiffly beaten
½	cup firmly packed light brown sugar
1	cup chopped pecans
½	cup chocolate chips (optional)

- Heat oven to 275°F and line baking sheet with wax paper.
- Gradually add brown sugar to egg whites. Continue to beat.
- Add pecans and chocolate chips ¼ cup at a time.
- Drop meringue by teaspoonful on wax paper.
- Bake 20 minutes. Turn off oven.
- Leave in oven to completely dry, 1½ - 2 hours.

Kisses will keep a long time in tight container.

CHEF'S NOTE

Meringue will not set in high humidity. Always check weather report before baking.

APPLE TART

Make in food processor

Tart pastry:

1½	cups all-purpose flour
1	tablespoon sugar
½	teaspoon salt
6	tablespoons cold butter
2	tablespoons shortening
3	tablespoons ice water

- Place flour, sugar and salt in food processor.
- Add butter and shortening.
- Start processing, pouring water slowly through feed tube until dough starts to form a ball.
- Roll out dough and carefully arrange in 10-inch tart or pie pan.

Filling:

3	tablespoons flour
¼	cup firmly packed brown sugar
½	cup sugar
½	teaspoon ground cinnamon
¼	teaspoon ground nutmeg
4-5	apples or 7 - 8 peaches, peeled, sliced
➤	juice of ½ lemon
¾	cup heavy cream
2	tablespoons butter

- Heat oven to 375°F.
- Sprinkle flour and brown sugar over unbaked tart pastry.
- Mix sugar, cinnamon and nutmeg in small bowl.
- Toss fruit with lemon juice.
- Overlapping slices, arrange fruit in layers, sprinkling each layer with sugar/cinnamon mixture.
- Pour cream evenly over fruit.
- Dot with butter.
- Bake 1 hour. Cover lightly with foil if crust is browning too much.

RHUBARB CUSTARD PIE

1⅓	cups sugar, divided
3	tablespoons flour
¼	teaspoon salt
3	eggs, separated
3	tablespoons frozen orange juice concentrate
2	tablespoons butter or margarine, softened
3	cups fresh rhubarb, cut in ½-inch pieces
9	inch unbaked pie shell
⅓	cup chopped pecans

- Heat oven to 350°F.
- Combine 1 cup sugar, flour and salt.
- Add egg yolks, orange juice concentrate and butter.
- Beat until smooth. Stir in rhubarb.
- Beat egg whites to soft peaks. Slowly add remaining sugar. Beat to stiff peaks.
- Gently fold into rhubarb mixture.
- Pour into pie shell. Sprinkle with pecans.
- Bake 55 minutes. Garnish with whipped cream if desired.

Strawberries may be substituted for 1 cup rhubarb — really delicious!

PECAN PIE

Easy

9	inch unbaked pie shell
1¼	cups pecan halves
3	eggs
⅓	cup butter, melted
1	cup light corn syrup
1	teaspoon vanilla
1	cup firmly packed brown sugar
1	tablespoon flour
½	teaspoon salt

- Arrange pecans in pie shell.
- Beat eggs well. Add butter, corn syrup and vanilla.
- In separate bowl, combine sugar and flour.
- Add to egg mixture. Beat well.
- Pour over nuts in pie shell. Nuts will rise to surface.
- Put in cold oven. Bake 45 minutes at 350°F or until knife inserted 1 inch from edge comes out clean.

HISTORY NOTE

Suzanne Eady, who was much loved at Oxford for many years, is credited with this recipe. Her husband, Virgil Young Cook Eady, was Dean of Oxford College from 1944 to 1966. He said to the students of 1957: "Let us run with patience the race that is set before us; and let us make sure that we are running toward the proper goals."

GEORGIA PEANUT PIE

🕐

20	round buttery crackers, finely crushed
1	cup sugar, divided
¾	cup chopped roasted peanuts
3	egg whites
¼	teaspoon cream of tartar
1	teaspoon vanilla
➤	whipped cream
➤	bitter chocolate, shaved or grated

- Heat oven to 350°F.
- Mix cracker crumbs with ½ cup sugar and peanuts.
- Beat egg whites until stiff, adding cream of tartar, remaining sugar and vanilla.
- Fold into cracker mixture. Pour into 9-inch pie pan.
- Bake 25 minutes. Cool. Refrigerate 3 hours before serving.
- Top with whipped cream and sprinkle with chocolate.

OLD FASHIONED BUTTERMILK PIE

½	cup (1 stick) butter
1½	cups sugar
3	tablespoons flour
3	eggs
1	cup buttermilk
1¼	teaspoons vanilla
¼	teaspoon ground nutmeg or 1 tablespoon lemon juice
9	inch unbaked pie shell

- Heat oven to 350°F.
- Cream butter and sugar. Beat flour into mixture.
- Beat in eggs, one at a time; gradually add buttermilk.
- Add vanilla and nutmeg or lemon juice.
- Pour into pie shell.
- Bake 40 - 50 minutes.

COCONUT PIE

Easy

4	eggs
1½	cups sugar
½	cup (1 stick) butter or margarine, melted
2	cups shredded coconut
2	cups milk
1	teaspoon vanilla
½	cup flour

- Heat oven to 350°F and grease 10-inch pie plate.
- Combine ingredients in order given. Pour into pie plate.
- Bake 45 minutes. Cool. Serve warm or cold with sweetened whipped cream.

This pie makes its own crust while cooking. It is especially good made 1 day ahead.

CALIFORNIA CHOCOLATE PIE

3	ounces unsweetened chocolate
½	cup (1 stick) butter
4	eggs
2-3	tablespoons honey
1½	cups sugar
¼	teaspoon salt
1	teaspoon vanilla
9	inch unbaked pie shell

- Heat oven to 350°F.
- Melt chocolate with butter. Cool slightly.
- Beat eggs until light. Mix in honey, sugar, salt and vanilla.
- Add chocolate mixture and mix. Pour into pie shell.
- Bake 25 - 30 minutes until top is crusty but filling is soft. Do not overbake.

This pie has custard-like center when first out of oven. Best served warm with ice cream or whipped cream.

CHOCOLATE CHESS PIE

1½	ounces unsweetened chocolate
½	cup (1 stick) butter
2	eggs
1	cup sugar
1¼	teaspoons vanilla
¼	teaspoon salt
9	inch unbaked pie shell

- Heat oven to 325°F.
- Melt chocolate with butter. Cool slightly.
- Beat eggs, sugar, vanilla and salt.
- Stir chocolate mixture into egg mixture. Pour into pie shell.
- Bake 45 minutes or until filling puffs. A crispy crust will form on top; it will crack.
- Cool before cutting.

Easy — and a chocolate lover's delight!

SINFULLY DELICIOUS CHOCOLATE TORTE

½	cup (1 stick) unsalted butter
1	cup ground almonds
¼	cup fresh bread crumbs
⅔	cup sugar
3	eggs
➤	grated peel of 1 orange
¾	cup semi-sweet chocolate chips, melted

Glaze:

2	teaspoons honey
2	ounces unsweetened chocolate
¼	cup semi-sweet chocolate chips
4	tablespoons unsalted butter

- Heat oven to 350°F and grease 8-inch cake pan.
- Line bottom with wax paper.
- Cream butter. Add almonds, bread crumbs and sugar.
- Add eggs, one at a time, beating well after each.
- Add orange peel and chocolate. Pour batter into pan.
- Bake 30 - 35 minutes (do not overbake). Cool in pan 5 - 10 minutes. Turn out onto serving plate.
- Melt glaze ingredients and pour over warm cake.
- Refrigerate. Remove from refrigerator 30 - 60 minutes before serving.

PERFECT CHOCOLATE 3-LAYER CAKE

🕐 *Must be refrigerated*

1	cup unsweetened cocoa
2	cups boiling water
2¾	cups sifted all-purpose flour
2	teaspoons baking soda
½	teaspoon salt
½	teaspoon baking powder
1	cup (2 sticks) butter or margarine, softened
2½	cups sugar
4	eggs
1½	teaspoons vanilla

- Heat oven to 350°F.
- Grease and flour three 9-inch cake pans.
- Mix cocoa and water until smooth. Set aside.
- Sift flour, baking soda, salt and baking powder.
- In large bowl, cream butter and sugar until light and fluffy. Beat in eggs and vanilla.
- Add dry ingredients and cooled cocoa mixture alternately; begin and end with dry ingredients.
- Divide mixture evenly among 3 pans. Bake 25 - 30 minutes or until tests done.
- Cool 10 minutes in pans. Remove to racks.
- Meanwhile prepare filling and frosting.
- Place 1st layer of cake on plate, top side down. Top with half of filling.
- Place 2nd layer, top side down. Spread on remaining filling.
- Place 3rd layer, top side up. Frost sides first, covering any whipped cream that may have come from between layers. Frost top of cake.
- Refrigerate 1 hour before serving.
- Use a very thin knife or bread knife to cut cake. Slice with a sawing motion.

Filling:

1	cup heavy cream, chilled
¼	cup powdered sugar
1	teaspoon vanilla

- Whip cream until soft peaks form.
- Add sugar and vanilla. Continue whipping until mixture holds shape. Refrigerate 1 hour before using.

Frosting:

6	ounces semi-sweet chocolate pieces
½	cup light cream
1	cup (2 sticks) butter or margarine
2½	cups powdered sugar

- In saucepan, melt chocolate with cream and butter over low heat, stirring until smooth.
- Remove from heat. Blend in sugar.
- Place pan in bowl of ice. Beat mixture until thickened to spreading consistency.

This cake is absolutely delicious and well worth the time and effort.

DIVINE DEVIL'S FOOD CAKE

🕐   *Must be refrigerated*

8	ounce can julienne beets, undrained
½	cup (1 stick) unsalted butter, softened
2½	cups firmly packed light brown sugar
3	large eggs
2	teaspoons vanilla
3	ounces unsweetened chocolate, melted
2	cups sifted all-purpose flour
2	teaspoons baking soda
½	teaspoon salt
½	cup buttermilk

- Heat oven to 350°F.
- Grease and flour two 9-inch cake pans.
- Drain beet juice into small bowl and set aside.
- Chop beets finely. Return to juice and set aside.
- Beat butter, sugar, eggs and vanilla until fluffy, about 5 minutes.
- Reduce speed and beat in chocolate.
- Combine flour, salt and baking soda.
- Alternately add flour mixture and buttermilk to butter mixture; begin and end with flour. Mix 1 minute.
- Add beets with juice. Mix until blended, about 1 minute. Batter will be thin with pieces of beet.
- Pour into pans. Bake 30 - 35 minutes or until tests done. Cool completely.
- Meanwhile prepare frosting.
- Assemble layers, frosting each layer and sides.
- Cake must be refrigerated.

Frosting:

2	cups heavy cream
16	ounces semi-sweet chocolate, chopped
2	teaspoons vanilla

- In saucepan, heat cream to boiling. Immediately remove pan from heat.
- Add chocolate and vanilla. Stir until smooth.
- Transfer to glass bowl. Refrigerate. Stir every 10 minutes until mixture is as thick as pudding (about 50 minutes).

HISTORY NOTE

Emory's first museum of art and archaeology found a permanent home in a historic building redesigned by architect Michael Graves. The current museum, the Michael C. Carlos Museum, was custom-designed by Mr. Graves and includes twenty-nine exhibition galleries.

Mocha Pecan Torte

🕐

Cake:

6	eggs (room temperature), separated
1	cup sugar
1	teaspoon vanilla
3	tablespoons cold water
1	cup sifted all-purpose flour
1	teaspoon baking powder
½	cup finely chopped pecans

- Heat oven to 350°F.
- Grease and flour two 8-inch cake pans.
- Beat egg whites until soft peaks form. Add sugar slowly and beat until stiff.
- In separate bowl, beat egg yolks until thick and pale colored.
- Blend in vanilla and water. Using wire whisk, fold carefully into egg whites.
- Fold in flour and baking powder. Pour into pans.
- Bake 20 minutes. Cool 10 minutes. Remove to wire rack. Cool completely.
- Meanwhile prepare filling.
- With serrated knife cut each cake layer horizontally to make 2 layers.
- Stack (4) layers, spreading coffee mixture between.
- Spread chocolate mixture on top and sides of cake.
- Sprinkle nuts on top. Refrigerate until 1 hour before serving.
- *Variation:* Walnuts, hazelnuts or almonds may be substituted.

Mocha Filling:

1	cup (2 sticks) unsalted butter
1½	cups powdered sugar
2	eggs
2	tablespoons strong coffee
2	ounces semi-sweet chocolate, melted
1	cup heavy cream, whipped

- Cream butter. Add sugar.
- Add eggs, one at a time, beating well after each. Add coffee slowly.
- Place ⅓ of mixture in separate bowl. Add chocolate. Fold in ⅓ of whipped cream.
- Fold remaining cream into coffee mixture. (Beat well again if mixture separates.)

This cake is best made 1 day ahead.

Coca-Cola Cake

2	cups sifted all-purpose flour
2	cups sugar
1½	cups small marshmallows
½	cup (1 stick) butter or margarine
½	cup vegetable oil
3	tablespoons cocoa
1	cup Coca-Cola
1	teaspoon baking soda
½	cup buttermilk
2	eggs
1	teaspoon vanilla

Frosting:

½	cup (1 stick) butter
3	tablespoons cocoa
6	tablespoons Coca-Cola
16	ounces (4 cups) powdered sugar
1	teaspoon vanilla
1	cup chopped pecans

- Heat oven to 350°F and grease 13x9x2-inch pan.
- In large bowl, combine flour, sugar and marshmallows.
- In saucepan, mix butter, oil, cocoa and Coca-Cola. Bring to boil and pour into dry ingredients; blend well.
- Mix baking soda and buttermilk. Add to batter with eggs and vanilla.
- Pour into pan and bake 35 - 45 minutes or until tests done.
- During last 10 minutes of baking time, prepare frosting: In saucepan bring butter, cocoa and Coca-Cola to boil.
- Blend with powdered sugar.
- Stir in vanilla and pecans. Spread on hot cake.
- When cool, cut into squares and serve.

An Atlanta original!

FRESH APPLE CAKE

2¼	cups sugar
2	eggs and 2 egg whites
1¼	cups applesauce
¼	cup vegetable oil
1½	cups sifted all-purpose flour
1½	cups whole wheat flour
2	teaspoons vanilla
1	cup chopped nuts
1½	teaspoons baking soda
1	teaspoon salt
1	cup coconut
3	cups finely chopped apple

Glaze:

½	cup (1 stick) butter or margarine
1	cup firmly packed brown sugar
¼	cup milk

- Heat oven to 325°F and grease 10-inch tube pan.
- In large bowl, beat sugar, eggs and egg whites.
- Add remaining ingredients; beat until smooth. Pour into pan.
- Bake 1¼ hours or until cake pulls away from sides of pan and toothpick comes out clean.
- Just before cake is done, boil glaze ingredients in small pan 2½ minutes.
- Remove cake from oven. Pour hot glaze over top.
- Cool in pan. Loosen with metal spatula or knife to remove.

GEORGIA PEACH POUND CAKE

1	cup (2 sticks) butter or margarine, softened
3	cups sugar
6	eggs
3	cups sifted all-purpose flour
¼	teaspoon baking soda
¼	teaspoon salt
½	cup sour cream
1½	teaspoons vanilla
½-1	teaspoon almond extract
3	cups peeled, chopped fresh peaches, drained

- Heat oven to 350°F and grease and flour 10-inch tube pan.
- Cream butter and sugar until light and fluffy.
- Add eggs, one at a time, beating well after each.
- Sift flour, baking soda and salt in separate bowl.
- Add to creamed mixture alternately with sour cream; begin and end with dry ingredients.
- Stir in vanilla and almond extract. Fold in peaches.
- Pour batter into pan. Bake 75 - 80 minutes or until cake tests done. Cool 10 minutes before removing from pan.

To use frozen peaches, thaw and drain.

CREAM CHEESE POUND CAKE

1½	cups (3 sticks) butter or margarine, softened
8	ounces cream cheese, softened
2½-3	cups sugar
⅛	teaspoon salt
1½	teaspoons vanilla
¼	teaspoon almond extract
6	large eggs
3	cups sifted all-purpose flour

- Heat oven to 325°F.
- Grease and flour 10-inch tube or bundt pan.
- Cream butter, cream cheese and sugar.
- Add salt, vanilla and almond extract.
- Beat on high until light and fluffy, about 4 minutes.
- Add eggs, one at a time, beating well after each.
- Reduce speed and gradually add flour.
- Spoon into pan. Cut through with knife to eliminate air bubbles.
- Bake on middle rack of oven 90 minutes or until tests done.
- Cool in pan until slightly warm to touch.
- Remove from pan and cool on wire rack.

CHEF'S NOTE

Cake tests done when toothpick inserted in center comes out clean or when cake begins to pull away from sides of pan and feels springy to touch.

COCONUT POUND CAKE

Freezes well

1	cup (2 sticks) butter
½	cup shortening
3	cups sugar
5	eggs
1	cup milk
3	cups sifted all-purpose flour
½	teaspoon baking powder
2	teaspoons vanilla or coconut extract
1	cup coconut
➤	powdered sugar
➤	fresh strawberries or raspberries

- Heat oven to 325°F.
- Grease and flour 10-inch tube or bundt pan.
- Cream butter, shortening and sugar. Beat in eggs and milk.
- Sift flour and baking powder; add to butter mixture.
- Add extract and coconut.
- Pour into pan. Remove air bubbles (see note).
- Bake 75 minutes on bottom rack of oven. Do not open oven during baking.
- Let cool in pan 15 minutes. Remove to rack.
- To serve sprinkle with powdered sugar and fill center with fresh strawberries or raspberries.

CHEF'S NOTE

To remove air bubbles in cake batter, run knife in zigzag fashion through batter in cake pan.

KENTUCKY BUTTER RUM CAKE

1	cup (2 sticks) butter
2	cups sugar
4	eggs
1	cup milk
1	tablespoon lemon juice
2	teaspoons vanilla
3	cups sifted all-purpose flour
1	teaspoon each baking powder and salt
½	teaspoon baking soda

Glaze:

2	cups sugar
½	cup water
1	cup (2 sticks) butter
6	tablespoons dark rum

- Heat oven to 325°F.
- Grease and flour 10-inch tube or bundt pan.
- Cream butter. Add sugar slowly.
- Add eggs, one at a time, beating well after each.
- Combine milk, lemon juice and vanilla.
- Combine flour, baking powder, salt and baking soda.
- Alternately add flour and milk mixtures to butter mixture. Mix well.
- Pour into pan. Bake 1 hour or until tests done.

- *Glaze:* Bring sugar, water and butter to boil. Lower heat. Cover until sugar dissolves. Cool. Stir in rum.
- Remove cake from oven. Pierce top of cake with skewer.
- Spoon glaze over cake. Leave in pan until glaze is absorbed.
- Loosen cake carefully with metal spatula or knife and remove from pan. Cool on rack.

ANGEL L'ORANGE

🕐 *Serves 16-20*

3	envelopes plain gelatin
½	cup cold water
2	cups sugar
2	cups boiling water
➢	juice of 2 lemons
12	ounces frozen orange juice concentrate, thawed
2	cups heavy cream, whipped
34	ounces angel food cake (about 2 cakes)

Frosting:

1	cup heavy cream, whipped
¼	cup flaked coconut

- Grease springform pan.
- Dissolve gelatin in cold water.
- Dissolve sugar in boiling water.
- Add gelatin mixture, lemon juice and orange juice concentrate.
- Refrigerate until thickened.
- Add whipped cream.
- Scrape brown off cake. Break cake in pieces and fold into mixture.
- Pour into pan. Refrigerate, covered, overnight. Remove cake from pan.
- Frost with whipped cream and coconut.

A light, refreshing summertime dessert.

CRANBERRY SWIRL CAKE

½	cup (1 stick) butter, softened
1	cup sugar
2	eggs
2	cups sifted all-purpose flour
1	teaspoon each baking powder and baking soda
½	teaspoon salt
8	ounces sour cream
16	ounce can whole cranberry sauce
1	teaspoon almond extract
½	cup chopped walnuts

Glaze:

1	cup powdered sugar
½	teaspoon almond extract
2	tablespoons warm water

- Heat oven to 350°F and grease and flour 10-inch tube pan.
- Cream butter and sugar. Add eggs. Mix well.
- Sift dry ingredients. Alternately add flour mixture and sour cream to butter mixture, mixing well.
- Add almond extract. Blend.
- Spread half of batter in pan. Top with half of cranberries. Repeat layers. Top with nuts.
- Bake 50 - 55 minutes.
- Cool cake 10 minutes in pan before removing. Cool completely.

- Combine glaze ingredients and drizzle over cake.

Festive fall holiday cake!

GRANDMOTHER'S GINGERBREAD

½ cup (1 stick) butter or margarine, softened
1⅓ cups firmly packed brown sugar
⅔ cup dark molasses
1 egg, beaten
1 teaspoon each ground ginger and cinnamon
½ teaspoon ground cloves
1 cup coffee
½ teaspoon baking soda
2½ cups sifted all-purpose flour
1 teaspoon baking powder
⅛ teaspoon salt

- Heat oven to 375°F and grease 13x9x2-inch pan.
- Cream butter and brown sugar.
- Add molasses, egg and spices. Mix.
- Dissolve baking soda in coffee.
- Sift flour, baking powder and salt.
- Add flour and coffee alternately to sugar mixture.
- Bake 35 - 40 minutes until tests done.

Adapted from a great grandmother's recipe from the 1800's using ½ cup bacon fat and baked in a wood-burning stove.

CHEF'S NOTE

Serve Grandmother's Gingerbread with Lemon Crème Fruit Sauce (page 272), Lemon Filling (page 273), lemon yogurt, slivers of crystallized ginger, sweetened whipped cream or simply with powdered sugar.

PUMPKIN CHEESECAKE

Crust:

¾	cup graham cracker crumbs
½	cup finely chopped pecans
2	tablespoons sugar
2	tablespoons brown sugar
¼	cup butter, melted

- Combine crust ingredients.
- Pack into springform pan. Freeze 30 minutes.
- Heat oven to 350°F.

Filling:

3	8-ounce packages cream cheese
1	cup plus 2 tablespoons sugar
¾	cup canned pumpkin
1	egg plus 4 egg yolks
1½	teaspoons ground cinnamon
¼	teaspoon ground nutmeg
½	teaspoon ground ginger
¼	teaspoon salt
1	tablespoon cornstarch
½	teaspoon vanilla
➢	whipped cream for garnish

- *Filling:* In large bowl, combine all ingredients except whipped cream in order listed. Beat well.
- Spoon into crust.
- Bake 50 - 55 minutes.
- Refrigerate when cooled.
- Garnish with whipped cream to serve.

   A fall favorite but good year 'round.

FABULOUS CHOCOLATE SAUCE

Easy

2	ounces unsweetened chocolate
½	cup sugar
½	cup half and half
½	teaspoon vanilla
⅛	teaspoon salt

- Chop chocolate in food processor or blender.
- In small saucepan, heat sugar with half and half.
- Add to chocolate and process.
- Add vanilla and salt.
- Store in refrigerator.

This is wonderful! Serve warm over ice cream or sliced pound cake.

CARAMEL EXTRAVAGANCE

1	cup (2 sticks) butter, melted
2	cups firmly packed dark brown sugar
¾	cup light corn syrup
14	ounce can sweetened condensed milk
¼	teaspoon salt
1¼	teaspoons lemon juice
½	cup half and half
1½	teaspoons vanilla

- In double boiler, mix butter, sugar, corn syrup, milk, salt and lemon juice.
- Cook 1 hour, checking water level occasionally.
- Stir in half and half and vanilla. Cook additional 30 - 40 minutes.
- Cool in pan. Refrigerate tightly covered.

Absolutely fantastic when served as dip with Granny Smith apples! Superb as ice cream sauce! Tastes like candy!

CHEF'S NOTE

To prevent discoloration of freshly sliced apples or pears, cover with fresh grapefruit juice or diluted lemon juice.

LIQUEUR CREAM SAUCE

★   *2 cups*

3	egg yolks
½	cup plus 1 tablespoon powdered sugar
¼	cup Grand Marnier liqueur
1	cup heavy cream, whipped

- Beat egg yolks, sugar and liqueur in mixer or food processor until smooth.
- Fold in whipped cream. Refrigerate minimum 1 hour.
- Spoon over fresh fruit.
- Can be stored 24 hours in refrigerator. Mixture will separate; gently refold.

LEMON CRÈME FRUIT SAUCE

3 cups

2	eggs
1	cup sugar, divided
⅓	cup fresh lemon juice
1	tablespoon cornstarch
½	cup water
1	teaspoon vanilla
1	cup heavy cream (do not whip)

- Beat eggs, ½ cup sugar and lemon juice until foamy. Set aside.
- In saucepan, mix remaining ½ cup sugar, cornstarch and water.
- Cook over medium heat. Stir until clear and thickened.
- Remove from heat. Slowly beat in egg mixture.
- Cook over low heat until thickened. Remove from heat. Stir in vanilla.
- Cool before folding in cream. Refrigerate 2 hours.

This sauce is a wonderful dip with fruit as an appetizer. It rates a "wow!" served over fruit as a dessert and may be used as a salad dressing as well. An easy make ahead recipe.

LEMON FILLING

1½ cups

2	eggs and 2 egg yolks
½	cup sugar
⅓	cup fresh lemon juice
¼	cup butter, cut in bits

- In double boiler, lightly beat eggs and yolks.
- Mix in sugar and lemon juice.
- Cook over simmering water, stirring constantly, about 5 minutes until thickened. Do not allow to boil; it will curdle!
- Remove pan from water. Stir in butter a few bits at a time until melted.
- Strain and refrigerate.

Use as sauce or filling for cake or tart. Wonderful on toast or Grandmother's Gingerbread (page 269).

ITALIAN CREAM

Easy   3 - 4 cups   Serves 12 - 15

1	pound Mascarpone (Italian cream cheese found in specialty food stores)
1	cup sugar
¼	cup rum or orange liqueur
2	cups heavy cream

- In food processor or blender, mix Mascarpone, sugar and rum, a small amount at a time, until smooth.
- Gently stir in cream. Blend until smooth.
- Serve with fresh fruit such as strawberries, raspberries or blueberries.
- Store in refrigerator.

Easy Tiramisu: Layer cream with lady fingers or cake slices. Sprinkle with cocoa and shaved chocolate.

BOURBON BALLS

½   cup (1 stick) butter
16   ounces (4 cups) powdered sugar
¼   cup evaporated milk
¼   cup bourbon whiskey
2   cups finely chopped pecans
8   ounces unsweetened chocolate
1   inch cube paraffin

- Cream butter and sugar. Add milk, bourbon and pecans.
- Chill 1 hour. Roll into 1-inch balls. Freeze.
- Melt chocolate in small pan. Add paraffin.
- Cool slightly; keep melted by placing pan in warm water.
- Pierce frozen candy balls with toothpicks. Dip balls in chocolate to coat.
- Place on wax paper to harden.

Chocolate coating makes these different!

PRALINES

Easy   *2 dozen*

1   cup sugar
1   cup firmly packed brown sugar
½   cup evaporated milk
¼   cup butter or margarine
2   cups broken pecan pieces
1   teaspoon vanilla

- In saucepan, bring first 5 ingredients to boil.
- Let mixture boil 3 - 5 minutes, stirring constantly.
- When candy reaches soft ball stage, remove from heat. Add vanilla.
- Stir 1 minute (no more!). Drop by tablespoonful on wax paper.

Soft ball stage is 238°F on candy thermometer.

This recipe was contributed by Mrs. C. K. Radford of Memphis, Tennessee, mother of Mrs. James T. Laney.

CHOCOLATE TRUFFLES

🕐

8	ounces dark sweet chocolate, chopped
5	tablespoons water
1	tablespoon instant coffee granules (optional)
½	cup (1 stick) cold unsalted butter, cut in ½ tablespoons
¼	cup orange liqueur or rum
½	cup ground hazelnuts (optional)
½	cup sifted cocoa

- In double boiler, combine first 3 ingredients over medium heat.
- When chocolate has softened, beat until smooth and creamy.
- Remove from heat. Beat 1 minute to cool.
- Gradually beat in butter, piece by piece, until smooth.
- Beat in liqueur slowly. Refrigerate 1 - 2 hours until firm.
- Form into 1 - 2-inch balls. Roll in cocoa to coat.
- Place in paper candy cups to keep truffles separated. Refrigerate.

CHEF'S NOTE

Candy is best stored in tightly covered container in refrigerator or freezer.

SNOW BIRDS

Easy

1½	pounds white chocolate
3	cups pecan halves

- In double boiler, melt chocolate slowly. Stir in pecans.
- Drop by teaspoonful on wax paper. Cool.

PEANUT BRITTLE

Easy

2½	cups raw peanuts
2	cups sugar
2	cups light corn syrup
1	teaspoon salt
1½	teaspoons baking soda

- Grease jelly-roll pan.
- In heavy pan, boil peanuts, sugar and corn syrup until honey colored.
- Add salt and baking soda. (Mixture will foam.) Stir until mixed.
- Pour quickly onto pan. To spread, tilt pan (do not use spoon).
- Cool completely. Break in pieces.

This is a tasty one-hundred-year-old recipe originating in Hanover, Pennsylvania.

EPICUREAN FALL SEATED DINNER FOR 12

PEAR CUSTARD TART

Serves 12

Pastry:

6	tablespoons butter
1½	cups all-purpose flour
1	egg yolk
½	teaspoon salt
4-6	tablespoons cold water

- Cut butter into flour until mixture resembles coarse crumbs.
- Mix egg yolk and salt with 4 tablespoons cold water.
- Add to flour mixture and stir to form ball. Add extra water if necessary. Chill 30 minutes.
- Roll out and fit in 10-inch tart pan. Prick bottom and line with wax paper. Add beans or rice to weight paper down.
- Bake 15 minutes at 400°F. Remove beans and paper. Bake 5 more minutes.

Filling:

½	cup (1 stick) butter
½	cup sugar
2	large eggs
¼	cup flour
1¼	cups finely ground almonds
1	teaspoon vanilla
4	pears, thinly sliced (Bartlett good variety to use)
4-8	tablespoons apricot jam
2	tablespoons dark rum

- Cream butter. Add sugar then eggs. Beat.
- Add flour, almonds and vanilla. Beat until smooth.
- Pour into tart pastry. Arrange sliced pears in fan on top.
- Warm apricot jam and rum; stir until smooth. Strain if necessary. Brush over pears.
- Bake 35 - 40 minutes at 425°F until done.

HISTORY NOTE

The William R. Cannon Chapel, adjoining the Candler School of Theology, built in 1981, was designed by noted architect Paul Rudolph.

Epicurean Winter Buffet for 36

Chocolate Nut Cake with Hot Fudge Sauce

Serves 36

⅔	cup whole pine nuts, toasted
1	cup (2 sticks) unsalted butter
8	ounces unsweetened chocolate
4½	cups sifted all-purpose flour
1	teaspoon salt
1	tablespoon baking soda
3½	cups sugar
1	cup walnut oil
3	cups milk, divided
2½	teaspoons baking powder
6	eggs
2	teaspoons vanilla
1	cup minced toasted pine nuts

- Heat oven to 350°F and grease two 10-inch bundt pans.
- Sprinkle whole pine nuts in bottom.
- In double boiler, melt butter and chocolate.
- In large bowl, mix flour, salt, baking soda, sugar, oil, chocolate mixture and 1½ cups milk.
- Mix 2 minutes on medium until blended.
- Add baking powder, eggs, remaining 1½ cups milk and vanilla.
- Mix 2 minutes, scraping sides. Add minced pine nuts.
- Divide batter evenly between pans.
- Bake 40 minutes until cake begins to pull away from sides of pan and feels springy to touch. Cool on rack.
- Invert cake on serving platter. Pour hot fudge sauce over cake just before serving or serve sauce on the side.

Hot Fudge Sauce:

1	cup (2 sticks) unsalted butter
8	ounces unsweetened chocolate
4	cups sugar
2	cups evaporated milk

- In double boiler, melt butter and chocolate.
- Add sugar and milk alternately, stirring constantly.
- Continue to cook over boiling water until sugar is melted.
- Store sauce, covered, in refrigerator.
- Reheat in double boiler.

Chef's Note

Pine nuts can be purchased in bulk from farmers' markets or specialty food stores.

Epicurean Spring Cookout for 30

Lemon Pound Cake with All Berry Topping

Double recipe to serve 30

2	cups (4 sticks) unsalted butter
1	teaspoon salt
3⅓	cups sugar
10	eggs
2	tablespoons lemon extract
1	tablespoon vanilla
1	tablespoon lemon zest (optional)
4	cups sifted cake flour

- Have ingredients at room temperature. Grease 10-inch nonstick bundt pan.
- Cream butter and salt. Beat 4 minutes.
- Gradually add sugar, continuing to beat until fluffy.
- Add 8 eggs, one at a time, beating well after each.
- Add lemon extract, flour and remaining 2 eggs. Beat until blended.
- Pour into pan. Place in cold oven and set temperature at 300°F.
- Bake 1½ - 2 hours.
- Remove from oven and cool 15 minutes. Remove from pan.

All Berry Topping:

4	cups frozen blueberries, divided
2⅔	cups sugar
⅔	cup fresh lemon juice
4	teaspoons lemon zest
4	teaspoons cornstarch
1	teaspoon salt
½	cup brandy
6	cups frozen raspberries
4	cups frozen blackberries
6	cups sliced fresh strawberries

- Combine 2 cups blueberries, sugar, lemon juice, lemon zest, cornstarch and salt in non-aluminum saucepan. Bring to boil.
- Reduce heat and simmer until blueberries are soft.
- Remove blueberries with slotted spoon.
- Simmer until sauce thickens.
- Cool sauce to lukewarm before adding brandy.
- Place all berries in large serving bowl. Stir in sauce; leave at room temperature to thaw for serving.

Acknowledgements

EMORY SEASONS COOKBOOK COMMITTEE 1988-1993
Nancy Elsas, chair
MaryKay Wilcox, co-chair and editor
Georgia Parks, recipe collection
Martha Catherwood, word processing and co-editor
Bette Walton, treasurer

Jean Bergmark
Peggy Brann 1989-1990
Chris Cannon 1992-1993
Olympia Conant
Neva Fisk
Suzanne Freed
Beth Garrettson
Michelle Hall 1992-1993

Barbara Hund
Becky Hunter
Eleanor Joslin
Elizabeth Joyner
Carolyn Lollar
Sue Lueptow
Blair Major 1989-1990
Peggy Noble 1990-1992

Pat O'Shea
Ruby Patterson 1989-1990
Dot Per-Lee
Betty Ricks
Ruth Rohrer
Leigh Schmickel
Lynn Vogler
Bette Walton

E.U.W.C. PRESIDENTS:

1988-1989 MaryKay Wilcox
1989-1990 Becky Hunter

1990-1991 Donna Culler
1991-1992 Margot Eckman

1992-1993 Nancy Elsas
1993-1994 Becky Hunter

SECTION CHAIRS:

Appetizers   Sue Lueptow
              Pat O'Shea
Salads   Dot Per-Lee
Soups   Betty Ricks
Breads   MaryKay Wilcox

Vegetables   Lynn Vogler
Cheese, Eggs, Pasta, Grains
              Becky Hunter
              Elizabeth Joyner
Chicken   Beth Garrettson
Fish   Ruth Rohrer

Meats   Bette Walton
Desserts   Nancy Elsas
              Suzanne Freed
              Carolyn Lollar
              Georgia Parks

EDITING AND PROOFREADING ASSISTANCE:

Jean Bergmark
Chris Cannon
Olympia Conant
Margot Eckman
Eileen Finlayson

Neva Fisk
Sharon Gunn
Michelle Hall
Vicky Holifield
Barbara Hund

Marguerite Ingram
Eleanor Joslin
Charlotte Keller
Dandridge Penick
Jean Steinhaus

Thank you: to Cassie Fahey and Alison Creagh of the Emory University Bookstore for help and encouragement.
to Ruby Patterson, who helped to catalyze our efforts.
to Sara Gregory for Oxford history.
to our E.U.W.C. members, friends and families, who contributed favorite recipes and then tested recipes many times while encouraging us to the finish!
to Joe Alcober and Meredith Himebaugh at Emory Publications.
to Ann Borden and Annemarie Poyo for photography.
to Epicurean and Houston Mill House staff.

ACKNOWLEDGEMENTS

We thank all those people who so generously contributed recipes for our collection. We apologize if we have inadvertently omitted any name of a contributor or tester. In some instances recipes were combined or adapted after extensive testing. Friends and family, sometimes even at great distances, were particularly helpful testers.

Linda Adams	Dorothy Brown	Mary B. DeLoach	Sherry Fort
Jane Alexander	Jean Brumley	Deede DeLorme	Iris Frank
Eden Anderson	Charles Buckley	Martha Devis	Carolyn Frazier
Georgia Andrews	Susan Buckley	Adelle Dickey	Ruth Fredrickson
Jeanne Andrews	Nancy Bull	Margie Dietz	Suzanne Freed
Maria Are	Ellen Burt	James T. Dooley	Eleanor Ganey
Mona Arnold	Judy Butker	Lee Ann Doty	Beth Garrettson
Jimmie Artley	Claydean Cameron	Rose Doty	Brooke Garrettson
Betty Atwood	Christine Camp	Karen Denham Downen	Honey Gfroerer
Glen R. Avant	Chris Cannon	Carole Drvaric	Mrs. S. T. Ginsberg
Louanne Bachner	Marian Carlson	Lucy Duke	David Ginsburg
Ellen Bain	Jane Carney	Virginia Dunbar	Mary Glassick
Arlene Bard	Betty Carringer	Wilma Durpo	Jan Gleason
Mary Bauslaugh	Candy Casarella	Mary Ellen DuVarney	Audrey Goldstein
Ruth Becker	Mildred Casey	Mary Eberhart	Subie Green
Dorothy Bell	Martha Catherwood	Jim Eckman	Pat Gregerson
Beth Bennett	Carolann Charen	Margot Eckman	Sara Gregory
Jean Bergmark	Irene Check	Nancy Elsas	Joseph Guillebeau
Zahava Berkowitz	Mrs. James D. Clements	Patricia I. Erickson	Michelle Hall
Ruth Berman	Honor Cobbs	Naib Evans	Jean Halstead
Ellen Bernstein	Cynthia Cohen	Rhonda Evans	Barbara Hana
June Bishop	Marian Compans	Cassie Fahey	Robin Harbuck
Norma J. Bishop	Olympia Conant	Cornelia Ferrell	Joan Harmon
Marilyn Bonkovsky	Virginia Cook	Abbott Ferriss	Priscilla Harris
Eva Bookman	Jill Corson	Ruth Ferriss	John Hartley
Ruth Boozer	Alison Creagh	Eileen Finlayson	Margie Hartley
Priscilla Boskoff	Susan Crist	Jana Frances Fischer	Ann Hazzard
Jane Boswell	Donna Culler	Neva Fisk	Elaine Henderson
Anne Brake	Peggy Cundiff	Ildi Flannery	Genie Hilliard
Peggy Brann	Mary Carolyn Currie	Melanie Fleek	Nancy Hilyer
Marlene Bright	Jolene Davis	Mary Louise Fleming	Pauline Hoch
Carolyn Broucek	Edna Deckbar	Cheryl Fletcher	Vicky Holifield

Donna Holladay
Frits Hommes
Greet Hommes
Lane Hubbard
Kathryn Huddleston
Suzanne Hugueley
Helen Huguley
Barbara Hund
Jeanette Hunt
Becky Hunter
Robert L. Hunter
Margaret Hyatt
Marguerite Ingram
Carol Issa
Rachel Jeffrey
Helen Jenkins
Katrina Jensen
Catherine Johnson
Stella Johnson
Clare Boisfeuillet Jones
Lois N. Jordan
Eleanor Joslin
Elizabeth Joyner
deForest F. Jurkiewicz
Virginia Kafoglis
Edith Kellum
Bobbie Kenitzer
Betty Kerner
Bill Kerner
Fanny King
Carol Knopka
Mary Jo Knutson
Lonna Beth Kral
Dru Kring
Fareez Krishnaswamy
Jenny Lambert
Mary Landt
Berta Laney
James T. Laney
Mary Laney
Maggie Lawson
Betty Lehner
Barbara Licznerski
Karen Lindsay
Elizabeth Littrell
J. Paul Littrell
Carolyn Lollar
Marion Lord
Anne Lueptow
Susan Lueptow

Alice Lunn
Bonnie Lyle
Jean MacKay
Blair Major
Sheila Mallon
L. & J. Manley
June M. Mann
Judy Martin
Mary Martin
Frances Mathis
Gene May
Penny McCroan
Milah McDavid
Nancy Mchova
Valerie J. McKibben
Nancy McLaren
Irene McMorland
Jean Megenity
Elizabeth Menger
Karen Menton
Cora Meyers
Gwen Michienzi
Caroline Minter
Alexandra Mitch
Ruth Money
Charlotte Moran
Nancy Murdy
Edith Murphree
Bridget Murphy
Cheryl Murphy
Laura Murphy
Nancy D. Murphy
Rocky Mutter
Cora Myers
Nelly Naib
Mrs. Ed Nebel
Kay Nicolaysen
Lynn Nicolaysen
Anne Nicolson
Peggy Noble
Marshall Norman
Mary Norwood
Kaaren Nowicki
Pat O'Shea
Ami Offenbacher
Terri Olson
Georgia Parks
Lois Parris
Marzia Pasquali
Ruby Patterson

Dandridge Penick
Carol Penn
Allison Per-Lee
Dot Per-Lee
Joni Per-Lee
Sarah Phythyon
Karen Pooler
Anne Porr
John Preedy
Marilyn Prevor
Mrs. C. K. Radford
Shirley Rauber
Anne Belle Ray
Neva Redfern
Clara Redmond
Helen G. Richardson
Marian Richardson
Betty Ricks
Henry C. Ricks, Jr.
Joyce Ringer
Mrs. Alan Ritter
Lauralee Robertson
Terri Robertson
Anne Rodig
Jean Rogers
Ruth Rohrer
Betty Roy
Dorothy Rozier
Terri Rumple
Cindy Runyon
Beverly Schaffer
Mary Willson Schill
Karen Schindler
Leigh Schmickel
Jane Schrum
Betty Schulte
Louise Scranton
Mary Ann Seavey
Marlys Sell
Maria Sgoutas
Madhu Sheth
Lois Shingler
Patricia Shropshire
Lani Sibley
Alida Silverman
Helen Simmons
Ruth Simmons
Eva Sitton
Jacqueline Slack
Hazel D. Steel

Kathy Steinbruegge
Jean Steinhaus
Eycke Strickland
Carol Swetman
Heather Tangren
Georgann Tatman
Kim Teague
Ouida Temple
Margaret M. Thrower
Jean Thwaite
Alice Tinkley
Babette Tipping
Albert Tobuku-Metzger
Mattie Trimble
Lu Trump
Charky Tucker
Sandra Tucker
Joan Turcotte
Mrs. William T. Turner
Sue Turner
Mrs. Herbert Tyler
Joni Tyson
Kay Vogler
Lynn Vogler
Lisa Walker
Helen Wall
Bette Walton
Carol Ward
Dwight Weathers
Jean Weathers
Valerie Webster
Susan Weitman
Sally West
Joan Whitcomb
Luisita Whitman
Penny Whittington
Aileen Wieland
Ben Wilcox
MaryKay Wilcox
Rebecca Wilcox
Sarah Wilcox
W. Dean Wilcox
Helen Williams
Marion Williams
Jo Wood
Anne Yobs
Lori Zirnring
Caroline Z'Berg-Roblin

Emory University Woman's Club member Vicky Holifield graciously contributed the following illustrations to EMORY SEASONS:

D

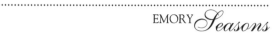

EMORY *Seasons*
Emory University Woman's Club
849 Houston Mill Road N.E.
Atlanta, Georgia 30329

Please send _____ copies of *Emory Seasons*   at $21.95 each $ _____
            Add postage and handling   at $ 3.00 each $ _____
            Add gift wrap (if desired)*   at $ 1.00 each $ _____
            Georgia residents add 5% sales tax   at $ 1.10 each $ _____
                                                       Total enclosed $ _____
                    Please make check payable to: *Emory Seasons*

Ship To:

Name _____

Address _____

City _____ State _____ Zip _____

Telephone number _____

* Gift card to read _____

MAILING LABEL — PLEASE PRINT.

From: Emory Seasons
849 Houston Mill Road N.E.
Atlanta, Georgia 30329

To:
Name: _____
Address: _____
City: _____ State: _____ Zip: _____

EMORY *Seasons*
Emory University Woman's Club
849 Houston Mill Road N.E.
Atlanta, Georgia 30329

Please send _____ copies of *Emory Seasons*   at $21.95 each $ _____
            Add postage and handling   at $ 3.00 each $ _____
            Add gift wrap (if desired)*   at $ 1.00 each $ _____
            Georgia residents add 5% sales tax   at $ 1.10 each $ _____
                                                       Total enclosed $ _____
                    Please make check payable to: *Emory Seasons*

Ship To:

Name _____

Address _____

City _____ State _____ Zip _____

Telephone number _____

* Gift card to read _____

MAILING LABEL — PLEASE PRINT.

From: Emory Seasons
849 Houston Mill Road N.E.
Atlanta, Georgia 30329

To:
Name: _____
Address: _____
City: _____ State: _____ Zip: _____

EMORY *Seasons*
Emory University Woman's Club
849 Houston Mill Road N.E.
Atlanta, Georgia 30329

Please send _____ copies of *Emory Seasons*   at $21.95 each $ _____
            Add postage and handling   at $ 3.00 each $ _____
            Add gift wrap (if desired)*   at $ 1.00 each $ _____
            Georgia residents add 5% sales tax   at $ 1.10 each $ _____
                                                       Total enclosed $ _____
                    Please make check payable to: *Emory Seasons*

Ship To:

Name _____

Address _____

City _____ State _____ Zip _____

Telephone number _____

* Gift card to read _____

MAILING LABEL — PLEASE PRINT.

From: Emory Seasons
849 Houston Mill Road N.E.
Atlanta, Georgia 30329

To:
Name: _____
Address: _____
City: _____ State: _____ Zip: _____